KEY  *to the* SACRED PATTERN

THE AUTHOR Henry Lincoln began his career in the theatre and first wrote for television in the early 1960s. After two hundred or so drama scripts, he encountered the Mystery of Rennes-le-Château in 1969, which led to his first BBC documentary film. In the three decades since he has concentrated, almost exclusively, on writing historical documentary scripts, the most notable of which have been his four films on Rennes-le-Château. In addition he has, with Michael Baigent and Richard Leigh, co-written two best-selling books on the subject, *The Holy Blood & the Holy Grail* and *The Messianic Legacy*.

In 1991 he took the Mystery of Rennes-le-Château into a new dimension in *The Holy Place*, moving on from hypothesis and concentrating on a demonstrable and provable thesis on which the enigma of Rennes-le-Château has been overlaid.

Now, in *Key to the Sacred Pattern: The Untold Story of Rennes-le-Château*, he sets down, for the first time, the extraordinary story of his thirty years of delving into one of the strangest mysteries of modern times, and the astonishing discoveries to which it has led.

By the same author
The Holy Blood & the Holy Grail, co-authored with
Michael Baigent and Richard Leigh
The Messianic Legacy, co-authored with
Michael Baigent and Richard Leigh
The Holy Place
The Templars Secret Island, co-authored with
Erling Haagensen

KEY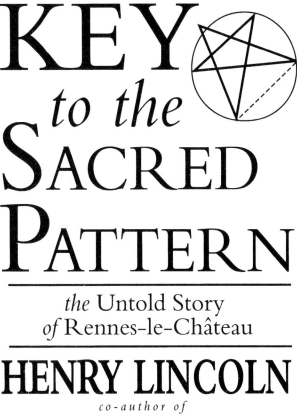
to the
SACRED
PATTERN

the Untold Story
of Rennes-le-Château

HENRY LINCOLN
co-author of
THE HOLY BLOOD AND THE HOLY GRAIL

CASSELLPAPERBACKS

A Windrush Press Book

First published in the United Kingdom in 1997 by
The Windrush Press.
This edition reprinted in association with
Cassell Paperbacks, 2002

A CIP catalogue record for this book is available
from the British Library
ISBN 1-84188-206-2

Designed and Typeset by
Carnegie Publishing, Chatsworth Road, Lancaster

Printed and bound in the United Kingdom by
the Bath Press Group

The Windrush Press
Windrush House, Adlestrop
Moreton-in-Marsh
Gloucestershire GL56 0YN
Telephone: 01608 658758
Fax: 01608 659345

Cassell Paperbacks, Cassell & Co
Wellington House, 125 Strand
London WC2R 0BB

A

mon cher ami
Michel,

qui trouva
Le Tomple

CONTENTS

PART ONE: THE DISCOVERING

PART TWO: THE DISCOVERY

Part One

THE DISCOVERING

INTRODUCTION

EVERYBODY loves a mystery story. When the mystery is not fictional but is set in a real place, at a real time and with real people, then the fascination becomes laced with a desire to know 'the truth'. When the story is further seasoned with the allure of buried treasure and when, furthermore, the events are not wrapped in an aura of long ago and far away, but occurred in a fairly recent past and in an easily accessible location – then the appeal is well-nigh irresistible.

The Mystery of Rennes-le-Château began in this way. A penniless nineteenth-century French village priest apparently finds something in his church. Suddenly, he is rich. Certainly, he begins to spend large sums of money. It follows therefore, people said, that he must have found a treasure.

In 1969 I set out to solve that mystery. It seemed to be an intriguing and very localised treasure hunt. Almost three decades later I can look back on four films and three books which have generated worldwide fame for the tiny Pyreneean village. From all around the globe, visitors now flock to Rennes-le-Château. Some are interested, some fascinated. Others are obsessed, filled with wishful thinking, searching for their own private holy grail and some for the Holy Grail itself. Distortions born of subjective non-reasoning have endowed the little hilltop with 'treasures' ranging from the lost wealth of the Knights Templar, through buried flying saucers to mummified bodies of Christ.

But, most curious of all, has been the ardent desire of some people to prove – or, at least to insist – that the story is a fraud. That there *is* no Mystery of Rennes-le-Château. For it is now no longer the mere and mundane search for the treasure of the priest, Bérenger Saunière. That 'simple' hunt has turned into the quest for an understanding of something much more profound. Rennes-le-Château has shown *itself* to be a mystery.

A sacred place, marked out and seemingly venerated by our remote ancestors. Marked out, moreover, with a skill and with an expertise that we, their 'enlightened' descendants, did not suspect they possessed. Why does the unexpected – the remarkable – the unprecedented – cause certain people so much disquiet and discomfort? Why do they wish the unfamiliar to be untrue?

To claim that there is no substance to the astonishing discoveries which have been made, is to demand the denial of empirically provable facts. To insist that the newly detected and extraordinary assemblage of data is the result of nothing more than meaningless coincidence is to show a wilful refusal to acknowledge that the past may yet have startling lessons to teach us. Such denials have been growing more vociferous of late. Some writers have even begun to propagate bizarre accounts of how I have 'invented' the story or been 'given' the details by shadowy and mysterious *éminences grises*.

I have decided, therefore, that I should at last set down the history of the unravelling of the threads of this tale. Even without the guess-work and fantasising of some reporters of my story, it is sufficiently colourful. My copious notes, diaries, photographs and recordings, assembled over years of research and filming, have enabled me to retrace my steps down the long trail with its many detours and stumbling blocks. I hope that this recital will demonstrate how the logic of the evidence led to its own final and ineluctable conclusion. A conclusion that is perhaps more startling than the original mystery. A conclusion, moreover, that is itself a new beginning, for to know is not necessarily to understand. I hope, above all, that the tale, stripped of the wishful-thinking, the delusions and the misconstructions which have been draped upon it, will prove entertaining.

The great geographer Alexander von Humboldt said: 'First people deny a thing. Then they belittle it. Then they decide it was known all along.' In the past thirty years, I have moved this story toward the second of those stages. I shall be happy if this book can contribute to its progress into the third.

H.L., 14 August 1997

'You're mad,' I said.

Patricia and Cécile had last met when they were sixth-formers. More than a decade had passed, with a friendship maintained solely by a regular correspondence. 'One day we must get together again,' had been a constant *leitmotiv* in their letters. But now, each girl had a husband and a bunch of children, five of the French variety and four English. Now – they had decided – was the time for the two families to spend a summer holiday together. 'But how do we know that Michel and I will get on?' I protested. 'How do you know the kids won't detest each other on sight? We'll be trapped in a French farmhouse for a month. And we could have a juvenile Third World War on our hands.' But we were committed. Michel and Cécile had already booked the farmhouse. It was called *Le Tomple* which, though I didn't realise it at the time, could not have been a more suitable name for my launchpad into a totally unexpected future.

Foreseeing what I considered to be an unquestionable need, I bought a handful of paperbacks in which I hoped to find escape from nine rampaging children and a French couple whom I knew no better than I did General de Gaulle. In the event, a miracle occurred. For Patricia and Cécile, their girlhood friendship proved to have survived intact. Michel and I took to each other at once. And the children, communicating effortlessly in a strange Anglo/French *patois* of their own invention, formed themselves into an adventurous and happy tribe. Of all my paperbacks, I found the time to read only one. It was called *Le Trésor Maudit* by Gérard de Sède. And it landed me with a life's work.

Chapter One

AUGUST 1969: SUMMER IN THE CEVENNES

THE CHILDREN yell, splash and scream at imaginary *vipères* in the stream by the house. Michel is ferrying the wives to the village in search of culinary essentials. I fulfil my appointed rôle of baby-sitter in the shade of the chestnut trees, drowsily leafing through my paperback. *'Le Trésor Maudit'* – 'The Accursed Treasure'. It's a good title for a desultory holiday read. Slowly I find myself beginning to tease at the unanswered questions in the book. To wonder, in fact, why some of the questions had been raised in the first place – and why other more basic questions had not been asked at all.

The sun glares on the water where the children play. I screw up my eyes and peer at the page in front of me. It is a reproduction of one of the mysterious parchments which apparently conceal clues to the 'accursed treasure' – a treasure waiting to be found somewhere down near the Pyrenees. I stare blankly at the page, feeling myself drift off into sleep.

Suddenly I'm wide awake again. The chestnut trees have gone, the children's voices faded. All I am aware of is the curious writing of the parchment. Suddenly I can *see* the message. There it is ... simple ... a 'boy-scout' code. I begin to spell it out.

'This treasure belongs to ...'

But ... this is *too* simple. Why hasn't the author of my paperback said anything about it? It's fun – it's exciting – it doesn't give away any vital details. Surely he must have found it. He has hinted at much more complex ciphers waiting to be found. If he has looked at all, he can't have missed this one. After all, what I've found is merely a carrot – a teaser. Something that says: 'You're on the right lines. There *are* hidden messages. Keep looking.' I look. I count letters. I try reading them backwards – then vertically – then every second one – then every third one. But the sun is hot.

There is a yell and something thuds into the grass beside me. The children have left the stream and I'm in imminent danger of being brained by a missile from the over-enthusiastic game of *pétanque* which has started. 'Sorry. We didn't realise you were working.' Working? Hell – they're right. Already my ever-present pad is covered with scribbled notes. I abandon *The Accursed Treasure*. After all … I *am* supposed to be on holiday. I ought to know myself better. This sort of puzzle is not one I can leave alone.

After dinner we sit under the canopy of vines on the little terrace, looking out across 'our' empty, peaceful valley. The nine children continue to expend their limitless energy by the stream, communicating in their extraordinary, but to them perfectly comprehensible mixture of the two tongues. The conversation of the adults is light, inconsequential and at the same time absorbed and attentive.

The beginnings of what will become a deep friendship are growing between we two couples. It will increase each year in the few short summer weeks we shall henceforth spend together. These after-dinner conversations are the time for filling in the history of the past years; exploring each others' thoughts, reactions, feelings; building a store of memories to tide over till the next *grandes vacances* – and perhaps starting a train of common interest which we can carry through into the letters we will write during the winter.

My 'discovery' of this afternoon is an inevitable topic. I show them my paperback – tell them I have found a message in the parchment – one that's not revealed in the book. Cécile is a crossword addict, I know this sort of game with words will appeal to her. She and Michel take no longer than I did to crack the code, once I have shown them the key. Patricia, as I expect, is more interested in the background story than in the specific puzzle. I sketch in for them the curious tale of the Lost Gold of Rennes-le-Château, as I have gleaned it from the book. The children wander back and sit listening. My older boy asks if this is 'something new I'm cooking up for kid's TV?' He is the only one old enough to remember the fictional treasure hunt serial I wrote some years ago. The youngsters' eyes widen when I tell them: 'No. This time the treasure seems to be for real.' Buried treasure! A *real* buried treasure – and Dad's solved one of the clues! The children examine my evidence, then go into a huddle with the book to see what they can find. Somebody asks if I intend to write a programme about it. At this early stage I certainly have no such plan. But the idea has been planted – it is bound to grow.

For the remainder of the holiday *Le Trésor Maudit* is passed from hand to hand. Everybody hopes to be the first to find the next clue. But nothing materialises. With the end of summer in the Cévennes, the drive home with our friends to their lovely little city of Vendôme on the Loir and then the sadness of parting till next year – everything is moving me back to my 'ordinary' pressured world of television. *The Accursed Treasure* is becoming one of the parcel of holiday memories. The 'reality' of scripts and deadlines is about to take over again. But … packed into a grip and into one of the corners of my mind is that paperback with its strange half-told story. Sometime or other I will have to come back to it.

Chapter Two
1970: CHRONICLE

FOR MORE THAN A YEAR, the story simmers in the back of my mind. Occasionally I pick up the book and amuse myself for an hour or two, teasing at the puzzle. But more and more clearly I see that research – and fairly deep research – will be necessary if I am to arrive at any of the answers to the rapidly multiplying number of questions in my mind. Then, a hardback illustrated edition of the book comes my way. Now I have photographs of the village, the people, the countryside, the curious church where the mysterious parchments were found. This new visual material and the very captions to the pictures themselves raise a totally new crop of questions. The idea of a television programme on the story begins to take a firmer hold.

Certainly, if the mystery could move from the 'amusement' to the 'work' side of my life it would provide the opportunity for the necessary research. I would no longer need to feel the twinge of guilt when I allow the story to occupy time which should have been spent more 'productively'. But thus far my writing has been devoted to the fictional world of the television drama series. This programme – even more unlikely-seeming than some of the wilder of my own plots – must be treated factually. A documentary approach is the only possible way.

The BBC's *Chronicle* programme seems to be the right place for this story. *Chronicle* deals with subjects of historical and archaeological interest, investigating current work and exploring interesting stories, characters, events of the past. Paul Johnstone is in charge. Fortunately, I have known Paul for a number of years although we have never worked together. I telephone his office and make an appointment 'for a chat about a possible programme idea'. I realise that many of the slightly sensational and speculative aspects of the story are not suitable for *Chronicle*'s format – but there is sufficient interest in the history and background. And I am certain that my decipherment of the parchment's 'schoolboy' code can be splendidly visualised on the small screen. So, in mid-November 1970, I settle down in Paul's office with a cup of coffee and a list of half-a-dozen notes. The facts as I need to recite them at this stage are relatively simple.*

In 1891, Bérenger Saunière the impoverished young priest of the tiny French village of Rennes-le-Château found four parchments in a hollow pillar in his church. Shortly after the discovery he made a trip to Paris to consult experts on the content of the mysterious documents.

Thereafter, and for the twenty-five years until his death in 1917, the priest lived the life of a millionaire. He bought land, built houses, renovated his church, made charitable gifts, etc. etc. etc. Did the parchments lead him to the discovery of a treasure? Did he in some way cash in on it? And – more importantly from the point of view of a possible *Chronicle* programme – what could the treasure have been?

Not surprisingly, this is the aspect on which Paul questions me most closely. I outline the historical trail that is there to be followed. It provides a very startling answer to the question of what the treasure might possibly be. And it provides my suggested title for the programme: *The Lost Treasure of Jerusalem . . .?* But Paul has sat behind his desk listening on countless occasions to equally startling but utterly unfounded theories. One vital question still needs to be answered. Even accepting that a valid historical case can be made out for the theory that a tiny French village may be the hiding place of an important historical treasure – is this enough to make a television programme? Theories do not necessarily make pictures.

Now comes my *pièce de résistance*. I show Paul a copy of one of the mysterious parchments reproduced in my now well-thumbed paperback. The text is Latin – clear and not at all ambiguous – a passage from John's Gospel. He examines it for a few moments, then looks up at me with a slow grin. 'Come on, Hen. What have you got up your sleeve?'

I show him the simple key to the hidden message and leave him to work it out for himself. A couple of minutes of silence while Paul jots down letters, then reads the result. A DAGOBERT II ROI ET A SION EST CE TRESOR ET IL EST LA MORT – (This treasure belongs to Dagobert II king and to Sion and he is there dead).

---

* The quarter century and more that has passed has wrought many changes in the basic 'facts'. At this first meeting I knew little more than what de Sède had written. H.L.

(11)

Bérenger Saunière, in all his finery, on the day of the dedication of his flamboyant new church decorations.

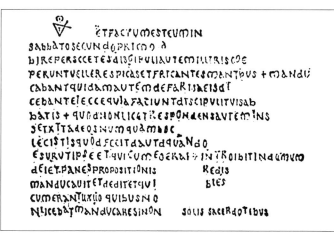

The parchment with the Dagobert message.

'Well, well ...' 'Intriguing, isn't it?' 'It's certainly that, my boyo.' 'And that decipherment will make a marvellous sequence for animation.' Paul nods and thinks. 'All right. There's enough to gamble on a trip to Paris. Let's talk to the author of your paperback. If it still sounds good, we'll think about a possible programme.'

CHRISTMAS WEEK 1970: PARIS

Gérard de Sède, the French author, has been tracked down and has agreed to see us. On the Monday I fly over, having arranged to meet him at the *Deux Magots* Bar near St Sulpice. Paul is to follow on the Tuesday. I make my way to the *Deux Magots* for my 6.30 appointment. Paris is looking as beautiful as ever and, in Christmas week, the festive air adds to my feeling of exhilaration at what might prove to be the start of an interesting and exciting project. At the bar I enquire of one of the waiters and de Sède is pointed out to me. He is a stocky, well-built man, dark, with an open-seeming face and questioning eyes. He looks up as I approach his table and smiles. 'M. Lincoln ...?' The brief formalities are soon over – some wine appears and we begin to sound each other out.

The second parchment.

Like myself, he is a professional writer and so cannot but be interested in the possibility of the BBC wishing to enlist his co-operation on a programme to be based on his *Trésor Maudit*. He expresses his willingness to co-operate and we talk in general terms about the way I intend to handle the programme. This leads me nearer to one of the key questions

I have been longing to ask ever since, under the chestnut trees of the Cévennes, I had seen the 'hidden message' staring me in the face. The inevitable preliminary formality has slipped away. We are now two writers having a professional discussion. I judge the moment to be right and put my question: 'M. de Sède – why didn't you publish the message in the parchment?'

And now occurs the first of the curious tiny hints that the story of the treasure of Rennes-le-Château is not going to be such a straightforward piece of television reportage. He looks at me for a moment. There is a barely perceptible fraction of a pause. Then: 'What message …?' Suddenly I find myself reluctant to speak the message aloud. 'The message that is very, very easy to find.' We are each aware of the cautious fencing that has begun. We continue the game for a little longer until each is sure that we are both speaking of the same message – that we both know it – and know also that the other knows it. I repeat my question: 'Why didn't you publish it?' Again there is a pause. Finally I get my answer: 'Because we thought it might interest someone like you to find it for yourself.'

What on earth can he mean? And who are *we*? Something tells me not to pursue this oddity any further at this stage. This is after all only a preliminary meeting, getting to know each other, sizing each other up. Instead I show him another little decipherment which I have attempted. One which I don't take altogether seriously, but which is nonetheless interesting.* It is based on a reproduction in de Sède's book of a very strange inscription once on a grave in the cemetery of Rennes-le-Château. My interpretation of the grave inscription seems to take him completely by surprise. This is evidently something new to him. An animated discussion develops on the validity and significance of my reading. At last we part amicably enough, having arranged to meet for lunch on the following day, when Paul will have arrived from London.

There is a slightly unreal air about the Tuesday lunch. De Sède finds the idea of sampling English pub food amusing – and so we rendezvous at the newly opened 'Red Lion' in the Champs Elysées. Pints of English bitter beer and shepherd's pie … a discussion sometimes in French, sometimes in English, on the problem of presenting a very French story in the very English terms of the BBC.

As I stand at the bar ordering more beer, I find myself thinking that

---

* For this questionable 'decipherment', see *The Holy Place*, pp. 49–50. H.L.

this must be a foretaste of Britain's entry into the Common Market. Ah well ... I suppose there's something to be said for being a pioneer ... though I have a wistful longing for a cosy bistro lunch and a decent bottle of wine.

Over lunch, de Sède shows us some new documentation on the story. Paul listens and asks his careful questions while I file away in my mind the fresh snippets of information. Time is running short – my plane leaves at 6 p.m. – but I know that Paul will make no snap decisions. As I expect, when the meeting breaks up, Paul has promised to get in touch with de Sède 'when a decision has been made.'

Paul is staying in Paris for meetings on other *Chronicle* projects. We grab a cup of tea before I race for the airport and he voices some minor reservations which are still in his mind. Nevertheless, we both see a possible twenty-minute item for insertion in a magazine programme. We agree to think over the problems and consult on Paul's return to London. If the decision is to be 'yes', then it will mean immediate pressure to prepare for shooting in the early spring.

In the plane on the way back to London, I have the first opportunity for quiet reflection. I suddenly realise what I may be letting myself in for. This is no fictional drama script. I can't push this story around to suit myself. There can be no altering of plot to avoid difficulties. This story must be told in dramatic terms, yet fixed rigidly within the framework of known, provable facts and reasonable hypothesis. No cheating allowed. There's a lot of work to do ... and I haven't yet seen the village which is our prime location.

Two days later, Christmas Eve, Paul is back in London. He telephones me.

'Now that we've both had a chance to sleep on it – what are your feelings about the Rennes-le-Château story?'

'I still think it'll work, Paul. A lot depends on the locations and what visual material we can turn up.'

'I agree. Right. We'll go for a twenty to thirty minute magazine item. Come in to the office next week; you'd better meet the laddie who'll direct it for you. Young, enthusiastic – you'll like him. I think you'd better aim for a recce trip to the village early in February. We'll shoot end of March.'

'As soon as that?'

'Soon? You've got all of six weeks to sort things out. Merry Christmas.'

I put down the phone and take a deep breath. I'd better start thinking about a draft script. I'll have to have something to discuss with my director when I meet him. Suddenly it's stopped being chat. I've got a documentary to write. Merry Christmas, indeed!

The festivities are coloured for me by my preoccupation with the mystery of Rennes-le-Château. Even so, I enjoy the usual over-large Christmas dinner and the fun of gift distribution around the decorated tree. But later in the afternoon the family notices my increasingly abstracted air and at last I slip away to my papers. Over the months to follow, they will grow used to a father who, even when he's present in the body, seems to be permanently miles away. Even at the very beginning, when I knew in fact very little of the story, I found it difficult to shake free of the mystery. It was all too easy to allow it to become an obsession.

As soon as the official holiday is over, I have my first meeting with my director. Andrew Maxwell-Hyslop is a tall, eager, intelligent young man. To my vast relief I discover that he can speak French and has taken the trouble to read de Sède's book during the Christmas break. No need to waste time explaining the story. He already has a mass of questions to ask, which I deal with as best I can. We discuss a possible shape for the programme and I promise to have the draft script roughed out before we make our recce trip – which is now fixed for the 19th to the 24th of February.

As I work on the draft I begin to learn the problems of writing a true story set in a real location. I can't invent pretty pictures to suit myself. The setting for this programme exists and I must write my script in such a way that full advantage is taken of what is there. I find myself threshing around in a morass of ignorance. Exactly how big is Rennes-le-Château? Where is the church in relation to the château? Can I get them both into the same shot? And where, for example, is the Devil's Armchair – the strange rock which apparently has some mysterious significance? Is it close to the village? Or will we have to devote an entire half-day to getting to it, filming, and getting back? Our shooting time will be limited.

If any of the locations are impossibly remote, I may have to cut them from the script. A new crop of purely practical questions begins to grow. And there is no way of finding the answers until I have actually seen the village with my own eyes.

FEBRUARY–MARCH 1971: RECONNAISSANCE TRIP

I can feel the excitement bubbling beneath the surface when I meet Andrew at the Airport Coach Terminal on the afternoon of 19 February. For both of us, the excitement is mixed with an eagerness to get on with the job – and a certain trepidation. We're on our way – committed – but what are we going to find?

The BBC is allowing Andrew to try his wings for the first time alone. There will be no senior eye to keep watch on this trip. But Paul feels that, with 'an old hand' like myself for company, there shouldn't be any really major problems. The 'old hand' doesn't altogether share Paul's confidence. This may be my one hundred and fourth script for television – but the story is still in a totally new area for me. One hundred and three drama scripts don't necessarily teach one how to set up a good documentary. Especially with a story as complicated as this one. As we fly to Paris, director and writer are both aware that this is the beginning of the testing time. Neither of us can afford to mess up this programme.

The plan is to spend a relaxed evening in Paris before taking an early train next morning as far as Toulouse, where a hired car will be waiting for us. Simple. But I'm about to learn that trips abroad with a lot of work to cram into a limited time are never simple. Minor annoyances can develop into major crises – and plans can be upset by a change in the weather. I'm to learn to thank God for my peculiar sense of humour.

The first 'nonsense' occurs – though we're not aware of it at the time – as soon as we set foot on the pavements of Paris. It's late. I'm first off the airport coach and am hailing a taxi as the luggage is being off-loaded. The taxi pulls up, I grab my grip, Andrew his case and we're off to our hotel. We book in, dump our bags and set out to find a cosy restaurant for a quiet dinner. At about 1 a.m., pleasantly relaxed, back to the hotel. I prepare for bed and suddenly Andrew finds that he can't unlock his suitcase. We examine the key and the case. The awful truth dawns. It's not his case. Same size – same colour – but unquestionably not the same case. Andrew sinks slowly onto his bed.

'All my notes … the stills camera … the view-finder … What the hell can we do?'

'At one thirty in the morning? Nothing. Get to bed and sleep.'

'But, Henry – you don't seem to understand. Someone's got my case. They might be travelling on anywhere. All my stuff might be half-way across Europe by now!'

'Unlikely. Whoever it is will have stood by the coach waiting for his case to be unloaded. When all the luggage had been claimed, your case would have been left over. He – or she – will have realised what's happened. Your case will be locked in the coach terminal office. And I'll bet there's one rather fed-up traveller who's hung about hoping you'll realise your mistake and get back there.'

'I'd better do that.'

'Now? It's too late. Phone by all means – but I think you'll find the terminal will be shut for the night.'

It is. Nothing more can be done until, we guess, about 7.30 in the morning. Our train leaves at 08.57. We agree that, should there be any trouble about retrieving Andrew's case, I will travel on alone, pick up the car at Toulouse, try to do some racing around on my own and then get back to collect Andrew at the end of the day. Already our carefully worked out timetable is beginning to look not quite so reliable.

After a sleepless night, Andrew hares off to the coach terminal while I check us out of the hotel and make my way to the Gare d'Austerlitz. I'm not exactly looking forward to a solitary seven-hour train journey, but at least I'm learning a valuable lesson. With the story of Rennes-le-Château, nothing is ever going to be simple and straightforward. In the event the case is indeed locked in the coach terminal office. Vastly relieved and looking remarkably fresh despite his lack of sleep, Andrew arrives at the station in good time, clutching his suitcase and having left a note of profuse apology to the other unfortunate traveller.

The train journey through France is enjoyable but fatiguing. At 4.30 we reach Toulouse and set off immediately to find our hire car. Luckily the Hertz office is close by the station and I notice, with some alarm, that already the evening rush hour is beginning. We can't afford to wait for it to subside. We have to get to Carcassonne, almost a hundred kilometres away. There is someone we need to see – this evening, if possible.

As I've had more experience of driving on the 'wrong' side of the road, Andrew suggests that I should take the wheel. Suddenly I realise that I'm faced with yet more practical problems. Although I've driven many miles on the Continent, it has always been in my own, English, car. Now for the first time I'm to plumb the mysteries of the left-hand drive – and in a strange city – and in rush hour. First, however, there is another small difficulty to resolve. The BBC has failed to provide the correct letter of authority for the car hire firm. Complicated negotiations ensue, but after half an hour or so (more precious time dribbling away), we get the keys and are taken to the car. It's parked with inches to spare in a narrow side street leading straight out into the busy main concourse in front of the railway station. I settle behind the wheel, grope for the gear lever with the unaccustomed right hand and edge my way out into the maelstrom of traffic. Andrew's touching faith in my ability to cope with car, traffic and French driving gives me a certain determined confidence. In a surprisingly short time, thanks to Andrew's inspired navigating and signpost spotting, we are out on the empty open road and bowling down to Carcassonne.

'One must not die without seeing Carcassonne,' goes the old saying – and for years I had been determined one day to pay a visit to that incredible walled citadel. Now, here I am on my way – yet all my thoughts are concentrated on a tiny, unprepossessing hill-top village just a few miles further on up the valley of the River Aude. Even so, in the evening light, that first glimpse of Carcassonne is breathtaking. Battlements, towers and turrets – a mediaeval fairy-tale city silhouetted against a green-gold sky. One feels almost cheated when the sudden glinting in the massive gateway is not the gleam of armour, but the headlights of a car. The twentieth century sits incongruously within those massive walls. Andrew and I indulge in five minutes of being 'tourists'. We take photographs, admire the view and react in that especially euphoric way which all travellers experience when they come upon a place like Carcassonne for the first time. But five minutes is all we can spare. We have a call to make.

We have been given an introduction to Mme Lily Devèze who is guide historian in the Old City and who is naturally steeped in the history of the region. This evening we intend merely to introduce ourselves and ask when it will be convenient for her to grant us an interview. But we have not reckoned on her generous hospitality. Within moments, we are settled in arm chairs, enjoying a glass of wine and the friendliness of Mme Devèze's welcome.

Yes, she knows a little of the 'Mystery of Rennes-le-Château', though she has never visited the village. I voice my small worries and ask her advice on a problem I have been thinking about ever since we left London. It is essential for us to see the interior of the church, but I know that often in small villages – and especially remote and isolated villages – the inhabitants can be very suspicious of strangers. Rennes-le-Château must inevitably have had its share of treasure hunters and we know that they are not welcome. What sort of reception will we two foreigners get? In February we can hardly pass as chance tourists. If the doors are closed to us, what strategy can Mme Devèze advise? The answer is simple. Mme Devèze, as an accredited guide, carries official papers which give her access to all Public Monuments. To our great delight, she offers to accompany us on our first visit to Rennes-le-Château. The only question remaining is – when? With limited time at our disposal, we had intended making for the village first thing tomorrow morning – Sunday. Happily this suits. She has the day free and is prepared to devote it to us.

Chapter Three
RENNES-LE-CHATEAU:
FIRST IMPRESSIONS

AFTER A COMFORTABLE NIGHT in a pleasant hotel in Carcassonne, we duly present ourselves at 10 a.m. to collect our guide. Five minutes later we are on our way. At long last I am about to see Rennes-le-Château for the first time. The hour-long drive seems a fitting introduction. As we follow the valley of the Aude, the countryside grows wilder and more rugged. It is climbing towards the distant snow-capped Pyrenees. The road hugs the riverside, curving and twisting through craggy gorges of harsh grey rock – dull olive coloured vegetation and occasional glimpses of the racing grey-green river spattered with chopped white foam around scattered rocks. Thickly wooded hillsides skirt the road – filled with secret shadows beneath the bright sunlight. One can believe that nearby, yet out of sight, may lie an unguessed world of mystery. We pass through Limoux – a pleasant little town which produces a delicious sparkling white wine, *La Blanquette de Limoux*, which deserves a far greater fame than it enjoys. Then on through Alet-les-Bains, much smaller and much prettier than Limoux and with the ruins of an impressive and ancient cathedral. And then, at last, Couiza.

I know that we are almost there and yet, so far, there has been no indication – no distant view of Rennes-le-Château – no signpost with its name. No hint that one is now only minutes away from what must be one of France's most curious villages. I slow down as we enter Couiza, turning right into the town, crossing the bridge over the river almost at walking pace as we search for the signpost to direct us to Rennes-le-Château. And suddenly, there it is. A tiny road slips off to the left between a stone wall and a high bank ... 'RENNES-LE-CHATEAU – 4.4km'. Immediately the road

The Tour Magdala.

begins to climb steeply upward. As it turns and turns on itself, hugging the mountainside, an amazing view begins to open up. To the south, the great bowl of a plain, rimmed in the distance by mountains and behind them, far off, the Pyrenees, their snowcaps startlingly fiery in the clear sunlight. To the east and much closer – a few miles only – soars the Peak of Cardou, 'The Eagle's Nest', with strange craggy rock outcrops hanging on its flanks. The river below us winds towards Cardou. On the other side of the valley to the north is the enormous shattered ruin of the Castle of Coustaussa, once guardian of the valley approach.

But at each new bend in the road, our eyes turn upward, looking for that first glimpse of Rennes-le-Château. One mile. Two. Still we climb and still no sight of the village. This is truly '*une ville perdue*' – a lost city. Then – totally unexpectedly – a little battlemented tower juts from the hilltop, poised delicately over the valley. The tower doesn't seem to belong. It hasn't yet grown into the landscape. It looks like what it is – a rich man's folly. I recognise it immediately from the photographs I have seen. It is the Tour Magdala, built by the principal character in our story, Bérenger Saunière, the impoverished country priest who became '*Le Curé aux Milliards*'. A twist in the road and the tower has disappeared again. A few more turns and there are the houses. Unprepossessing – a typical village of Southern France.

Except for the sign on the wall. Crudely painted, blue scrawl on a white board: 'Fouilles Interdites' – 'Excavating prohibited'.

Excavating? To the casual visitor not knowing the golden legend, there must come immediately the question: what could there possibly be to dig for amongst this tiny cluster of ramshackle houses which huddle round their equally tiny church and unimpressive château? But we, who already know part of the amazing story, have come – like so many before us – to find the answer to that question. To see, on his home ground, if we can gain sufficient insight into the character of Bérenger Saunière to unravel any more of the Mystery of Rennes-le-Château. As I edge the car round the last bend and into the village itself, I am surprised to find how tiny the place is – and how apparently deserted. The streets are empty and silent, save for a couple of watchful cats. A small board nailed to a wall indicates a parking place. It directs us up a narrow road. The car has only inches to spare between the houses. Then, suddenly, ahead of us, I see the entrance to the church. It is much smaller than I had imagined from the photographs. Even so, it is not a disappointment. A few yards before reaching the church door, the road turns sharp left and we are driving past the Villa Bethania, another familiar building. This is the large house built by the Abbé Bérenger Saunière and in which he entertained his guests. Now it is the Hotel La Tour. Just beyond the Villa is the small car park, beyond which is the extraordinary folly, the Tour Magdala. I park the car and we get out and look around us.

High above the valley, the village enjoys an amazingly beautiful panorama. In every direction, but especially southwards towards the Pyrenees, there is a vista which alone makes the long climb worth while. Rennes-le-Château has two treasures – the curé's gold and its breathtaking mountain-top setting. From the film-maker's point of view this is an incredibly valuable bonus. Saunière, after all, might have been the priest of a grubby and uninspiring industrial parish. The backdrop to our story is everything that could be wished. But for almost every visitor, the view is only of secondary importance to the mystery. And on this, my first visit, I have to admit that my mind turns away from the beauties of the landscape in search of the traces of Bérenger Saunière.

As we stand by the car, the door to Saunière's Villa Bethania opens. A small, dark, neat and smiling man comes towards us – the first human being we have seen in the village. Here is a man who is to become a dear friend. Charming, affable, well-read and, of course, steeped in the story of Bérenger

The newly built Villa Bethania with the church tower to the right. Saunière and his housekeeper, Marie, are beside the fountain and in the background his dog, Pomponnet, can be glimpsed in his kennel.

Saunière, this is Henri Buthion, hotelier, the present owner of the Hotel La Tour.

Mme Devèze, in her role as guide, takes over the formalities. Identities are established and we arrange to lunch at the hotel after a preliminary look around. My fears of possible difficulties prove groundless. M. Buthion produces the key to the church and we begin our tour. He is an accomplished guide around his domain. In the couple of years since the publication of *Le Trésor Maudit*, he has grown used to the small summer crop of French tourists, each clutching his copy of the paperback and each with his own theory on the whereabouts of the curé's treasure. However, for the moment, we are not looking for treasure. Andrew and I are hunting for camera angles and locations. We already have an idea of some of the things we are to see from the illustrations in de Sède's book. But yet again I am to find that even my apparently straightforward ideas and deductions from this evidence are not totally reliable. My first few hours at Rennes-le-Château are to provide yet more of those curious tiny hints that the story is not by any means straightforward.

Before going into the church we visit the little graveyard. Like all French cemeteries, it has an alien air to English eyes. The bare brown earth and imitation flowers present a gloomy picture of death. Nowhere is there the green charm and ordered calm tranquillity that can be found in some English country churchyards. At the far end, against the wall, M. Buthion tells us, is the grave of Bérenger Saunière himself. From a distance I think I can recognise it. De Sède's book has a picture which, according to the caption, is the tomb of Saunière with, in front of it, an excavation made in 1966. Featured prominently in the photograph is a large rectangular tomb – in the foreground is a deep hole ... the excavation of 1966. I had imagined that this large tomb was that of Saunière. I stroll over to it and immediately I am taken aback to see the memorial inscription for quite a different person. M. Buthion sees my puzzlement. Smiling he indicates a spot some yards away to my right. 'He's over there.'

And, indeed, there is the curé's resting place. Small – a simple stone cross raised above a narrow flat stone which lies along the grave. Broken, partly overgrown; weathering and accumulated earth and leaves make the lettering hard to decipher: 'ICI REPOSE BERENGER SAUNIERE', but it's at the *other side* of the hole which, the photograph's caption implies, could be an attempt at 'tomb robbing'.

Looking again at the book, I see that Saunière's grave is not even visible in the illustration. An error? Perhaps. It's certainly another of the odd anomalies which I'm beginning to collect.*

We move on to visit the church. It is dedicated to St Marie-Madeleine – Mary Magdelene – who, legend tells us, came to France bringing the 'true Cross' and the Grail. Her statue, bearing in her arms the Cross and Grail, stands above the church entrance. Beneath her feet, Saunière has carved the daunting admonition: TERRIBILIS EST LOCUS ISTE – This place is terrible.† (More thought-provoking is another phrase carved upon the porch: DOMUS MEA DOMUS ORATIONIS VOCABITUR – My house shall be called the House of Prayer. This quotation is completed in Matthew 21 xiii with the words: 'But ye have made it a den of thieves.')

---

* Saunière's simple grave is now, inevitably, somewhat embellished. The stone is embedded in an uncompromising raft of concrete, upon which a large bas-relief of the good curé looks quizzically down. H.L.

† Some visitors to Rennes-le-Château read an unnecessarily sinister meaning into these words, which are taken from the Book of Genesis 28 xvii and refer to the place where Jacob dreamt of the ladder ascending into heaven. The Mass for the dedication of a church begins with this phrase. I have also seen it affixed to the wall of the Temple Mount in Jerusalem. H.L.

Just inside the church door, the holy water stoup is supported by a devil of startling ugliness. Hideous and deformed, he crouches by the entrance, his glass eyes wide and staring, his face contorted into a silent scream of hate. To come upon him unexpectedly would be something of a shock. However, again de Sède's illustrations have prepared us and I am surprised to see how small he is. I had pictured him as being life-size, but he is barely half my height. The decrease in size seems to diminish his menace.

The church interior is very small and very dark, with just the tiny blood-red glimmer of the lamp at the altar. Henri Buthion turns on the lights for us and immediately everywhere there is the gleam of gold. All around us is an incredible, detailed mass of decoration. Statues, pictures, every wall surface – everything is painted and where possible gilded. The total effect is overpowering and bordering on vulgarity. There is no delicacy here. Rather a flamboyant expression of enormous vitality, sliding toward bad taste, garish, yet somehow retaining an odd attraction. In its flamboyance and gaudy charm, it seems to echo Saunière's character. Perhaps it should. All this decoration was done to his directions. This is his statement.

We spend half an hour or so examining the details. I begin to make notes and take photographs. Andrew concentrates on the directorial problems of camera angles and lighting. Then, while he goes outside with the others to look for his exterior shots, I settle myself into one of the pews. Here, at last, is my first opportunity to sit quietly and soak up the atmosphere of Bérenger Saunière's church.

These few minutes of solitary silence produce the most surprising and unexpected of my discoveries so far. My attempt to absorb atmosphere is fruitless. There is none. I am puzzled. Every ancient building – and in particular every old place of worship – that I have ever visited imparts its own 'feel'. That purely subjective, but nonetheless tangible, sense of the past; of the weight of years which the stones have accumulated. Like many people who visit this now famous little church for the first time, I had half expected an air of menace, perhaps. Or a sense of something sinister. Or, at the least, of something 'uncomfortable'. Certainly I expected the centuries of prayer to have left their mark. But here ... nothing. The place is a blank. Inert and dead, the faces of the statues are blind and remote. Their staring painted eyes are truly sightless. There is nothing for them to see. The phantasmagoric mass of garish detail swamps any sense of meaning. There is no coherence – not even in the fourteen Stations of the Cross. Each detail seems separate, as if each has its own separate meaning to

Saunière beside the pillar.

convey, but of atmosphere – nothing. The church stands calm and filled with emptiness, as though it has been sucked dry.

At last I escape into the bright February sunlight. The others are looking at the Visigothic pillar in whose hollow interior Saunière supposedly found his mysterious parchments. The pillar has been moved to a small garden in front of the church porch, where it serves as support for a statue of the Virgin.* Looking at the intricately carved stone, I am struck by the incongruity of the new carving which Saunière has added to its surface. 'PENITENCE PENITENCE' 'MISSION 1891'. I find it hard to understand why anyone with a sense of history, as Saunière apparently had, should wish to deface so ancient a relic in this way. An odd, but simple explanation comes

---

* Moved again in 1994 to the village museum, for fear of vandalism (or worse). The move established again the unreliability of de Sède's information. The pillar is *not* hollow. The shallow mortice-hole in its surface is too small for the concealment of the hollow tube which, allegedly, contained the parchments. A wooden newel-post is now displayed in the museum as the 'real' hiding place. But this too, lacking proof, is very questionable. H.L.

into my mind. By carving writing onto it, he has given it a 'top' and a 'bottom'. Now there is only one 'right way up'. Perhaps he is making us look at it 'wrongly'? (This rather foolish-seeming thought leads me later to check on Visigothic and Merovingian art – of which I am totally ignorant. My hunch is proved to be possibly correct when I discover that the carved Cross with pendant Alpha and Omega is a recurrent device in Visigothic art – and here, indeed, Saunière's inscription is making us look at it upside down. Another oddity.)

Over lunch we discuss the story with Henri Buthion. He is delighted by our plan to make a film for the BBC and is quite sure that we will receive full co-operation from the village. Problems and uncertainties seem to be growing less. We talk on as the afternoon slips away. The food is too good to hurry over and, besides, it is important to us to have M. Buthion's good will. He is full of anecdotes and local stories concerning Bérenger Saunière and the hunt for his treasure. Some interesting new ideas are added to my list of notes. At last we leave, more than satisfied with our first visit to Rennes-le-Château, made undeniably easier by Lily Devèze's skilled 'oiling of the wheels'. Andrew and I arrange to return early next morning, to spend a long working day reconnoitring the relevant sites. To our great delight, a room is to be prepared for us in the Villa Bethania. Tomorrow night we shall sleep *chez* Bérenger Saunière.

CAMERA PROBLEMS

Any detailed investigation will throw up odd coincidences. The preparatory work on the story of Rennes-le-Château is no exception, though some months are to pass before 'coincidence' piled on 'coincidence' begins to make me look for some other explanation. But, coincidence apart, this long Monday is to produce the first of a small crop of odd occurrences which I have always firmly left in the pigeon-hole of 'pure chance'. This is the attempt to photograph details in the church of a neighbouring village, which demonstrates yet again the apparent inevitability of snags on every facet of this story.

The day we have planned is to be a very active one. A lot of ground must be covered – numerous sites checked for accessibility and visual usefulness. Very early in the morning, Andrew and I leave our hotel in Carcassonne and return to Rennes-le-Château to deposit our bags and check exact map references with Henri Buthion. There is to be some scrambling over rough mountainous country, so we change into stout walking shoes and pack our gear into rucksacks. As we sit in the car making last minute checks before leaving the village, M. Buthion appears with a picnic to sustain us until we return in the evening. And what a picnic! Yet a third treasure of Rennes-le-Château is Henri Buthion's superb cuisine.* Our day is loosely planned. It is impossible to tell how long some of the sites may take to reach.

The village of Rennes-les-Bains is high on our list of priorities. Its church and cemetery have pictures, grave inscriptions and memorials of interest. Rennes-les-Bains is a health resort where hot springs and mineral rich water serve a modern hospital, as they once served the baths of a Roman spa. Saunière's story has threads which reach back into the distant past and so visual evidence of ancient occupation of the area is of great value to us.

Rennes-les-Bains proves to be a complete contrast to her sister village of Rennes-le-Château. Here there are no immense mountain-top views. The spa hugs the river in the depths of a steep and wooded valley. Quaint bridges link the straggling lines of houses on either side of the river. Beneath the run-to-seed Victorian *Thermes Romains* hotel the river steams where hot springs pour into the icy water, providing a still useful place for the local housewives to do their weekly wash. The tiny square with its dusty trees is quiet and sleepy. Elderly people sit in doorways or on stone parapets. Invalids in wheelchairs, patients at the hospital, gossip quietly in the shade. Even in February, the days can be bright and warm in this part of the world.†

We find the church just off the little village square. We make a hurried inspection, but it is very dark inside and the paintings which, it has been suggested, may have details of interest to us, are all but invisible. We decide to waste no more time here for the moment, but to set off immediately to find the Devil's Armchair – a rock on the plateau above Rennes-les-Bains which seems to have links with the strange devil in Saunière's church. As we will have to pass through Rennes-les-Bains on our way back, we decide

---

* Henri Buthion, as well as his *Hotel & Restaurant la Tour*, are now long gone from Rennes-le-Château. H.L.

† Rennes-les-Bains was struck by a disastrous flood in September 1992. The level of the river rose from 8 centimetres to 8 metres in the space of a couple of hours. Behind the village church, the cemetery was devastated. The side was ripped from the *Thermes Romains*, as well as from many other buildings. The hotel has now lost its air of decay and has been repaired and fiercely modernised. H.L.

to revisit the church and take our photographs when, we hope, the light may have improved.

Just outside the village we find the tiny, almost invisible track up the mountain side which Henri Buthion has marked on our map as the way up to the Devil's Armchair. I tuck the car into a patch of shade by a small stone parapet and, shouldering our gear, we set off up the tree-canopied path. The going is hard and rough, the track dividing constantly, heavily overgrown and growing steeper with every turn. Pauses for breath become more and more frequent and I can feel my sweater becoming sodden with perspiration. I curse at not having brought any lightweight summer clothing – but then, this *is* February. My rucksack gets heavier and conversation dries up as we save our breath for the dogged slog up the hillside.

During one of our pauses, Andrew helps me find a new burst of energy by remarking: 'You seem to be quite fit for a man of your age.' A man of my age? One would think I was in my dotage! The rucksack is suddenly lighter. I charge on ahead at a speed which borders on folly, muttering into my beard a string of clichés on the general theme – 'as old as one feels'. However, as my pace begins to slacken again, I decide to accept Andrew's remark in the complimentary spirit in which it was intended. After all, I *am* almost old enough to be his father. Not quite … but almost. And my sole exercise is usually the daily walk to my car. Yes, I suppose I *am* quite fit for a man of my age. Here I am, halfway up a Pyrenee and not totally in a state of collapse. Not yet. Even so … *my* age, indeed!*

The trees thin out into a clearing. There it is. A huge grey boulder hollowed out very neatly into the form of an armchair. Its size gives almost the impression of a throne. Momentarily, I am uncertain if we have found the right spot. Somehow the rock doesn't look quite as I remember it from the illustration in de Sède's book. But Andrew finds a small and rotting wooden notice nailed to a tree: *Source du Cercle. Fauteuil du Diable.* 'Spring of the Circle. Devil's Armchair'. The small spring is beside us and there is nothing else around that could be the rock we are looking for. I walk around it, looking for an angle which will match my memory of the photograph while Andrew ferrets in the rucksack for the book. But from no point does it look quite right. Andrew finds the page and immediately the explanation is obvious. 'Try standing on your head,' he says, 'de Sède's printed the picture upside down.' No wonder it doesn't look right. Probably another

---

* I was a youthful 41. H.L.

mistake – but certainly yet another addition to my now rapidly growing list of puzzling oddities.

The Devil's Armchair is a strange object. The hollow cut into it to form the seat is far too neat and regular to be natural. But why laboriously carve a seat into a rock on a remote and deserted hillside? There is no view of interest to be had from here. Perhaps it was once the site for meetings of some sort? A witches' coven perhaps? Or a druidic assembly? Who can tell? Nevertheless, from our point of view it is visually interesting and I know that I can link it into the pattern of treasure clues which will be part of our film. We discuss the feasibility of getting the camera crew and equipment up to the spot. It won't be easy and will take most of half a day to arrive, set up and film. We make our decision to include it in the shooting schedule and feel that we've earned a breather. I settle in the Devil's Armchair to demolish a good part of Henri Buthion's picnic. Then we take a few photographs and set off back to the car.

I am the first to arrive, to find a quartet of amiable old gentlemen sitting in the shade on the stone parapet beside which I have parked. I call out a *Bon Jour* to them, raising my hand in greeting. I am aware that my small camera is hanging from its strap around my wrist. I lean against the bonnet of the car and chat with the old men as I wait for Andrew to arrive. At last I hear him calling me from a short distance away up the hillside. He has found a possibly interesting angle on Rennes-les-Bains. I climb the short distance back along the path to join him. We consider the shot, decide against it and return to the car. In three minutes we are back in the square at Rennes-les-Bains. For the second time we will try to photograph the interior of the church.

As we begin to sort out our gear, I find that my camera is missing. We hunt methodically through the car. Nothing. More wasted time. I must have dropped it back where we had parked. Back into the car and up the road. The four old gentlemen are still taking the sun on the stone parapet. I park beside them again and ask if they have seen my camera. Yes, one of them says, he remembers it being on a strap around my wrist. The only possibility seems to be that I must have dropped it on the path when Andrew called me back to look at the view. We climb back to the spot. Not a trace. These first few yards of path are neat and bordered by short, stubby grass. Nowhere for a camera to lie concealed by undergrowth or rocks. But … nothing. We rejoin the old men who have been scouring the area around and under the car. But the camera has totally disappeared.

This is disastrous. Apart from the loss of the half dozen or so shots I've just taken, there is now no point in revisiting the church at Rennes-les-Bains. I must buy another camera. But where? The only hope, the old men tell me, is in Esperaza, a village back beyond Couiza. This is going to cost a good hour. I have never realised how precious time can be. And the loss of the camera will remain a totally unsolved mystery. However, this cloud proves to have the proverbial silver lining. The small photography shop in Esperaza is owned by the mayor of the village, Georges Basset. He is to become a good friend and provide some very useful information on the Saunière story. The purchase is hurriedly made and we race back towards Rennes-les-Bains. The light is going, so we decide to abandon the church until tomorrow. There are other locations still to find. Some strange standing stones and a couple of local springs are apparently related to the 'treasure clues'. Searching unsuccessfully for a spring called *La Source de la Madeleine*, we eventually spot a sign indicating *Fontaine des Amours* – the Lovers' Fountain. Could this be an alternative name for the spring we are hunting? It doesn't seem likely, but I decide to sprint down the hillside to look, while Andrew turns the car.

As soon as I see it, I know that this is not *La Source de la Madeleine*. However, as I am here, I decide to photograph it. I take one shot, but the light is bad and the angle worse. There is a large rock beside the river into which the spring flows. I clamber onto the rock – and find myself confronting my first independently discovered piece of local 'evidence' in support of the story as reported in de Sède's *Trésor Maudit*. The book had implied some sort of 'liaison' between Saunière and Emma Calvé, a world-famous prima-donna of the period. And here unexpectedly, at the Lovers' Fountain, I find that the rock onto which I have climbed bears a classic lovers' inscription – a heart transfixed by an arrow. Beneath it – E. CALVE with the date 1891. Strange. 1891 is the year of Saunière's alleged discovery of the parchments. It wasn't until a year or so later, apparently, that he met Emma Calvé. Even so, the inscription is a charming link with the story. I take photographs and, very pleased with my little discovery, I call Andrew to look at it. He is as pleased as I am and suggests that we return tomorrow, time permitting, to re-photograph when the light will be better.*

---

* The *Fontaine des Amours* is one of the most delightful of the locations in the area. There is no prettier spot for a picnic. H.L.

The inscription at the Lovers' Fountain.

This incident at the *Fontaine des Amours* is to prove rather more significant – and even disturbing – than we imagine. It is to be the first evidence
that our movements are being watched. And the watching eyes, it seems,
are unfriendly and even unscrupulous. Our return visit produces a shock.
The inscription is no longer there. It has been hacked from the rock. My
photograph (above) is the only evidence that the inscription ever existed.

But for now, unaware, we set off again, to find *La Source de la Madeleine*
in the fading light, to take our last photographs of the day and turn the
car in the direction of Rennes-le-Château. Tonight we shall sleep in Saunière's Villa Bethania.

A magnificent meal awaits us and an all-too-short evening of absorbing
Henri Buthion's first-hand knowledge of Rennes-le-Château. We must have
an early night. Tomorrow is to be the last day of our reconnaissance trip
and there is still a lot of ground to cover.

UN PETIT MIRACLE

I am awake with the dawn. The air is fresh and still. The view from my windows is almost too beautiful to be real. To the east, I find myself looking out at Saunière's tiny church, almost within touching distance. My other window looks south and a gentle pearly light of limpid clarity seems to pick out each tiny detail of the immense landscape. In moments it will be day. I dress hurriedly and make my way to the terrace beside the Tour Magdala. Sunrise at Rennes-le-Château is bound to be worth seeing.

In fact, as the light grows and the bright morning sun begins to spread sharp shadows across the countryside, I find a visual effect which is to become my favourite shot of the film. In the valley below the terrace to the west, a green field slowly conjures up a sharp black silhouette of Rennes-le-Château on its mountain-top. The crenellated Tour Magdala, the terrace, the conical glass Orangerie – all are laid out on the bright green with intense sharpness of detail. I photograph the view and at breakfast startle Andrew by begging him to undertake the persuasion of our camera crew to be out of bed before dawn in order to capture the 'shadow village' for the programme. I feel optimistic about the day. It has started well.

We still need to find a good 'long shot' of Rennes-le-Château with which to open the programme. We ask Henri Buthion where we can find a really interesting distant view which will show the isolation of the village. There's a spectacular one, he tells us, well to the south and on a range of hills at the far side of the plain. It's possible to drive almost all the way directly to it, though he doubts that our rather delicate hired car will enjoy the trip. Before we even have time to wonder if we might dare suggest it, Henri offers to take us in his own, rather more robust, vehicle. The final three-quarters of a mile must be climbed on foot. There is no track up the mountainside, but the going is relatively easy. Strung out in a line, we make our way up a not-too-steep slope towards a group of impressive stark white rock needles, which tower up on the crest. The view of Rennes-le-Château far off across the plain and framed between the jutting bare rocks, is perfect. Unfortunately, the location is too remote and time-consuming to include in our shooting schedule. We decide to compromise by losing the framing rocks, but getting a nearer view from below, on the plain. I begin to take the usual photographs which are my vital visual note-taking. Andrew moves off to take some shots from further along the ridge. Time, as ever, is limited.

Today we must try, for the third time, to photograph the interior of Rennes-les-Bains Church.

There is a sudden sharp cry of consternation from Andrew. He has taken his first shot and discovered that a knob has been lost from his camera. It is impossible to wind on the film. But this is ludicrous. I begin to feel that we are the victims of some mad conspiracy. Are we *never* to get our photographs of Rennes-les-Bains? We hunt about on the hillside, but the task is obviously hopeless. How to find a small black and silver object, one inch in diameter, on a rocky slope, when we can't even retrace our path with certainty? Without a track to follow, we had climbed haphazardly. I couldn't begin to pick out my own steps, let alone Andrew's. In any case, we have no idea at what stage of the climb the tiny part had been lost. Dejectedly we begin the scramble back down the mountainside.

More time must now be lost in the forlorn hope of tracking down a replacement for the missing part. Henri Buthion trudges beside me in silence. Then he says, in a matter-of-fact tone: 'Perhaps we should ask St Antoine l'Ermite for help? He's very good at finding lost things.' I have already, in my conversations with Henri, realised that he is a man of simple and honest piety. But the suggestion of invoking the aid of a saint to find a lost camera knob seems to me to be verging on superstition. I fleetingly consider making a joke on the lines: 'Why not? We've got nothing to lose.' But I'm not sure that the feeble humour will work in French and, anyway, as a joke it's pretty pathetic and I suspect that it would probably offend Henri. He meant what he said. We walk on for a while discussing practical matters. When do we expect to return with the camera crew? How many bedrooms will we require? Will we need to use the mains electricity for our lights?

Abruptly Henri breaks off the conversation and veers off across the rocky slope. I wonder where he is going. And then I see something glinting on the ground ahead of him, some fifteen or twenty feet away. Henri approaches it, then bends to examine the shiny object. He looks back at me. 'I told you St Antoine would help.' We hurry over to him as he bends to pick up the camera knob. This was unquestionably an enormous stroke of luck. Or was it? Smiling, Henri drops the tiny, glinting object into Andrew's hand. '*Voilà! Un petit miracle.*' There doesn't seem anything more to say.

And so – back to Rennes-le-Château. We say our farewells to Henri Buthion, happy in the knowledge that we will now find a firm friend in the village when we return in a few weeks for the filming. With another of Henri's gourmet picnics stowed in the car, we set off for our final reconnaissance. The enormous shattered ruin of Coustaussa Castle provides another distant view of Rennes-le-Château, framed in crumbling walls and ideal for our closing sequence. Then, at last, Rennes-les-Bains – and more curiosities.

De Sède's book has provided a plan of Rennes-les-Bains Church to illustrate an alignment of features which are, supposedly, significant. One of these features is a painting of Mary with the dead Christ.* This is known as *Le Christ au Lièvre* (the Christ of the Hare) as, according to de Sède, the right knee of Jesus resembles a hare's head. In conversation, he has given me the additional information that this painting has the curious detail of a hidden spider. This, he says, is a treasure clue in the form of a rebus. (Spider in French is *araignée* – and so, in the local accent – *à Rennes* which means 'at Rennes.') The 'hidden spider' is, he says, the Crown of Thorns in the bottom right-hand corner of the painting.

The first oddity which we notice is that de Sède's plan places the painting on the eastern wall of the side chapel, whereas it hangs on the western wall (and appears always to have done so). The walls of the church are black with the grime of decades. There is no reflected light, in fact, almost no light of any kind. The painting is all but invisible. Hoping for the best, I take flash photographs and trust they will enable me to examine the details later. De Sède's suggested 'alignment', already questionable with the mis-placing of the painting, supposedly begins from a lime tree in the cemetery. We hunt for the tree without luck. True, there are the stumps of trees which have been cut down in years past. But in the appropriate spot ... nothing. Yet another anomaly. It seems clear that we can take none of de Sède's account at face value. Everything must be checked and if it's not verifiable then, as we now see, it must be treated with extreme caution. Our recce trip has provided most of the answers we were looking for. It has also produced a host of new questions. This, as we are to learn, is the normality of Rennes-le-Château research. But for now, we are satisfied and head for home and the detailed work of preparing the script and shooting schedule.

Back in England, my photographs at last allow me to examine the interior details of Rennes-les-Bains Church. De Sède has told me that the rebus of

---

* This was later found to be a reversed, mirror-image copy of a painting by Van Dyck which is in the museum of Anvers. H.L.

the hidden spider is to be found in the bottom right-hand corner of the misplaced painting. My photograph shows that the Elements of the Passion – the three nails, the sponge etc – are indeed in the indicated place. According to de Sède, the Crown of Thorns is painted to resemble a spider. Now that my photograph enables me to see it clearly, it seems that an enormous effort of the imagination would be required to see the crown in this way. But, as I examine the details, I notice that there is, indeed, a spider-like form 'in the bottom right-hand corner'. A weed growing in the cleft of a rock can certainly be interpreted as 'spider-ish'. Such an interpretation is unquestionably subjective and therefore, in my terms, unreliable. Nevertheless, the correct shape in the place suggested by Sède, even though he has specified the wrong detail, gives me pause for thought. When I look for the supposed 'hare's head' on Christ's knee, I find that, again, such a subjective interpretation is possible from the shading in the paint. But I also notice that there is an even more prominent 'hare's head' in the blatantly unnatural depiction of Christ's right armpit. Why has no mention been made of this? And what possible significance can be wrenched from all these bizarre – and dubious – details? I begin to wonder how much of his information stems from his own knowledge and how much is simply the passing on of information provided by someone else. In my mind I hear the echo of his enigmatic statement at our first meeting: '*We* thought it might interest someone like you ...' Certainly, the hints are growing that the increasing number of anomalies may be indicating that de Sède is not the prime source of the story in his *Trésor Maudit*.*

As I work on the script, I spend much 'thinking time' in staring at Saunière's parchments, which are pinned to the wall above my desk. I notice that there are some irrelevant-seeming crosses interspersed among the letters of one of the documents and it is thus that I stumble upon a strange new addition to the dossier of 'secret messages'. The lay-out of the crosses leads me to the discovery of a remarkable geometric design upon which the writing has been ingeniously overlaid. The carefully structured pattern is that of a five-pointed star enclosed within a circle.† Why is it there? And what can it mean? At one of our frequent meetings, I show the new

---

* My photographs also reveal a wonderful detail in Rennes-les-Bains Church which has nothing to do with the Mystery. To the left of the door, is the Font in a small niche. In the gloom I have sensed rather than seen its details. Above the Font, the flash of my camera in the darkness has recorded a superb bas-relief of The Baptism of Jesus. A treasure 'worth the detour' H.L.

† For an explanation of the logic of this superlative design, see *The Holy Place*, pp. 27–31. H.L.

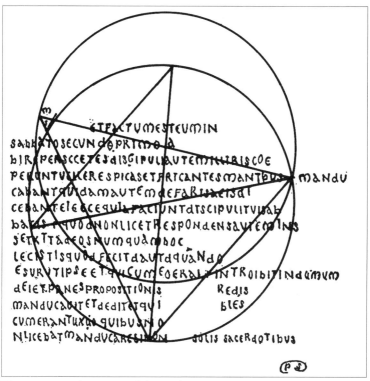

The geometric sub-structure of the parchment.

discovery to Andrew. He is as impressed as I am by the logic of the construction. But, like me, he can guess at no explanation, other than the well-known – and somewhat dubious – occult significance attached to the design in relation to magical operations, such as the 'raising of spirits'. This interpretation would seem rather to be raising an unnecessary hare, as far as our story is concerned and neither of us can see a way of incorporating it succinctly into the film. Years are to pass before the significance of this geometry is to become apparent. For the moment, it is a loose end and we must leave it dangling.

Chapter Four

FILMING:
AND A CHANGE OF PLAN

IN MARCH 1971, Andrew and I set off with our crew to film the short magazine item which Paul Johnstone is planning to use for a *Chronicle* programme later in the year. We have no idea that new revelations are to move the mystery of Rennes-le-Château in unexpected directions.

The first hints of what is to come pass almost unnoticed in the general flurry of activity. De Sède makes a fleeting visit to the village to watch us at work. In one of my conversations with him, he refers to a passage in his book which has always seemed to me to be an odd irrelevance. The passage describes how, during a fateful trip to Paris for the decipherment of the parchments, the priest Saunière had bought copies of a few paintings. One of these was the seventeenth-century masterpiece, *The Shepherds of Arcadia*, by Nicolas Poussin. This is the depiction of three shepherds and a shepherdess who contemplate a tomb in a mythical, Arcadian landscape.

When I had first read this in the paperback edition of de Sède's book, I had barely noticed it. The story seemed no more than a fleeting glimpse of one facet of Saunière's character and interests. The illustrated edition of *Le Trésor Maudit*, however, had drawn my attention more closely to this apparently simple anecdote. 'Throwaway' minor item it might be, but the author had seen fit to include the painting among the illustrations. Why go to the trouble and expense of having the picture reproduced when its relevance to the story merited only one short sentence? Now, de Sède tells me, someone has apparently found the location painted by Poussin. The tomb and landscape are not at all imaginary, it seems. Moreover, they are somewhere near Rennes-le-Château. De Sède claims to have no more precise information, however. His informant has promised to provide further details which he will send to us 'as soon as he has them'. This new curiosity is to be the bombshell which is to affect all our plans. The fuse is to be lit while we wait for the 'further details'.

Filming uneventfully over, the editing process now remains. Back in London, we begin to assemble all our carefully shot footage into a programme. As we do so, more information arrives from de Sède. This is in the unexpected form of a 'new' decipherment. My original 'boy-scout' code had been found in the shorter of the two documents supposedly found by Saunière. Now de Sède sends us the text of a message concealed in the scores of meaningless interpolated letters which I had long ago detected in the longer document. Once again, the earliest of all my questionings of the mystery echoes in my mind. 'Why do no decipherments appear in de Sède's book?' There was, it is true, a passage relating to work supposedly done by 'cipher experts'. Their conclusion was that the documents contain ciphered texts with 'a double-key substitution and a transposition worked on a chess-board pattern, with additional complications in the form of intentional errors designed to lead the decipherer onto false trails'. But how, I had wondered, could these conclusions have been reached without making a successful decipherment? And if such a decipherment had been made ... again ... why was it not published?

What are we to make of this new message? It is bizarre and largely incomprehensible. But it contains one vital and – now – resonant phrase: 'Poussin holds the key.' Here is the link with the artist and Saunière's alleged purchase of a copy of *The Shepherds of Arcadia*. The fuse has been lit – and it is rapidly followed by the detonation. De Sède's promised 'further details' arrive. They are photographs of a tomb in a pastoral landscape. The location, he informs us, is a mere couple of miles or so from Rennes-le-Château – 'on the right of the road, between the villages of Serres and Arques'. Both tomb and landscape seem, beyond question, to be identical to those depicted in the Poussin painting.

Exactly at this time and independently of de Sède, I stumble upon another link with Poussin and his painting and learn an important lesson. 'It is not enough to look. One must also see.' My work on this story began when I looked at Saunière's parchment and saw the hidden message. I have even eventually 'seen' the complicated geometric pattern hidden beneath the letters. Yet there is another simple message staring me in the face and, though I have looked at it many times, it is only now, when its significance is screaming at me, that I see it. It is on a gravestone inscription reproduced

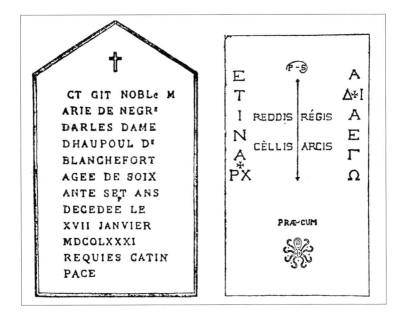

in *Le Trésor Maudit*, which de Sède tells us, Saunière was careful to efface (though a copy, apparently, has survived.)

This slab lay upon the grave of Rennes-le-Château's *grande dame* of the eighteenth century. She was Marie de Blanchefort, who died in 1781, and this inscription, together with the accompanying one upon her headstone, are integrally linked with the secret messages of the parchments.*

The two vertical lines bordering the inscription have been nagging at me for months. There doesn't seem to be anything terribly complicated about them, yet I can find no satisfactory meaning. The central text is Latin, as is, apparently, the left hand vertical column. The right hand column seems to be Greek. But, so far, my 'small Latin and less Greek' has got me nowhere. 'ET IN PAX' seems to be as much as the first column can suggest. But my Latin, rusty though it is, tells me that 'PAX', the nominative case of the noun 'Peace' is grammatically incorrect after the preposition 'IN'. Even accepting bad Latin merely gives: 'AND IN PEACE' – which is not very helpful. The right-hand Greek column seems to make no sense at all. But now thoughts of Poussin are in my mind and

* See *The Holy Place*, Chapter 5. H.L.

the 'decipherment' of the vertical columns leaves me ashamed of my blindness.

The whole text is Latin – but the vertical columns are written in a form of the *Greek* alphabet. The 'concealment' is as simple as that. All that is necessary is to transliterate into the Roman alphabet. E, T, I, N and A remain the same. But P becomes R; X becomes K (or hard C) ... and so on. The two columns simply read: 'ET IN ARCADIA EGO' ... the inscription on the tomb which is being contemplated by the shepherds in Poussin's painting. Here was our link.

All these suggestions that a 'key' to the mystery lay in the works of Poussin, and the startling and filmable discovery of the *Shepherds of Arcadia* tomb and landscape can no longer be ignored in terms of our programme. Andrew and I have a long, anxious but excited discussion. The framework of the programme on which we have been working and the screen time available to us, does not allow space for this new material. In any case, our filming trip is over and we have no visual material to illustrate the 'Poussin discovery'. Certainly we can reproduce the painting in our film. But the landscape? The new locations? The new facts and theories? We have not an inch of suitable visual material. We must speak to our producer.

Paul listens to our account of the new information and is as impressed as we are by the photographs of the tomb. He agrees that the story has gained a new dimension, even if the eventual solution to the riddle seems to be even more shrouded in mystery than before. Paul feels, as we do, that the Poussin aspect cannot be ignored. It is dramatic and visually exciting. Moreover, in terms of what is known of Poussin's life and work, it is a true discovery. Somehow it must be included in the film. In the world of television, however, the decision cannot be as simple as that. We already have a projected transmission date for the programme. To allow time for another filming trip and the shaping of a new programme, means that our 'slot' will have to be filled by something else and a new date found for our transmission. This however, is not a problem for Andrew or me. Paul, having agreed with us that the new material merits an expanded film, delights us by making the decision that we can have an entire *Chronicle* programme in which to explore Saunière's story. He will solve the administrative problems. It's for us to make the film. Now, suddenly, we have space to breathe. The full-length film we are now to make cannot be transmitted until the early spring of 1972. There will be time for me to do a great deal more research. We will not be returning to Rennes-le-Château for filming until September, when the tourist season and the height of the summer heat will be over.

ANOMALIES

Meanwhile, there is a great deal of work to do. An obviously fresh line of enquiry has been opened by the complex new decipherment sent by de Sède. It becomes the subject of much debate. How is it to be incorporated into my new and expanded script? The message is weird and, superficially, whimsical: BERGERE PAS DE TENTATION QUE POUSSIN TENIERS GAR-DENT LA CLEF PAX DCLXXXI PAR LA CROIX ET CE CHEVAL DE DIEU JACHEVE CE DAEMON DE GARDIEN A MIDI POMMES BLEUES – (Shepher-dess no temptation that Poussin Teniers hold the key. Peace 681. By the cross and this horse of God I complete this daemon guardian at midday blue apples.) What on earth are we to make of it?

De Sède claims that the decoding has been done by the computers of the French Army Cipher Department. But as I struggle to verify the con-voluted workings of the encoding method, I become less and less satisfied by this bald claim. I cannot imagine how *any* computer programme, no matter how sophisticated, can possibly make the arbitrary, illogical – not to say irrational – leaps which this code demands. I need expert advice. Fortunately, the BBC is in the process of making a series on *The Code-breakers*. A lead to a cipher expert requires no further effort than a dozen steps down the corridor from the *Chronicle* offices. A couple of telephone calls and I am in my car on the way to visit a retired member of the British Intelligence code-breaking fraternity.

I show him the coded parchments, the encoding system and the final message. He is intrigued and questions me closely on the provenance of the documentation and the possible dating of the cipher. I give him as much information as I have been able to glean from de Sède and voice my doubts about the reliability and frankness of my sources. The hint of possible skulduggery added to the extraordinary nature of the ciphered message seems to intrigue him even more. 'Leave it with me for a few days,' he says. Within the week I have his expert reaction. 'It's one of the most complex ciphers I've ever encountered,' he tells me. 'The system is perfectly valid but laborious. It would have taken months to prepare.' I ask if it would be possible to break the code by computer. 'Absolutely not,' he says. 'It just isn't a valid problem for a computer. It is, effectively, unbreakable.' 'So, how come we have the decoded message?' I ask. 'Whoever gave you the decipherment must have the key.' 'Or have an informant who has the key,' I muse. 'That's a different problem,' says the cipher expert.*

While I am working on the new leads and following up my fresh lines of research, yet another curiosity appears in the basic 'de Sède-given' story. I come across a second hardback version of his book. This is a Book Club edition. At first, it appears identical to the illustrated hardback which I have already acquired. But, true to the form of this story, I spot an apparent anomaly. Both books have the same illustrations – with one odd exception. The first book had already caused me to wonder about a seemingly irrelevant photograph, apparently of a wooden panel, with a carved bee in each corner and, in the centre, a winged female figure standing on a small globe and holding a wreath above her head. The caption to this illustration is, to say the least, unclear: '*Rennes-les-Bains – Thermes Romains (detail)*.' The text of the book makes no mention of it. One should not, however, invent unnecessary mysteries. Perhaps, I thought, there had been an explanation of this 'detail' which had been cut from the book during final editing? If the illustrations had already been prepared, then perhaps it had been too late to delete the photograph? As an explanation, this is not totally satisfactory; but it is, at least, possible.

The Book Club edition suggests otherwise. In the first hardback, the illustration is a half-tone photograph. The Book Club version is a line-block drawing. It follows that the mysterious 'detail' is not there in error. The illustration is clearly intended. Why? And why is no hint of an explanation to be found in any of the available texts? This is a mystery which is never to be resolved. When questioned, de Sède is unable (or unwilling) to give any sort of explanation. A tiny glimmer of light is eventually to be shed upon this peculiarity. De Sède has promised to supply visual material for our film. A dossier eventually arrives from his publisher in Paris, containing photographs of Saunière, his housekeeper, his church etc. In fact – all the book illustrations. And here are both the half-tone and line-block drawing of the Rennes-les-Bains 'detail'. My notes record my puzzlement:

---

* The full workings of this extraordinary cipher are to be found in *The Holy Place*. H.L.

On the back of the half-tone:– *Hotel des Termes Romains – Rennes-les-Bains – Porte de la Salle à Manger – Motif = Europe et les Abeilles – sur la Boule et tenant le cercle – (Taureau = Apis = Apiculture).*

So it's the dining-room door. What the Hell does that tell us? But … if the female is Europa … then that's a fascinating (if wild) link with the bees.*

I also note: 'The backs of almost all the illustrations are stamped in purple with the word – PLANTARD. What – (or who?) is Plantard?' Several years are to pass before I find the answer to that question. As I struggle with these and other more practical scripting problems, the summer slips past. Before I know it, our second filming expedition to Rennes-le-Château is upon us.

SEPTEMBER 1971:
FINDING THE TOMB

The BBC's customary budgetary restraints mean that this trip is going to be rushed. Paul can only provide a film crew for a brief couple of days. Worse – there will be no time for Andrew to make a reconnaissance. True, we now know the area in general extremely well, but we have seen no more than photographs of the 'Poussin Tomb' and are even uncertain as to its precise location. Preparing the script has presented no problems. I know what I want to say in words. But in picture terms, we will need matching shots of tomb and background to show as clearly as possible the exact parallels in painting and landscape. This means finding exact camera positions and, with limited filming time, it's better to know such things in advance. Our practical problems are solved, at least in part, by the increasing complexity of my researches. It has never been easy to follow up some of the leads from London. Most, if not all the documentation is in France. Paul eventually suggests that I should go ahead on my own for a few days of research on the ground. This will give me the opportunity to work on the story and, at the same time, reconnoitre the area for possible matching shots. This, with luck, should save Andrew hours of unproductive and

---

* The legendary Europa was seduced by Zeus in the form of a bull. Taurus = Bull. Apis is the Egyptian Bull God. Apis is also the Latin for bee. And Apiculture is bee-keeping. H.L.

exhausting mountain climbing. More to the point, my solo jaunt will not put too much strain on the BBC's purse.

In mid-September I set off for Victoria Station and the boat train. This time I am on my own. My feelings are mixed. There is a mass of work to do and I will have a few days alone in Rennes-le-Château. I have never enjoyed solitary travel and I wonder how the village will seem to a lone visitor. There have already been uncomfortable hints that there are some people who do not like strangers making too close an investigation of the mystery of Saunière's treasure. However, I expect to be too busy to become nervous. Even accepting that there is anything to be nervous about. The schedule is tight.

As I relax on the overnight train from Paris, I prepare a list of priorities. First and most obvious is to locate the tomb. I must waste no time as far as this is concerned. The train is due to arrive at Carcassonne at 6 a.m. A hired car has been ordered to meet me at the station. With luck, I shall be on my way by 6.15. I should be able to find the location, do a preliminary check on accessibility and still be able to breakfast at a not-too-unreasonable hour – say 8.30 – at Rennes-le-Château. The rest of the morning can be spent in dealing with any immediate problems and attempting to make contact by telephone with the few people I need to see. Most particularly, I must try to arrange meetings with local historians and experts, such as Professor Nelli of Toulouse University, who lives in Carcassonne. I'm hoping that someone will be able to give me some information on the tomb. This is an urgent priority as, apart from its appearance and approximate location, I still know nothing about it. I hope to devote the next two days to meetings and discussions with these experts as well as delving into the Departmental Archives. This will leave most of one day for examining the area around the tomb with some care, in order to identify possible camera positions. Then the long drive to Toulouse to meet Andrew who will be flying in late on the third afternoon. Paul has stolen a few days from his busy schedule to accompany him. Not surprisingly, he wants to share with us the excitement of our Poussin discovery. As usual, a lot to do. But I don't expect to be impossibly pressed for time.

Why will I never learn? There is no car waiting at Carcassonne Station. I make a decision. To hell with schedules and carefully worked-out time-tables. Rennes-le-Château dictates its own pace and I will just have to 'play everything by ear'. Even so, I am furious – as my scribbled memos at the time show:

7.00 a.m. Considerable difficulty tracing car hire firm. No office in Carcassonne ... no office in Narbonne. Concessionaire of some sort – not functioning till 8.00. Total waste of time! Object of exercise totally frustrated!! I'm bloody angry!!!

8.35 a.m. Call from hire firm. Car trouble. (I am convinced they just forgot!) Will be delivered in 1 hour. Excuses and apologies ... but the damage is done!

There is nothing to do but cool my heels at Carcassonne Station and wait. Offices of archivists and other people I might wish to see will hardly be functioning much before 9.00. There is absolutely no way to utilise the wasted time, other than in drinking interminable cups of coffee, writing enraged and useless memos and altering my plan of action. The car eventually arrives at 9.45.

I race off to the office of the town archivist. Nobody seems to know anything of our tomb. Promises are made to haul out relevant documentation for me to see later in the day. A telephone call to Professor Nelli sets up a preliminary meeting for tomorrow. A flying visit to the local Tourist Office again produces a blank as far as the tomb is concerned.

The day is dribbling away and I am still in Carcassonne. Until I have located the tomb, I will continue to feel myself working against a background of uncertainty. Finding the tomb, therefore, is still – at least subjectively – my first and most urgent priority. At last, having shaken the remainder of the day into some sort of projected order, I climb back into the car and head south. The road is now familiar and I drive fast. Limoux and Alet flash past. On the approach to Couiza, I suddenly notice a fleeting new glimpse of Rennes-le-Château through the trees on a bend in the road. Henri Buthion will be wondering where I am. But there is no time to call at the village. 'Find Arques and the tomb' has become an urgent, pressing demand, as though it might slip away if I don't quickly pin it down.

Into Couiza and then the left turn towards Rennes-les-Bains. Cardou ahead, where the road curves right. At the mountain's foot, the familiar right turn to Rennes-les-Bains. But this time straight on, following the signpost: 'SERRES – ARQUES'. The road winds with the river: never is there a long view ahead. The valley begins to broaden on the right. At last, on the left, the four-square stark shape of the Château of Serres. It can't be much further. I slow the car and begin studying the road ahead with care. The tomb should be 'beside the road to the right on a broad curve'. At each bend I slow to walking pace and scan the countryside. I seem to be driving for endless miles round countless curves and always – nothing. Have I missed it? Should I turn back and start again? I decide to press on, at least until I reach the village of Arques. Once there I will be certain that I have gone too far. The tomb is 'between Serres and Arques'.

Another curve in the road. Nothing. Another. This time there is a knoll topped by a clump of trees. I begin to accelerate past it, already concentrating on the road ahead. But, in the shade under the trees I seem to sense, rather than see, a hard-edged shape. Whatever it is, the feel of angularity registering in my mind is of something man-made. I stop the car and look back over my shoulder. And there it is. There can be no question. This is 'Poussin's Tomb'. In shape and size and colour, there is no doubt. Even the familiar splashes of ochre hue in the earth of the surrounding countryside echo the tints in the large photo-reproduction of the painting which lies on the seat beside me. I reverse the car and pull off the road onto a conveniently placed open patch of grass. The few yards I have travelled back are enough to conceal the tomb again behind the trees of the knoll. It may be near the road – but it is very easy to miss.

I get out of the car and look around me. There is a small ravine between the knoll and the road, steep-sided and quite deep. Beyond the knoll, the ground descends to where, some few hundred yards away, a couple of large and apparently ruinous buildings are crumbling back into the landscape. Back along the road and on the opposite side from the tomb is a small group of inhabited farmhouses. But nowhere is there any sign of movement or activity. I seem to be alone in a sleeping countryside. From where I have parked, a small track winds off in the direction of the knoll. Eagerly, I follow it. It leads me upwards and I find myself approaching the tomb from behind. 'Behind', that is, as I have been used to seeing it in the painting. But even from this angle, as I glimpse it through the trees, it 'feels right'. I take a firm grip on myself. There must be no wishful thinking. No colouring of conclusions. Now that I'm here, I've got to be sure that the similarity is more than a chance resemblance.

But the only tiny, fleeting sense of anything that might be called disappointment comes when I examine the front of the tomb. There is no trace of any inscription – not even any faint marks in the stone that might once have read ET IN ARCADIA EGO. But perhaps this is hoping for too much. I move away from the tomb, holding the colour reproduction of the painting in my hand, trying to place myself directly in relation to the structure as it was viewed by the artist. It is barely possible. One must move to the very

Paul Johnstone beside the Poussin tomb.

edge of the ravine which drops almost sheer. The little flattened top of the knoll ends abruptly only a few feet in front of the tomb. Once correctly positioned, though, the harmonious matching of image with reality becomes striking.

Through the trees, there is the glimpse of a towering rock pinnacle. This is placed with extreme accuracy in the painting. There is a clear difference, though, in the landscape to the left of this rock, which is a rising slope. In the painting, however, it falls, though I note that a line of cloud in the picture seems to follow the outline of the rising hillside. I mentally file away the fact for future consideration. The matching of the entire landscape to the right is most impressive. Cardou and the crest of Blanchefort fall into their correct places. Most exciting of all, I notice that a very distant low hilltop on the painted horizon is matched exactly in reality. And the hilltop is unquestionably Rennes-le-Château. Here is a bonus indeed. The village is visible from the tomb – and Poussin has placed it with such accuracy that a superb matching shot will be possible for the film.

Already there are enough resemblances to satisfy me in the broad overall impression. As I begin to study the smaller details even more convincing matches appear. Behind the right-hand corner of the painted tomb is a tree. A large and ancient holly-oak is growing in the right place. Could it be the same tree, three centuries older? Or a descendant of the original? Perhaps, but in any case, it isn't possible to be certain that Poussin's painted tree is, in fact, a holly-oak.* However, the placing is visually very satisfactory. Most unexpected and remarkable is the matching of another small detail. The shepherd to the right of the picture rests his foot on a small round rock. In precisely the correct spot, a matching round rock is incorporated in a ledge which has been added to the front edge of the tomb.

Everything about both tomb and setting is right. Now I am certain that all the delays and extra work have been worthwhile. The few minutes I have needed for confirmation have proved very exciting and I find myself regretting that I am alone. This has been an experience to share. However, there is no time for the luxury of indulging in moments, however brief, of private satisfaction. It's already lunchtime and my afternoon appointments are pressing. I take a few photographs, then turn the car back in the direction of Rennes-le-Château.

I drive with a feeling of exhilaration. The frustrations of the early morning are forgotten. I find myself singing loudly and tunelessly as I drive the last few kilometres up the winding steep ascent. I am looking forward to meeting again all my friends in the village. The discovery that the BBC has forgotten to forewarn Henri Buthion of my arrival is no more than an amusing side issue. It certainly doesn't prevent him from instantaneously producing one of his superlative lunches, which I have barely time to enjoy before I am on the road back to Carcassonne.

The town archivist's office has been unable to find any trace of the Arques tomb in their records. Nobody knows anything about it and there seems to be a general puzzlement at the lack of information. Although I am disappointed at not being able to unearth any background material for my script, I cannot prevent a feeling of private pleasure that we seem to be on to something quite new. Certainly, the prevailing ignorance seems

---

* Enquiries at the Botanic Gardens at Kew elicited the opinion that the tree in the painting 'looked like *Quercus Ilex*' (the holly-oak). H.L.

to imply that the significance of the tomb has never been noticed before. It is suggested that I talk to the curator of Carcassonne's library, a respected and knowledgeable local historian who has done much research into the history of the area.

I meet René Descadeillas, the curator, in his office and he examines the photographs of the tomb with interest. He knows nothing of it and is, at first, intrigued. He agrees that the structure looks worth investigation and makes a telephone call to a colleague who may, he thinks, be able to shed some light – but, again, a blank. By now I am beginning to find the widespread ignorance of a large roadside tomb quite extraordinary. M. Descadeillas, though, interprets the lack of knowledge as proof that the tomb can have no importance. 'The whole region has been gone over very thoroughly,' he says. 'If this tomb had any importance, then I or my colleague would know of it.' I find this statement a little sweeping, but when I steer the conversation on to Rennes-le-Château and Saunière, the change in his attitude, as I noted at the time, 'was peculiar to say the least'. Saunière, he insists was nothing but a crook. The only mystery lies in the identity of the three or four people who were giving him the money. 'Pious people who did not wish their families to know about it.' As an explanation, I find the suggestion that a small number of people should be willing to support 'a crook' in luxury, even more mysterious. 'Especially,' as my notes read, 'he didn't pursue the thought linking crookery with secret gifts and thus produce blackmail.'

M. Descadeillas's opinions are stated very clearly and forcefully. The parchments, he tells me, are rubbish. I ask about the secret messages. 'The message relating to Dagobert, for instance.' He roars with laughter. 'There are no such messages,' he insists, 'They are all pure imagination.' The documents, he tells me, are a patently inept attempt at reproducing ancient writing. They are so clearly not of the period they are trying to imitate that they must be worthless forgeries. I wonder if M. Descadeillas would consider his own writings to be 'rubbish' and 'pure imagination', if he were to be presented with them written out in an inept attempt at Babylonian cuneiform? The hidden messages are, after all, clearly embedded within the texts. The content is unquestionably of more significance than the manner in which it is conveyed. I find it strange that an historian should so adamantly refuse even to consider a concretely expressed possibility of which he is claiming to be ignorant.

There is no doubt that the mention of Rennes-le-Château has caused a marked change in his demeanour. Nevertheless, he offers to let me examine his own book on Saunière. This is a small unpublished work, a copy of which is kept at the library. It contains, he tells me, 'all the verifiable facts'. I may peruse it for half an hour – but the taking of any notes, he tells me, is expressly forbidden. He leads me to a small room, seats me at a table and disappears. The book will be brought to me. Again I am struck by this sudden change to what seems a curious suggestion of hostility. A functionary duly appears some few moments later and places the book in front of me, then sits at the table facing me impassively. He is there, presumably, to ensure that no clandestine notes are taken. In this slightly unreal and uncomfortable manner, I leaf through Descadeillas's book. My memo jotted on leaving the library tells me that Descadeillas's account of the Saunière story seems as bizarre as ever, but contains 'a meticulous assemblage of dates, costs, names of craftsmen, artists and firms involved in the various building projects etc.' Not very helpful. But, as the details are presumably available in the records, the embargo on note-taking seems even more mystifying.*

One aspect which strikes me forcibly is the book's insistence that Saunière acquired his wealth by trafficking in masses. I have encountered this accusation elsewhere, though never with any accompanying proof. One would think that if Saunière, as suggested, mounted a large campaign of advertising to attract commissions for the saying of masses in return for payment, then some trace of this would survive. M. Descadeillas's account, however, gives no supporting evidence for the accusation, nor is there any mention of his other suggestion of wealthy and anonymous benefactors. (A suggested possible enquiry in Saunière's own day apparently 'went as far as the Vatican', but the matter was dropped as 'non-proven'.)

All in all an interesting, if not terribly illuminating hour or so, though I am still no further on in my attempts to learn something of the tomb beside the road between Serres and Arques. I head back towards Rennes-le-Château, but with no further pressures upon me for today, I decide to indulge in some needful relaxation and leave the over-familiar main road to wander the byways from Carcassonne to Limoux. The countryside is magical, the villages content beneath their quilt of centuries in the fading autumn light.

---

* Months later, I discover that M. Descadeillas is, himself, one of Rennes-le-Château's small army of dedicated diggers for treasure – which explains, perhaps, his obfuscatory attitude. H.L.

In St Hilaire I find a wonderful abbey church with a cloistered garden made for peaceful contemplation. Inside the church, a superb twelfth-century carved marble sarcophagus makes an altar for a side chapel. This is one of those unexpected treasures which are tucked away in obscure hamlets throughout France and which, in guidebook terms, are 'worth the detour'.

In the last of the daylight, I pause in Alet-les-Bains. On each of my previous hurried journeys to Carcassonne and back, I have been aware of the impressive ruins of a great cathedral beside the road in the centre of the village. At last, I have the time to pause. Filled almost to the brim with the shadows of the end-of-day, the towering, ruined walls seem forlorn yet beautiful. I stand where wraiths of rich-robed priests seem still to make their reverence before the High Altar's silent, empty space. In place of incense, darkness rises to the vaulted roof. I feel an intruder upon the serene sleep of the years of abandonment and leave quietly to wander through the empty village streets.

During the quarter century of my many voyages of return, Alet-les-Bains has become for me a place of special enchantment and delight. The main road no longer leads the passing traveller to stumble unexpectedly upon this little jewel. Happily, perhaps, the village is now bypassed and the modern world races past on the other side of the river. But Alet has never released me from her spell. With her empty, tranquil, pretty streets, she seems to me to be the embodiment of a demure young lady from an age long past who watches, smiling beneath lowered eyelids, too shy to speak, but knowing that you will find her charming.

Reluctantly, I leave and drive the last few miles in darkness up the winding road to Rennes-le-Château, anticipating a peaceful evening for thinking time before an early bed. The evening though, as I should by now have grown to expect, does not turn out quite as I have anticipated.

UNEASY MIDNIGHT

Henri Buthion has prepared for me the room in Saunière's Villa Bethania that I am beginning to look on as 'mine'. Refreshed and looking forward to a quiet dinner, I make my way down to the kitchen, where I am now *persona grata*. Henri's wife, mother and children all concern themselves with the running of the hotel. It is pleasant, with the rush of the summer holiday-period now over, to be able to fall with them into the relaxed pattern of a small family hotel off-season. A pre-dinner drink in the kitchen, lending a willing hand in the preparation of one's own repast can be a pleasant way of passing a half-hour, provided one's presence is accepted in the sanctum. I think it possible that they find my 'Englishness', my writer's curiosity and my enthusiasm for the village's story to be both novel and, in some way, entertaining. Certainly I am freely accepted into their more private world and allowed, with much good will, to continue my incessant questioning and absorbing of atmosphere.

With my meal at last prepared, I adjourn to the hotel's dining room. (Some months are to pass before I am to be honoured by a place at the Buthions' own table.) The *salle à manger* is very long and narrow, partially below ground-level and had originally served as Saunière's winter garden.* Each table is illumined by dim, red-shaded wall-lights which add a cosy and intimate charm when the place is full. Empty as it now is, there is an almost gloomy, tunnel-like aspect. Henri has laid my place at a small table half-way down the room and I notice with surprise that another place has been set at the table by the door. I am not, as I thought, the hotel's only guest.

I have barely begun my meal when a tall, fair, well-built and youngish man comes in and, with a nod in my direction, settles into the other place. There seems a sense of strange self-consciousness in two solitary guests sharing so large a dining-room – especially as he is seated with his back toward me, tucked into a shadowy corner. It is impossible for either to ignore the other's presence and the silence, broken only by the soft clatter of cutlery, becomes almost uncomfortable. When Henri reappears with my next course, I murmur to him something about realising that it is, perhaps, too late to invite the stranger to share my table for dinner, but perhaps Henri might ask the young man if he would care to join me later for coffee and a *digestif*? Henri thinks this a good idea, as the man has already enquired about me and seems keen to find the opportunity for a talk. My invitation is duly passed on and accepted. The meal over, Henri brings the young man to my table, makes a formal introduction and discreetly withdraws, leaving us with a supply of coffee and cognac.

At first, the conversation is no more than the expected banalities – polite

---

* It has now become a village museum. H.L.

commonplaces about the hotel, the excellent food, the beauty of the countryside. For the last few years, he tells me, he has taken to visiting Rennes-le-Château for the odd weekend. His home town is no more than an hour or so's drive and he is attracted by the peace and quiet and, of course, the mystery of the village. News that 'a foreigner' is showing a more than usual interest has reached him and so he has taken the opportunity to make an out-of-season visit in the hope of meeting me and, perhaps, comparing notes. His manner suggests that he has something more specific on his mind than mere social chatter. The conversation moves more and more concretely toward treasure hunting. He implies that he has been told that I seem to have had a measure of success in unravelling some of the clues.

Experience has already taught me that those who delve into this story purely as a hunt after treasure are given to caution, jealous of their 'discoveries' and inclined to play everything 'very close to the chest', horse-trading odd snippets of information in return for leads in areas which they have not covered for themselves. Whatever they consider to be the most valuable of their discoveries, they keep very much to themselves. This treasure-hunting aspect, though fascinating and very productive from the point of view of entertainment, has always, for me, been secondary to the excitement of the unravelling of the historical mystery. Naturally, I – like anyone – would be thrilled to discover a real-life treasure. Treasure-hunters, however, are not willing to believe that I am genuinely not on the hunt for gold. That I would hand over anything found to the authorities and not disappear into the night with the loot would, in their eyes, be more than unlikely – as well as totally incomprehensible. Perhaps I am too cynical to cherish dreams of finding an Aladdin's cave of riches. But certainly, my conviction that the research and the making of the film are more valid channels for my energy than any treasure-hunt, has made me more open-handed with the fruits of my work than might otherwise be the case. Quite simply, I have nothing to hide.

My young friend, therefore, seems to find it a little novel that I am quite willing to go over the details of decipherments, possible angles of approach to the mystery, as well as a few of the new thoughts that I have had. I am hoping, of course, that this 'horse-trading' might produce some new thoughts for me – especially as I can see that most of my material is new to him. I am puzzled, though, as I begin to sense in him as much disquiet as excitement. As I finish the description of a possible interlocking of some of the clues, I can see that he is nearing some sort of decision. I wait for him to speak. The pause lengthens. I become aware of the utter silence which surrounds us. It is well past midnight and the village has been asleep for hours. We two, bent over our table in the shadowy gloom of the dining room, must be the only waking souls within miles.

The pause seems to become interminable. What is he thinking? He has seemed impressed by my reading of some of the clues. Does he think that I am about to reach the end of the trail? If so – why should that disturb him? Everyone who is chasing this treasure is aware that somebody else might get there first. This is one of the risks of the game so why should he be – even if only slightly – worried? The answer, when it comes, is more forthright and disconcerting than I expect. Suddenly he straightens in his chair and stares hard at me: 'Monsieur, I must tell you that I think I have located the treasure and I warn you that I shall be quite ruthless if you – or anyone – gets in my way.'

Rennes-le-Château has taught me to be ready for almost anything. Threats, however, are not part of my expectations. For all the scores of thrillers which I have written, it still comes as a shock to find myself playing a scene of thinly-veiled menace. This only happens in fiction. Or to somebody else. Certainly, until now, it has never happened to me – except in the pages of a script. I look at the young man, conscious of my five-foot-six-and-a-bit featherweight frame matched against this hefty six-footer. No question – there is not much I can do to prevent him bouncing me around the walls should he so choose. But is he serious? I consider a moment longer. He is. It is not only my innate cowardice that convinces me that I am in a situation that requires delicate playing.

My next move comes out of innumerable cliché scenes I have seen – and written – in the past. I reach out for the cognac and slowly top up his glass, then mine. True to the best traditions of the thriller, I note that my hand is as steady as the proverbial rock. The essential ridiculousness of the whole unreal situation strikes me and I realise that I am grinning like a fool. 'I believe you', is all I can think to say.

Perhaps my apparent amusement is as unexpected to him as his threats have been to me, for he relaxes a little and seems to be prepared to go on talking. He has said that he 'thinks' he has found the treasure; therefore he cannot yet have confirmed the fact. His worry obviously stems from his fear that my deductions will enable me to beat him to the prize. I, on the other hand, am perfectly well aware that I have no precise location in mind. In any case, the object of my visit is to film the 'Poussin Tomb'. What now begins to concern me is that he might, indeed, have located Saunière's hiding place. If he has, then he and any treasure he may find will unquestionably disappear, leaving nobody any the wiser, save possibly a 'fence' to whom he will eventually take whatever he may find that can be converted into cash. For the moment, the morality of this treasure-hunting mentality is not an immediate concern. I realise that there is nothing I can do to dissuade him.

I am made uneasy, however, by the fact that there is the chance that a possibly important archaeological find may disappear without a trace and, worse still, unrecorded. I know that, somehow, I must try to gain his confidence.

We talk on into the night as I attempt to convince him that I am not here to deprive him of 'his' treasure but that, should he make any such discovery, I would wish above all to see it. As persuasively as I can, I try to show him the necessity of making a record of such a find. I even make an absurdly forlorn attempt to persuade him to let me film any possible find before it is moved, or even touched. Perhaps my earlier willingness to share information has helped my persuasion. To my astonishment, he at last agrees to my request. He will allow me to film whatever he may find if I give my word to say nothing, nor to publish any photograph or film until a period of several months has passed. Mentally asking forgiveness of the powers-that-be for my offer to become an 'accessory after the fact', I try to pin him down to more than a mere vague promise. My problems are no concern of his, but he offers to send me a coded signal in the event of success. I am fully aware that the whole thing may be no more than a figment of his imagination. There have already been many before him who have thought they had solved the mystery – (and there are to be many more in the future). Sceptic I may be – but I am not prepared, through negligence, to throw away the faintest of possibilities. I have, and will continue to maintain an open mind.

I notice that my tentative 'pressuring' has brought back a little of the young man's edginess. Our discussion seems to be coming to an end. I am not sorry. It is nearly 2 a.m. and I've had a long and exhausting day. He sits contemplating me silently as I gather up the scribbled notes and sketches I have made during our talk. Then, as I am about to bid him good night, he says abruptly: 'Have you seen the excavation in the room under the Tour Magdala?' The sudden enquiry off-balances me. 'No. I thought that room was always kept locked.' He shakes his head with an air of faint amusement. 'Not always. Come on – I'll show it to you. Have you got a torch?' 'Er . . . no.' This is not, in fact, true. But suddenly I'm feeling nervous. I do not relish the thought of visiting an underground room in the depths of night. A room, moreover, where people have apparently been digging. Such an expedition, and with such an odd and alarming young man, strikes me as being not the wisest of undertakings. Discretion, at two in the morning, seeming to be unquestionably the better part of whatever valour I may possess, I decide against providing the means for a torchlight trip into the unknown. But I am not to be let off so easily. He smiles. 'That's all right. I know where there is one.'

He disappears, leaving me to wonder why he has asked for a torch if there is already one to hand. As I wait for him, alone in the shadows of the dining room, my nervousness increases and my imagination begins to work. If there is, indeed, an excavation in the subterranean room beneath the tower, then this would be a very convenient place into which I could be 'disappeared'. Andrew, Paul and the crew are not due for a goodly while. Again the ludicrous nature of the situation asserts itself and I begin a firm mental debate. 'If you're really nervous – then just refuse to go. Get into your bedroom and lock the door.' 'On the other hand, I'm supposed to be a writer in the process of researching a story. This is something worth exploring a little further. And anyway – I'm insured.' This foolish thought bolsters my spirits and appeals to my preposterous sense of humour. No – I'm not going to back out. In moments, my companion is back bearing a small torch to light our way and I'm committed.

We set off across the dark and night-changed garden. Theatrically sinister under the trees, the white-painted wrought-iron tables and chairs gleam in the feeble light like so many squat ungainly skeletons. The silence is absolute as I stand on the steps which lead down to the underground room and watch the young man as he fumbles with the door handle. In classic horror-film style, the door creaks open on its rusty hinges and he stands to one side to allow me through. I wonder how the door comes to be unlocked. Hoping that my momentary nervous hesitation doesn't show, I take a deep breath and make the few steps down into the darkness. He follows me in, then closes the door. The 'atmosphere' is crackling around us and my imagination is working at full stretch as he plays the beam of the torch around the room. It is small and bare. In the far left-hand corner is a huge mound of earth. Opposite a deep hole yawns, the feeble beam of the torch not reaching to the bottom.

KEY TO THE SACRED PATTERN

How deep is it? The amount of earth shows that a great deal of hard labour has been expended in the excavating. Somebody must have been totally convinced that they were on to something – though it seems a most unlikely place for a treasure to be hidden.

It doesn't take very long to examine a hole in the ground. In my present frame of mind, I have no great desire to linger. I express my marginal interest in the apparently fruitless labour and, in seconds, I am ready to depart. But my companion is now leaning his bulky frame against the door and showing no inclination to return to the hotel. He begins to chat in a half abstracted fashion. My uneasiness begins to increase. Imagination or not, I realise that I am in a potentially dangerous situation. And I don't like it one bit. The claustrophobic atmosphere of the dungeon-like room is heightened by the gape of the menacing hole behind me. I want to get the hell out of here. Somehow the simple expedient of elbowing him out of the way and opening the door doesn't, in the circumstances, seem to be the most reasonable of actions. His conversation meanders on, vague and pointless. Behind his words, he seems to be thinking of something else; coming to some sort of decision. I decide not to wait but to off-balance him – if I can. I try a long shot. 'Have you ever made any sense out of that very odd inscription behind the Calvaire in the churchyard?' Bull's-eye! He doesn't even know it exists and, of course, he won't miss an opportunity to pick up a new thread. 'Come on, then. My turn to show something to you.' I do not find creeping about in the churchyard in the dead of night a totally entrancing idea, but anything is preferable to remaining trapped in this sinister dungeon. I make a couple of determined steps straight towards him and, instinctively, he moves out of my path. I haul open the door, leap up the stone staircase and head back across the hotel garden. Behind me I hear him pulling the door closed and hurrying to catch up with my fleeting back.

The open cold night air has never been so welcome and I am almost beginning to enjoy the game. At least, I have regained some measure of control – of myself as well as of the situation. I show him the inscription behind the Calvaire. CHRISTUS A.O.M.P.S. DEFENDIT. He has no idea what the cryptic initials may signify.* As he begins to copy it into a notebook, I grab the opportunity to bid him an abrupt good night and make tracks for the hotel. Once in my bedroom, I lock the door and feel slightly foolish.

---

* When, some time later, I had encountered the mysterious Priory of Sion, I was able to make the suggestion that the letters may signify ANTIQUUS ORDO MYSTICUSQUE PRIORATUS SIONIS. De Sède offers AB OMNI MALO PLEBEM SUAM. H.L.

Has the undercurrent of threat and menace been entirely imaginary? Perhaps.

There is to be no concrete pay-off to this incident. The young man departs on the following morning after no more than routine social contact. He is never to communicate with me about any discovery, which is, in fact, no more than I expect. My belief is, that like so many others who think themselves on the verge of the great find he was, in the end, disappointed. Certainly he is not to disappear into the blue with his loot. He is still, I am told, to be seen in the village from time to time and for many years is always to contrive to coincide with my own visits. Obviously he has an informant among the watching eyes.

TWO AMERICAN LADIES

Sunday is to prove a more tranquil and more productive day. The general lack of information concerning the Poussin Tomb is still leaving me with a 'hole' in my script. I suspect that Professor Nelli will be no more likely than anybody else to provide any concrete information, though his opinion will certainly be worth having. So – back to Carcassonne yet again for my appointment. The professor proves to be a man of great charm and kindness, proud of his region and, justifiably, of his knowledge of it. We begin on a good-humoured note when he informs me that he is the 'colleague' telephoned by M. Descadeillas for help on my original enquiry. In complete contrast to his friend, Professor Nelli thinks that there is indeed something worth investigating in the Saunière story and he is vastly entertained by the fact that it should be a stranger – and a foreigner at that – who is drawing their attention to the hitherto unnoticed Arques tomb. 'Sometimes one needs a fresh eye to point out the obvious,' he says. He knows absolutely nothing of it, he tells me, but he agrees that the photographs show 'a structure of some importance – but probably not *seigneural*.' When I pinpoint it on the map, he is totally astonished. He knows the location extremely well, having visited the spot with M. Descadeillas, he says, 'dozens of times'. They are interested in an ancient standing stone which is on the hillside 'just across the road'. On each visit they must have parked their car somewhere in the vicinity of the tomb and have never registered it. 'René must be mortified. He is proud of his reputation as a local authority. I think it's a salutary, but amusing lesson. There is always something to learn.' He promises to investigate and to let me know if he turns anything up.

By now I am resigned to the possibility of gleaning no solid facts about the tomb. The last remaining hope lies with the owner of the land on which it stands, whose permission I need to film on private property. So far my efforts to track the owner down have been fruitless and the search has become one of my priorities. But, as is so often the case with the Rennes-le-Château research, light is shed from an unexpected source. Georges Basset, the photographer at Esperaza, who had helped out over my lost camera, has now become one of my network of local friends. I call in on him for replenishment of my film stock and, in the course of our brief conversation, Georges gives me my first – and most unexpected piece of information about the tomb.

He asks how my enquiries are progressing and I tell him of my conversation with Professor Nelli about 'a local tomb' and that the professor had seemed to arrive fairly quickly at the consideration of the necessity for opening it. (I mention this to Georges as a means of gauging the reaction of a local to such a suggestion.) Georges asks: 'Do you mean the tomb by the road near Arques?' 'Yes. Nobody seems to know anything about it.' 'But you don't need to bother about opening it. I know what's inside,' he says. 'Two American ladies.' 'You're pulling my leg. Two American ladies …?' But Georges Basset is not joking. His father had been the friend of a man who had arrived in the region just after the First World War – an American civil engineer named Louis Lawrence. Lawrence had bought the land on which the tomb stood and had lived there with his wife and his mother. Old Mrs Lawrence had died in 1920 and her son had had her laid to rest in 'the Poussin Tomb'. The younger Mrs Lawrence had joined her mother-in-law in about 1924. Lawrence himself had died in the hospital at Carcassonne, where he was buried.

Georges Basset's story seems odd enough to fit my growing pattern of unexpected details. But here, at least, is something concrete that can be checked and verified. At last I have a lead. When, later, I track down the elderly present owner of the land, he is able to confirm the account, with the additional substance that he had been present at the 1920 burial and had helped to open the tomb to receive the coffin of Mr Lawrence's mother. He is able to give me his assurance as an eye-witness that, when opened in 1920, the tomb had been completely empty. One is bound to wonder what could have brought an American civil engineer to what must, at the time, have been a remote and primitive part of the world. As for the tomb, the owner is able to give me no firm details concerning its history or purpose. 'My grandfather told me it had always been there,' he says. As my informant is a man in his eighties, this must take the tomb's existence back at least a century.* When I ask for his permission to film the tomb, he is quite happy to grant it. 'It's a favourite picnic place for many people,' he tells me. 'Nobody bothers to ask for my permission. But I certainly don't mind. It's a pretty spot and why shouldn't they? It does no harm. Film as much as you please.' It will not be long before his words re-echo in an unexpected fashion.

My day ends with a visit to the castle of Arques, which lies a few minutes drive beyond the tomb. It proves to be a wonderfully impressive *donjon*, its massive towered bulk rearing against the sky and seeming to epitomise all one's childhood fantasies of a toy fort made real. It will certainly be added to our list of filming locations. I make a note of an oddity concerning its setting. The castle lies almost half a mile away from the village, which nestles around its little church. The terrain between is flat and gently sloping and there seems no logic to the separation. Indeed, the *donjon's* function as refuge for the villagers in time of trouble, is hampered by the placing. For now I am simply noting a curiosity. I am years away from the realisation that the placing will itself prove of significance.

VANDALISM

Monday dawns grey and overcast. But the weather cannot dampen my spirits. My solitary reconnaissance trip has been as successful as I could wish. The morning can be spent making final checks around the tomb for camera positions before setting off on the long drive through sheeting rain to meet Paul and Andrew in the late afternoon at Toulouse Airport. The foul weather and the fatigue following days of concentrated effort make the drive less than pleasurable. I enter the outskirts of Toulouse to

---

* There have been various claims made for the age of the structure. Descadeillas said that it 'must be early twentieth century'. No solid evidence for dating has, thus far, been found. The owner's first-hand report of his grandfather's statement remains, therefore, the best evidence – such as it is. H.L.

encounter the end-of-day rush-hour, which purgatory is exchanged for nightmare when I find myself trapped mid-way along a flyover by a broken-down lorry. For nearly three-quarters of an hour, I fume as a massive grid-lock develops, seeming to envelop the city for as far as the eye can see from my elevated viewpoint. While I rage impotently, Paul and Andrew are panicking at the airport. Expecting to find me awaiting them, they have telephoned Henri Buthion for an explanation of my non-appearance. Having learned that I had left 'hours ago', they are in the process of imagining all kinds of dire vehicular fates which might have been visited upon me when I eventually find them, burdened by baggage and uncer-tainty. The film crew are travelling down by road and arrive *chez* Saunière some half-hour behind us. A convivial evening ends with the offering of fervent prayers for improved weather for tomorrow's filming.

Dawn brings scudding clouds, blustery winds but, mercifully, no rain, and I lead our small convoy of cars along the winding road to the 'Poussin Tomb'. Paul is delighted by the beauty of the landscape as Andrew takes on the role of guide. We make a few stops *en route* for Paul to see Coustaussa Castle, Cardou and Blanchefort, already familiar to him from the rushes of our spring filming. Beyond Cardou, Andrew is on unfamiliar territory and, for my companions, the excitement of discovery is again in the air. Serres Castle appears on our left. I slow the car. 'Not much further. It's on the right.' We drive on in silence and I can feel the slight building of tension. I am anxious to see Paul's and Andrew's reactions to the structure and its setting. I have tried very hard not to influence their expectations, merely saying that I am satisfied that the discovery is a genuine one. Will my producer and director agree that all our extra effort and expense have been worthwhile? I pull off the road onto the grassy parking space. The tomb is not yet quite in view. I want them to have their first sight of it as mine had been – a 'long shot' across the ravine, from the road. 'Just a few yards along the road,' I tell them. 'You'll see it from the parapet.' The others hurry on, Andrew clutching his reproduction of the painting. I hang back to watch their reactions – and I am not disappointed.

Andrew balances the picture on the stone parapet which edges the road and the others cluster round him to compare the painted scene with the landscape before them. A concentrated silence seems to stretch intermin-ably as I wait for their first comments. At last Paul turns towards me with a broad smile. 'I hoped it would be good, but I didn't expect it to be *this* good.' Andrew is elated. 'Everything's there,' he says, 'the landscape is a brilliant match. This has got to be Poussin's location.' '*Et in Arcadia Ego*,' Paul murmurs, 'We've found Arcadia.' I had never thought of our discovery in those terms before, but Paul is right. Here is the embodiment of a classical painter's vision of the ideal pastoral tranquillity. What has seemed an artist's bucolic fantasy is spread out before us along a valley of southern France. All that is lacking for the moment is the sunshine. 'It's incredible that nobody's spotted it before,' Andrew says. 'Who tipped off de Sède?' I wonder. I fancy that the original discovery was made, not by him, but by one of the shadowy figures I now suspect to be hovering behind him.

The crew sets up the camera equipment and we pass the morning in a state of euphoria and intense activity. We are able to make wonderful matches of Cardou and Blanchefort which lie precisely placed in painting and reality. The rock of Toustounes, directly behind the tomb, is also perfectly in its place. We have a lengthy conjectural discussion concerning the only mismatch – the ascending slope to the left of Toustounes, which Poussin has painted as a falling hillside. The painting is kept at the Louvre in Paris. I suggest that it might be worth checking there. The picture is bound to have been x-rayed. Perhaps Poussin had painted the correct slope and then, for some reason, changed it to cloud? There is obviously much more worthwhile research to be done. We end the morning's work more than satisfied with the film we have shot and make the brief drive back to Rennes-le-Château for lunch and preparation for the rest of the day's shooting. True to the pattern of the past months, the day has some surprises yet in store.

After a brief lunch break, we head off back to the tomb for the afternoon's filming. As we pull the cars off the road I am delighted to see the good-natured owner of the site coming down the pathway from the tomb. But, as I climb out of the car to greet him, my pleasure rapidly evaporates. He is in a towering rage. Shaking his fist as he approaches, he yells out to us to get off his land – or he will call the police. When he pauses in his tirade to take breath, I hurriedly ask what has made him change his mind. After all, I had asked for – and been granted his permission. 'Permission to film – yes. But not permission for vandalism!' Vandalism? What on earth can he mean? The careful professionalism of a film crew leaves no traces. He rages on incoherently while Andrew, Paul and the crew wait in puzzled incomprehension. Try as we might, we are unable to fathom what precise crime we are supposed to have committed. At last I persuade him to show us the cause of his fury. His anger is certainly real enough, but he is beginning to realise that my air of puzzled innocence is equally unfeigned.

KEY TO THE SACRED PATTERN

At the tomb, all is immediately made clear. During our brief absence, someone has made a determined effort to break through the roof of the structure. The stone top is badly battered in one corner and the large rock used to wreak the damage is still resting on it. My own anger at such monstrous barbarism needs no underlining. The owner can see that I am genuinely shocked, upset and worried by what has happened. In a few moments, good relations are restored and he readily agrees to the continuation of the filming. Nevertheless, the situation is disturbing. The timing of the incident can hardly be coincidental. To someone unversed in the tedious and time-consuming business of film-making, our departure after a long morning's work must have seemed a signal that the shooting is finished. Had we not returned, we would certainly have been held responsible for what must have appeared, at the best, a grotesque and arrogant ingratitude. This is patently an act of criminal vandalism designed to blacken our reputation. It would certainly have made any further co-operation from the locals highly unlikely. One could also suspect that the perpetrator might have been hoping that we had led him to 'the treasure'.

This upsetting incident serves to confirm a suspicion and a concern that has been growing in my mind ever since the destruction of the 'Calvé inscription' at the *Fontaine des Amours*. It is becoming obvious that my movements are being watched with some care. Henceforth, it is clear, if I show more than a passing interest in any site or object, then I will be exposing it to the risk of more tangible – and unwelcome – attentions. There is, of course, nothing I can, or would wish to do, to prevent others investigating the story. But an ominous tally is eventually to build up, of which this desecration of the Poussin Tomb is the worst.* I am to learn to become extremely circumspect; but the brute-force treasure-hunters are to leave an unpleasant trail at my heels. In the churchyard of Rennes-le-Château our spring filming had included the gravestone of Marie de Negri de Blanchefort, whose inscription had, allegedly, been effaced by Saunière. Now it is broken into three pieces, the result, presumably, of an attempt to find the treasure beneath.† I had also photographed the Standing Stone

---

* Attacks on this important and fascinating structure were to continue spasmodically for many years. At last, in the spring of 1988, a lunatic attempt was made to break into it with explosives. Tragically, but perhaps understandably, the owner sledgehammered it out of existence in the vain hope that the obsessive and outrageous attentions of the treasure-hunters would cease. H.L.

† Twenty years later, barely half the stone remains. H.L.

on the hillside above the Poussin Tomb. A return visit a mere couple of days later revealed that a deep pit had been excavated at its foot.

Rennes-les-Bains cemetery had an extremely interesting gravestone which Andrew and I had spent some time examining in the spring. Now we are to find that the stone has completely disappeared.

We were already uncomfortably aware that our film would probably bring many more treasure-seeking tourists to Rennes-le-Château. The village, we know, will risk the loss of its peaceful and unspoilt atmosphere. But this is a price which the villagers seem prepared to pay – and only with minimal reluctance. Tourists will unquestionably bring welcome and much-needed business to what is a comparatively impoverished area. However, innocent tourism is one thing. Quite another is the attention of unscrupulous gold-obsessed fortune-hunters who have no respect or concern for anything more than their own private fantasy of lining their pockets with what remains of Saunière's supposed treasure.

Chapter Five

THE SHEPHERDS
OF ARCADIA

APART FROM THESE disagreeable evidences of the unsavoury nature of our invisible observers, our second brief filming trip is completed without incident. Back in London, Andrew sets about assembling our material into a coherent film, while I finalise the commentary script. Paul fixes our transmission date – 12 February 1972.

A priority for this interim period is to seek advice on the significance of the Poussin 'discovery'. The acknowledged expert in the life and work of the painter is Anthony Blunt, Surveyor of the Queen's Pictures and Director of the Courtauld Institute of Art. Andrew is able to arrange a meeting for us and, armed with photographs of tomb and landscape, we meet in Blunt's study at the Institute in search of enlightenment. What we encounter is a brick wall. The painting depicts an imaginary tomb in an imaginary land-scape, Blunt tells us. We show him the photographs. He acknowledges that the structure is very like the tomb in the painting. We point out the exactitude of the match in the background landscape features. He ponders for a moment. The fidelity of painted detail to photographic image is undeniable. But Blunt shakes his head. 'This is a mere coincidence,' he says. 'An extraordinary coincidence, but a coincidence, nevertheless.' If I believe otherwise, Blunt insists, then it is up to me to produce a substan-tiating hypothesis. 'Poussin's life is extremely well documented,' he says, 'and he never visited this part of France.' When I query his dogmatic certainty concerning a life of three centuries ago, Blunt admits that there are gaps in the account of Poussin's early years. 'Is it possible,' I ask, 'that Poussin may have visited the area in his youth and made detailed sketches?' 'No.' 'Could somebody else have made sketches from which he produced the painting?' 'No. Poussin did not work from such sketches.' Here is the voice of the Expert. I can hardly, as an ignorant amateur, argue with the voice of authority. Blunt is retailing to us what he was taught – and what he continues to teach.

But I have stood in front of that extraordinary structure, and with my own eyes, seen and experienced a precise representation of Poussin's Arcadia. As an explanation, I find 'coincidence' less than satisfactory.

There is also the question of the 'Fouquet letter', found in the archive of the Cossé-Brissac family. Sent by the Abbé Louis Fouquet to his brother, Nicolas, Superintendent of Finances to the court of Louis XIV, it speaks of a meeting with Poussin in the spring of 1656. The letter is mysterious. Louis Fouquet writes of 'a secret' which he has learned from Poussin. 'A secret which kings would have great pains to draw from him.' Can Blunt shed any light on this? The letter has never been properly understood, he admits. It is his opinion, however, that it is to do with a commission for sculptures for Fouquet's garden. This explanation I find as unsatisfactory as the other. It is clear that I have more research – and more thinking – to do.

THE LOUVRE AND THE BIBLIOTHEQUE NATIONALE

Having drawn a blank with Blunt, I can only hope for better things from the Louvre who have promised to make copies of the x-rays of the painting available. Fortunately, we have arranged to film an interview with Gérard de Sède in Paris. The brief filming trip will give me the opportunity to visit the Louvre in order to see *The Shepherds of Arcadia* 'in the flesh' as well as in x-ray. The filmed interview is soon 'in the can' and I find myself with a free morning before my appointment with the Scientific Director of the Louvre. To my great delight, de Sède suggests that I might like to accompany him to the Bibliothèque Nationale where is deposited a considerable amount of documentation relating to the story.

There is one particular book which he is anxious for me to request at the library. This, he tells me, is a mysterious work on the ancient Celtic language, written by Saunière's friend, the Abbé Boudet, priest of Rennes-les-Bains. De Sède warns me not to expect to see the book, however. He knows of only two copies – one listed in the catalogue of the Bibliothèque Nationale, the other in a provincial library. But neither copy, he tells me, has ever been accessible. They are presumed stolen. He will be interested to see what response is made to my request to see it.

De Sède briefs me on the Bibliothèque's routine and I fill in the required forms. To his total astonishment, Boudet's book duly arrives. In the few moments which I can spare to study it, I can't see any immediate use for it in our film. However, I find de Sède's bewilderment at its appearance more than intriguing. Is this yet another example of his reliance on someone else's information?* Of the two other books which I have ordered at his suggestion, one appears. The other is reported as *communiqué*. This merely implies that it is presently being consulted by another reader. Clearly, I must return to the Library to continue my researches. For the moment, there are other demands upon my time.

I arrive at the Louvre to find that the scientist who has made the x-ray study has set up the radiographies for my examination and is on hand to deal with any queries I might have. But again I find myself confronting a seeming disappointment. The x-rays show beyond doubt that Poussin had made no essential alterations to *The Shepherds of Arcadia*. The anomalous slope and cloud to the left of the painting had been there from the very beginning. Whatever reason he may have had for the variation appears to be shrouded in yet more mystery. I spend considerable time contemplating the x-ray photograph in detail – such an opportunity comes but rarely – and, beyond any of my expectations, I notice yet another curiosity. There is a tiny detail, visible only on the underpainting and which seems to make no sense.

As can distinctly be seen, the staff held by the right-hand shepherd is overpainted by the roof of the tomb.

This seems to imply that the staff was painted first. Poussin appears to have worked backward from the foreground details – which seems an odd procedure. He has apparently fixed the placing of the staff before completing the painting of the tomb and the shepherd's head. When I point out this oddity I am given a surprising response. It seems that the anomaly has, until

---

* On my return to England, I ventured an order for Boudet's *La vraie langue celtique* at my local branch library. Amusingly, they were able to track down a copy within forty-eight hours. It was in the reference section of the library in the London suburb of Swiss Cottage. The book has now become a standard work for Rennes-le-Château enthusiasts and is available in more than one facsimile edition. (See *The Holy Place*, Chapter 9) H.L.

now, escaped detection. Perhaps, it is suggested, later overpainting may account for the peculiarity – though there appears to be no evidence of such overpainting. Another possible explanation is offered by the Louvre expert. The atomic density of the paint of the tomb may be heavier than that of the staff, which would have the effect of causing the staff to be blanked out. This however, does not explain why the lower part of the staff is not similarly blanked out. Such puzzles can be very tenacious. Although there is no way that I can use this fragment in our film, it will constantly resurface in my mind, demanding attention. For now, though, the loose end must be left dangling. I have yet one more task to fit into my day – a close examination of Poussin's visible depiction of *The Shepherds of Arcadia*.

THE DISAPPEARING SHEPHERDS

As with so many other aspects of the Rennes-le-Château research, even this seemingly straightforward matter provides its own crop of complexities. In normal circumstances, the painting would be on display in the Louvre's *Grande Galerie*. However, it has recently (and coincidentally) been on loan to the museum of Rennes. (Not Rennes-le-Château, but the town in Normandy.) It is now sequestered in the Louvre's vast store and is not accessible to the general public. While I have been examining the x-rays, the museum's Scientific Director has telephoned to arrange permission for me to visit *la réserve*. She hands me, in case of need, a slip of paper which she has signed as the necessary authority and then hurries off to a meeting leaving me to await the arrival of a guide to lead me through the endless and labyrinthine passageways of the palace.

This proves to be an extraordinary 'safari'. I am led along seeming miles of corridor; through doors which occasionally open onto public areas where tourists are gazing at the masterpieces which line the walls. Our dash through one such door finds us caught up in the throng surrounding Leonardo's *Mona Lisa*. Like Alice's White Rabbit, my guide elbows his way through the crowd, unlocks an adjacent door and we disappear again into yet more endless corridors. This time the walls are bare brick and I find myself gazing at yet another *Mona Lisa*. The sight brings me to a bemused halt. I stare hard, but can distinguish no difference from the painting on public display only yards away. I am aware that innumerable copies of Leonardo's masterpiece have been made, but this juxtaposition of a public and private *Mona Lisa* appeals to me. I gaze questioningly at my guide. 'Which is which?' He grins, shrugs, and gallops on along the dusty passageways.

THE SHEPHERDS OF ARCADIA

At last we reach the Aladdin's cave of the *réserve*. This is an enormous room which functions as a kind of 'filing cabinet'. On either side of a wide central aisle are rows of huge racks which reach to the ceiling. Each holds a number of paintings which are listed on cards on the visible, inner edge of the rack. My companion scans the cards on the left, while I check those on the right. I reach the end of the room without success and await the arrival of my guide. 'It's not on my side,' he says. 'Nor mine.' We must have missed it. We change sides and work back with rather more care. But, according to the file records, *The Shepherds of Arcadia* is not in the *réserve*. But this is ludicrous. Why is the Rennes-le-Château research so permanently dogged with problems and stumbling blocks? Where is the painting? 'If it's not indexed, then it's not here,' my guide insists. 'But it must be!' 'If it's here – and not listed – which is not possible,' he repeats, 'then it will take hours to find it. There are hundreds of pictures on these racks.' He clearly has no intention of embarking on a physical search of the Louvre's entire reserve collection of paintings and glares at me as if the breakdown in the museum's system was somehow my fault. 'I find it hard to believe that the Scientific Director would take the trouble to get me authority to see a painting which is not here,' I insist defensively, groping in my pocket for the little scribbled note of authorisation which she has given me 'in case of need'. I realise the futility of my gesture as I unfold the scrap of paper. It is hardly going to cause the Arcadian Shepherds to materialise from their present limbo. 'There you are,' I say, disconsolately. But in the bottom corner of the paper I notice a small scribble. It looks like the number 139. Clutching at the only available straw, 'Could it be Number 139?' I ask. 'The paintings aren't numbered,' he says, unhelpfully. I thrust the paper under his nose. He glowers at it. 'Ah!' he says, 'Thirteen g.' He turns on his heel and strides back down the rows of racks. Of course. '*Treize gauche*' – Thirteen left. He pulls out the thirteenth rack on the left. The Arcadian Shepherds slide coyly into view. We shall never know why – of all the paintings so carefully stored and docketed – this one alone should have slipped through the efficient net of the Louvre's record-keeping. It is simply one more example of the Rennes-le-Château rule which all researchers should take to their hearts: 'With Rennes-le- Château – *nothing* is ever straightforward.'

TRANSMISSION AND REACTIONS

Back once more in London, work on *The Lost Treasure of Jerusalem ...?* continues. Paul views Andrew's rough-cut of the film, and decides that de Sède's interview is unsatisfactory. De Sède has chosen to talk about aspects of the story which are not strictly relevant to our script. (An elaboration of the story of Saunière's possible liaison with an opera singer, while meriting a passing mention, is not the sort of detail which fits comfortably into *Chronicle's* historical/archaeological format.) In addition, de Sède's accent makes him difficult to understand and his subject-matter hardly merits the expense of sub-titles. Paul makes the producer's judgment to cut him from the film. I will have to fill the missing few minutes with a statement of my own. De Sède is furious. Unaware that such decisions are completely beyond the writer's control, he is convinced that it has been my personal wish to remove him from the film in order, as he puts it, 'to aggrandise myself'. No amount of explanation will convince him otherwise. A few years later, Paul's seemingly straightforward piece of editorial decision-making is to have unexpected and amusing – if violent – repercussions.

At 8.30 p.m. on Saturday, 12 February 1972, BBC 2 transmits *The Lost Treasure of Jerusalem ...?* Perhaps I should have expected it ... the Rennes-le-Château 'gremlins' are lurking in the wings. Great Britain is suffering 'a winter of discontent'. Militant trade union activity has succeeded in generating a power crisis. Halfway through the programme, electricity supplies are cut off. Across the country television screens go blank. Infuriated howls of frustration inundate the BBC's switchboard. And, from viewers in those areas unaffected by the power-cuts and who have managed to see the entire programme, there is a flood of interested mail. The strength of the reaction leads to a decision to repeat the programme. The second – and this time uninterrupted – transmission goes out six weeks later, on Good Friday, 31 March.

The public's response to the Rennes-le-Château Mystery is inestimably greater than I had anticipated. But then, as a journalist rightly commented: 'At the very mention of buried treasure, all the dream and greed muscles begin to tense.' Even so, I am completely unprepared for the vast number of letters which pour in. Such a reaction is, of course, hugely gratifying. What had started out as a 'brief filler for a magazine programme' has tapped a fascinated and productive current in the consciousness of the viewing public. Far from being a self-indulgence, further research into Saunière's story has become an imperative. At some time in the future, there will have to be a follow-up film.

INCONTROVERTIBLE PROOF ?

The Rennes-le-Château story elicits an immense range of reactions. The mail-bag produces ideas ranging from 'the whole story must be a hoax', to 'Why not simply find the treasure by overflying the area with an aerial magnetometer?' I also receive a couple of road maps each marked with a (different) location for Saunière's gold, identified by the ancient (and not one hundred per cent reliable) method of 'remote' dowsing. One letter requires an immediate response. A young Royal Artillery subaltern, stationed in Germany, writes to ask for the exact co-ordinates of the village. He has decided to give a squad of his soldiers an Easter break by taking them down to 'go over the area' and find the treasure. Andrew gently – but hurriedly – dissuades him. The local populace (not to mention the local authorities), will not be likely to welcome a rupture of their rural tranquillity by over-enthusiastic and highly questionable military manoeuvres.

The vast majority of the letters express fascination with the story and beg for more information, copies of the script and/or reproductions of the parchments. Best of all are those few letters which suggest new ideas and new leads. A teacher of Latin provides me with a wonderful anagram of *Et in Arcadia Ego* – the inscription on Poussin's painted tomb. He suggests *I tego arcana dei* – 'Begone! I conceal the secrets of God'. While the anagram is splendidly apposite, I can only remain aware that such word-play is no more than an interesting – if felicitous – chance. I am to learn that some 'solvers of the Rennes-le-Château puzzle' are prepared to base elaborate theories on such fragile 'evidence' – and then become quite angry when I refuse to be impressed by their wishful thinking. Anagrammatical games can produce apparently splendid results. Serendipity, however, is not the same as proof.

One letter in the early post is unlike any other. It is brief and startling and seems to be moving the story into a totally unlooked for direction. The writer is a retired Church of England vicar.

'May I advise you,' he states, baldly, 'that the "treasure" is not one of gold and precious stones, but a document containing incontrovertible evid-ence that Jesus was alive in the year 45 AD … This,' he goes on to say, 'would utterly destroy "Christian" dogma.'

My first reaction is that this is simply a communication from a crank and I toss it to one side. When, later, I again read it through prior to filing it away in my archive, I am struck by the vicar's dogmatic and quite uncranky style. I decide that a conversation with a priest who holds such extraordinary beliefs will prove more than interesting. I consider that an afternoon spent in such company will not be time wasted.

As the years have passed, I have come to realise that it is, perhaps, this attitude of mine that has contributed most to my ability to steer a way through fog-bound seas of uncertain material and into unsuspected harbours. Certain academic minds – especially of the Blunt variety – jump too readily to the conclusion that a given hypothesis is 'impossible'. They will not deign to waste even a moment of their time in consideration of *why* they are so certain and if, perhaps, there might not be among the dross at least the gleam of an interesting thought. It seems to me that what matters in the contemplation of seemingly outrageous ideas, is not so much whether or not one finds them acceptable, credible, or even likely. What matters more – and what is more illuminating – is the possibility that someone in the past may have held such a belief. Mariners, after all, once believed that the world was flat and that there was a danger of falling off the edge. The consequences of this belief merit study – even though one knows the belief to be absurd. I am *always* ready to devote a little time to the contemplation of even the most unlikely of suggestions. If it is utterly outrageous, then this will easily be seen. And I have certainly learned that some ideas, looked upon as crazy, have yet led to valuable insights. An open mind is a precious asset.

Although I cannot understand how anyone can claim to have 'incontro-vertible' documentary evidence of *anything*; although I cannot understand how the possibility that Jesus may have survived the crucifixion can have any relevance whatever to the story of Bérenger Saunière; I make my appointment with the Rev B and happily leave London to 'waste' an afternoon in his company.

He proves to be less dogmatic and less assertive in the flesh than he is upon the page. He gives me the impression that he now wishes that his letter had been lost in the post. He is unwilling to expand upon the tantalising tit-bit which he has proffered. I garner, however, two instructive scraps. The first is that, a long time ago, he had resigned his living and, still wishing to devote his life to service, he had turned to medicine and qualified as a doctor. Something made him leave the church – though he had returned to the fold in his old age. This man is clearly not a crank. I glean the second piece of information when I am probing to discover whence comes his extraordinary belief. He refuses to expand upon the simple statement in his letter, but confesses that the information came to him from one Canon A. L. Lilley. When, later, I turn my attention to the Canon, I discover that he had studied in Paris at the beginning of the century. He had apparently worked at St Sulpice and been involved with a young French scholar called Emile Hoffet. Now, suddenly, I glimpse a break in this fog of seeming irrelevancy. In his questionable account of the events at Rennes-le-Château, de Sède tells us that Saunière made a trip to Paris with his mysterious parchments. The documents were examined, he tells us, by experts at St Sulpice, including a certain Emile Hoffet. I hear the jaws of coincidence snap shut.

If the story is true and *if* the documents contain interesting information, then here is a possible train of transmission. Hoffet works on Saunière's parchments – Lilley is working with Hoffet. Lilley communicates 'something' to the Rev B, who loses his faith and quits the church. It's a tenuous and unlikely scenario. But it hangs together. And chimes with de Sède's other curious anecdote of the alleged death-bed confession of Saunière. The priest who heard it, he tells us, was deeply disturbed and refused to grant Saunière absolution. Whether or not these stories are true, there is certainly a consistency buried somewhere here.* For the moment, it appears no more than a fascinating, though irrelevant, side-track.

SHUGBOROUGH HALL

A more immediately productive new lead comes from a viewer who asks if I know of *The Shepherds' Monument* at Shugborough Hall in Staffordshire? This is a very large bas-relief of Poussin's *Shepherds of Arcadia* – but sculpted

---

* This was the first of the hints produced by the research, which eventually led to the creation of the hypothesis which was presented in *The Holy Blood & The Holy Grail.* H.L.

mirror-fashion, in reverse. Moreover, there is carved beneath the picture a row of cryptic letters which have never been satisfactorily interpreted. It seems worth the effort of a trip into the country to make some enquiries about this unexpected addition to my 'Poussin Dossier'. And it is to teach me a very valuable lesson.

Shugborough Hall is the home of the Earl of Lichfield. Now administered by the Staffordshire County Council, its stable block houses the County Museum, where I make enquiries. But little information is forthcoming concerning *The Shepherds' Monument*. It appears to date from the mid-eighteenth century and is the work of Peter Scheemakers. There seems to be no record of why it was commissioned, nor what its significance might have been. The letters beneath the bas-relief are:

$$O \cdot U \cdot O \cdot S \cdot V \cdot A \cdot V \cdot V$$
$$D \cdot \qquad\qquad\qquad\qquad\qquad M \cdot$$

These, too, remain unexplained. Only one possible suggestion seems to have been made. Anna Seward, an eighteenth-century poetess, known as *The Swan of Lichfield*, began a poem with the following lines:

> Out Your'n Own Sweet Vale, Alicia, Vanisheth Vanity
> 'Twixt Deity and Man thou shepherdest the way.

As can be seen, the initial letters of the first line (with the 'Y' of 'Your'n' excepted) match the inscription. And the letters, it can be suggested, lie 'between' the 'D' and 'M' of 'Deity and Man'. But, even accepting that Anna Seward's verse is linked with the Shugborough Monument, the connection cannot be said to shed any very clear light on the problem. Does the mysterious cipher simply record Anna Seward's verse? Or did Anna Seward write the words to match the enigmatic letters? In any case, this minor conundrum seems to be no more than a brief distraction from the Poussin and Saunière puzzle. It is in attempting to sever any possible links between the two stories, however, that I find myself facing yet another of the Rennes-le-Château coincidences.

In this account of the investigation springing from the ciphered parchments I have, thus far, concentrated on Poussin and his painting of *The Shepherds of Arcadia*. However, he is not the only artist to figure among the clues. The relevant part of the unravelled cipher reads 'Shepherdess – No Temptation – Poussin and Teniers hold the key.' The 'Shepherdess' has linked easily with Poussin in *The Shepherds of Arcadia*. But 'Teniers' still lacks certainty. De Sède has insisted that, with the reference to 'temptation' the relevant painting will prove to be a *Temptation of St Antony*. But the Teniers, father and son, had produced many variations on this theme. How are we to be sure which one is being indicated? Moreover, I am worried by the 'No Temptation' of the cipher. A vital indication is still missing. At Shugborough I glimpse the first faint gleam of a possible solution.

In attempting to clarify the reasons for the presence of the sculpted version in the Shugborough park, I ask if there is any evidence that it might have had some special significance to the family who commissioned it in the eighteenth century. 'Well,' says the curator of the museum, 'there is also a pencil sketch of the painting somewhere in the house.' I ask if I might see it and permission is readily granted. Someone is sent off to bring it down for my inspection. At last the messenger returns, holding a small picture frame. As he approaches, he says: 'I'm sorry, but it isn't the same painting.' He hands it to me, and I find myself gazing – not at the Louvre Shepherds, with which I am now so familiar – but at Poussin's earlier version of the same theme. This '*Arcadian Shepherds*' was painted about a decade before the Louvre rendering and is owned by the Duke of Devonshire. Far from being disappointed, I am more than intrigued. Evidently the '*Et in Arcadia Ego*' theme was of some interest in eighteenth-century Shugborough.

Taking a step further down this tantalising path, I ask: 'Did someone here make a habit of producing copies of Old Masters?' 'No,' I am told, 'There's only one other such copy – and it's not of a Poussin.' Still unaware of the approaching thunderclap, I innocently enquire which artist had been copied. 'Teniers,' comes the response. I can scarcely believe my ears. *Poussin and Teniers hold the key.* Coincidence can only go so far. Am I at last to discover which of the Teniers' *St Antonys* may be relevant? 'Can you give me the title of the Teniers copy?' I ask, trying to keep the excitement out of my voice. 'Oh yes. It's *Elijah and Elisha being fed by the ravens.*' The sudden elation evaporates. Oh well … perhaps one should not expect such an extraordinary chance to bear productive fruit. Nevertheless, in order to clear away the remains of this unexpected trail, I ask if I might see the picture. Unfortunately it is sequestered in the Earl's private apartment and he is not presently in residence. Yet another loose end which must be left dangling. I am disappointed, but not overly so. The reverberations of this particular thunderclap refuse to die away, however. In the back of my mind, the coincidence continues to nag. Fortunately Shugborough has an important lesson yet to teach.

The Shugborough pencil sketch of Poussin's 1630 version.

It is not until a considerable time has passed that I find myself back at Shugborough Hall, immersed in the preparatory work for the second Rennes-le-Château film, *The Priest, the Painter and the Devil*. Now, at last, I hope to be able to clear away the Teniers 'loose end'. Again I ask if it

(80)

might be possible for me to examine the painting, although I cannot see how the Old Testament story of *Elijah and Elisha being fed by the ravens* can have any definitive connection with the 'No Temptation' clue which should, it would seem, link in some way with Poussin's shepherdess and, presumably, St Antony.

This time Lord Lichfield is at home and he very willingly agrees that I may examine the Teniers copy. The picture is a quite large oil, I am told, painted by Anne Margaret Coke at about the same time in the eighteenth century that the *Shepherds' Monument* was erected in the grounds. When I am eventually taken through to see it, the painting has been set down in the centre of a handsome room, propped against a couch. As I follow the museum curator into the room I am unprepared for my reaction of sudden – if stunned – excitement. 'But that *can't* be Elijah and Elisha!' I exclaim. 'Why do you say that?' asks the curator, somewhat sharply, 'It's always been catalogued with that title.' 'But it can't be,' I insist, 'Look at it.'

'It can't possibly be an Old Testament subject. There's a crucifix in the centre.'

I have been taught two lessons in one. The first I should already have garnered from my brush with Anthony Blunt:– 'Never simply accept the word of an "expert". Check for yourself.' The second is confirmation of an earlier lesson:– 'One should learn, not only to look – but to see.' Brief further research reveals the subject to be *St Antony and St Paul in the desert*. Moreover, it is the only St Antony work by either of the Teniers in which the saint is not being tempted. Here, at last, seems to be confirmation that this could indeed be the painting referred to in the cipher. 'Shepherdess – No Temptation – Poussin and Teniers hold the key.' As additional confirmation, the artist has placed beside a tree in the background a shepherdess with a flock of sheep. How far must coincidence go? And why should this curious link with the Rennes-le-Château puzzle surface in England?

EXPERT OPINION

When, later, I check this Teniers painting in the catalogue of the Witt Library collection at the Courtauld Institute, I find it listed there, also, as *Elijah and Elisha being fed by the ravens*. I ask the assistant who is helping me to confirm that the painting has been wrongly named. He looks at the reproduction of the picture for some considerable time, but is unable to see why I will not accept the title in the catalogue. It is astonishing how the obvious can be invisible, even when staring one in the face.

My attitude to the reliability of 'expert opinion' is to be coloured yet further by another unforeseen result of the transmission of *The Lost Treasure of Jerusalem . . .?* Paul calls me to say that he has received a request and an invitation from a distinguished member of the 'Art World'. Would he and I be willing to attend a small and private *soirée* to discuss the Poussin question, preceded, if possible, by a showing of our *Chronicle* programme, so that all present might be *au fait* with our claims? As 'innocent lambs', we can see no objection to the plan. The evening is therefore arranged and, bearing a copy of the film, Paul and I duly and unsuspectingly enter the portals of the intended 'slaughterhouse' in a quiet and discreet Belgravia mews.

As we sip our sherry before the showing of the film, overheard snatches of conversation provide a hint of the nature of our audience. 'What did you think of the Rembrandt at Christies last week?' 'I bought it.' 'Ah ...' But the smooth and manicured veneer of our fellow guests is but thinly concealing some carefully sharpened claws. The showing is greeted by polite applause and compliments on the quality of the programme. Questions about Saunière and his possible treasure fill a half-hour or so of anodyne conversation. But, slowly, the conversation turns to 'matters artistic'. It is not long before I begin uncomfortably to realise that the 'Art Establishment' is out for my blood. An amateur enquirer is not welcome in the world of the *cognoscenti*. Especially when he is claiming to have made a discovery within the purlieus of their own professional expertise.

'Absolute rubbish, of course, trying to drag Poussin into this.'

'My dear boy, if Poussin had been involved in anything such as you are suggesting, then we'd know about it.'

'He can't possibly have painted your pretty valley, don't you see? He just never went anywhere near the place.'

'Do read up his life, dear boy. He worked in Rome – apart from one brief trip to Paris.'

I can feel myself, both literally and metaphorically, being backed into a corner. And, being cornered, I seek furiously for a way out. In such circumstances, I have found, the brain clears and the essentials present themselves.

'I know all this,' I say. 'The King summons him. He comes to Paris. He stays a couple of years – and then he goes back to Rome.'

'Precisely.'

'And when does this happen?' I ask, glimpsing a possibility.

'He's in Paris in 1640. Back in Rome in 1642.'

'And in what year did he paint *The Shepherds of Arcadia*?'

'About 1640.'

'Ah. So he's travelling at the right time.' My confidence is increasing.

'Can you tell me what route he took?'

'He took the usual route, of course.'

'That doesn't answer my question. Can you tell me what route he took?'

'He took the route that everybody took.'

'I'm sorry, but that still doesn't answer my question. What route did he follow from Rome to Paris and from Paris back to Rome?'

Five minutes of blustering later and my equilibrium is fully restored. The 'experts' have no idea of Poussin's itinerary. Their confident 'he never went near the place' has proved to be no more than an assumption. A short detour off 'the usual route' is therefore very possible. And the accuracy of his rendering of the landscape is convincing evidence that Poussin *did* make such a detour – and at exactly the appropriate time. An 'assumption' to the contrary is but a feeble counter-argument.*

It is my suspicion that, had I not been, in their eyes, an untutored amateur, their reception of this splendid addition to their knowledge of the life of the artist might have been a less hostile and dismissive one. As I make my way home after what has proved, in the end, an entertaining and illuminating evening, I can relax with the confidence of knowing that the quicksands into which I thought I had stumbled, have turned into far firmer ground. Our contentions have proved unquestionably more solid than the assumptions of the 'experts' – dogmatic though they may have been.

SECRET DOSSIERS ETC

The excitement engendered by the transmission and the reactions to the film begins to fade away. But I no longer consider time devoted to Rennes-le-Château to be a self-indulgence. I am now all too aware of the many and varying trails which have opened up before me.

My fleeting brush with the Bibliothèque Nationale, in the company of de Sède, has tempted me with a potential treasure-house of documentation. I decide that a trip to Paris for a few days of concentrated delving into the archives will prove worthwhile. And again I am confronted by the bizarre stumbling-blocks, false trails and smoke-screens which beset the seeker after Rennes-le-Château's 'truth'. Consulting a National Library should, one would think, be a relatively straightforward business. As one simple example of the convoluted contortions of the Rennes-le-Château material, I need cite only the curious case of the *Dossiers Secrets*. These 'Secret Dossiers' are supposedly the work of one Henri Lobineau. However, a search for this author in the Bibliothèque's catalogue will draw a complete blank. To track down this work, it is necessary to look under the name 'Schidlof'. How is the ordinary researcher to come by this recondite piece

---

* A decade later, attitudes were less entrenched and the facts were being faced. In Christopher Wright's *Poussin Paintings – A Catalogue Raisonné*, published in 1984, we read of the 'striking' similarities of the real and the painted tomb and landscape. *These similarities*, says Christopher Wright, *are undeniable and are unlikely to have been coincidental.* H.L.

of information? One might expect to find a card under 'Lobineau' with the indication: *see* 'Schidlof'. But there is nothing of the sort. In fact, no indication of any kind.*

I, of course, am in the privileged position of having been briefed by de Sède. He, hardly surprisingly, has been unable to explain to me why it is necessary to play this particular game – nor who had given him the needful key to the mystery.

Among the more intriguing publications which float in the muddy waters of the 'source material', there are a number whose authors are hiding their identities behind resonant pseudonyms. Madeleine Blancasall is clearly made up from a reference to Rennes-le-Château's patron saint, Marie-Madeleine, linked with the names of the two rivers, the Blanque and the Sals which conjoin just to the south of Rennes-les-Bains. Nicolas Beaucean is an obvious echo of the name bestowed upon the banner of the Knights Templar. The not very illuminating works by these two authors, I am able to consult with no difficulty. But another of the pseudonymous publications proves altogether more elusive. This is entitled *Un Trésor mérovingien à Rennes-le-Château*. The author cloaks himself with the saintly identity, Antoine L'Ermite (Antony the Hermit). This St Antony, by the way, is not to be confused with St Antony of Padua. Antony the Hermit carries a bell and a staff (the latter in the form of a Tau cross), and is always accompanied by a pig. He is the saint on whom one should call for aid in the retrieval of lost objects – as Henri Buthion had so happily demonstrated in the case of Andrew's missing camera knob. And he is, of course, the St Antony of the Temptations and of the Teniers' paintings.

A Merovingian treasure at Rennes-le-Château is the book which I had ordered during my visit to the Bibliothèque Nationale with Gérard de Sède. On that occasion, it had been *communiqué* – unavailable as another reader was consulting it. I am surprised to find, this few months later, that the book is still *communiqué*. On each of my three working days in Paris, I re-order the book. On each occasion I am informed that the book is *communiqué*. This is very frustrating – but the fact that other people, too, are delving into the Rennes-le-Château mystery is, perhaps, not surprising. For the moment, I must accept the frustration as 'part of the job'. But I gaze around the Bibliothèque's vast Reading Room and wonder which of

---

* The problem has presumably been solved in these modern days of microfiche and computerised catalogues. For full details of this questionable publication, see *The Holy Blood & The Holy Grail*. H.L.

those bowed heads is consulting my elusive quarry. Yet again, I return home to England with Antoine L'Ermite unconsulted.

A month or so later, a friend tells me that she is about to take a short holiday in Paris. Is there, she asks, any commission she can undertake on my behalf? I ask her to pay a visit to the Bibliothèque Nationale; to order up the evasive Antony Hermit and, if possible to photocopy a page or two. But she returns with the by now familiar lack of success. *Communiqué*. I am beginning to smell the proverbial rat. At the next possible opportunity, I must endeavour to trap it. Yet more months are to pass before I can make the attempt.

At last I find myself back at the Bibliothèque Nationale. Again I order the book. Again it is *communiqué*. I wonder if, perhaps, I should seek help from St Antony himself, but I am unsure if he will consider the task to fall strictly within his brief. After all, I haven't exactly *lost* the book. Would that I might be given the opportunity! I sit at my desk in the Reading Room and ponder upon the problem. If I can't ask St Antony, I can at least make enquiring noises at the librarian's desk. But – no, I am told, *communiqué* means *communiqué*. There's nothing I can do about it. Somebody is read-ing it. 'For months on end?' I query plaintively. But an unhelpful shrug is the only response. What seems a not unreasonable idea occurs to me. 'Can I, *madame*, order it up now for tomorrow morning, so that mine will be the first request of the day?' This suggestion is greeted by a glare of utter horror. This is not part of the Bibliothèque Nationale's routine. I must present myself at the desk each day, put in my order and await – with patience – until the other reader has finished with it. Clearly, I am going to get nowhere in the face of this bureaucracy. As a final desperate throw, I ask: 'Is it possible for you to indicate to me the desk of the other reader?' Total shock renders the librarian speechless. Her eyebrows pole-vault toward her hair line and her eyes close to block out the sight of such uncouth temerity. Duly chastened, I slink back to my desk. Obviously, I must devise another stratagem. I riffle abstractedly through the other books of my day's order, while my brain gnaws at my problem.

Here, for those unacquainted with such humdrum matters, I will explain the routine which must be followed in order to gain access to a book from the immense stock of France's National Library. First, it is necessary to track down the book in the library's main catalogue and make a note of its reference number. In the Reading Room, a form must be filled in, in triplicate, for each book requested and then handed over at the librarian's desk. One is required to enter one's name, the title of the book and the catalogue reference number. A desk number is then assigned. In due time, one's book – or books – will be brought to the indicated desk, where one is now free to begin work. Of the three copies of the form, one is retained at the librarian's desk, and the other two disappear into the cavernous recesses of the Library's store. When the book is found on the shelves, the second copy of the form is placed inside its cover so that it may now make its way to the appropriate reader's desk. The third copy – known as the *fantôme* – is placed in the space vacated by the book, where its 'ghostly' presence holds sway until the volume is restored to its rightful home. If the book is *communiqué*, then the *fantôme* is duly marked and placed on the reader's desk as notification of the fact. Is there any way in which I can take advantage of this elaborate routine?

'No' seems to be the only answer to my question. Lengthy discussions with functionaries of various sorts have always found me butting my head against the solid wall of the rigid rules and regulations. As I ponder upon this seemingly obdurate scenario, I begin to wonder if my command of the French language is not, for once, a disadvantage. I find myself remembering how helpful people used to be in the days of my *jeunesse*, when my fluency was less than adequate. Can I solicit aid by 'forgetting' the French language and presenting myself as a pathetically confused foreigner? Why not give it a try? Plainly, it will not work here, in the Reading Room where *Madame l'Ogresse* already knows to the contrary. I abandon my desk and, clutching my form emblazoned with the dread word *communiqué*, I make my way back to the Catalogue Room.

Two or three officials are to be found manning the catalogue, to provide assistance in case of need. I choose an elderly gentleman with a genial, smiling and helpful air. '*Excusez-moi, monsieur,*' I say, with as execrable an accent as I can muster, '*Parlez-vous anglais?*' 'A little,' he tells me. Taking shameless advantage of his limited English and my for-the-moment well nigh incomprehensible French, I laboriously explain that I am a writer, attempting to research within his hallowed walls, and finding difficulty in understanding the system. Can he help? 'But of course.' He will certainly do his best. I show him my *communiqué* form. He explains about *communiqué* and I explain that the damn book has been *communiqué* for months. The opacity of our mutual lack of fluency in the two tongues ensures that ten confusing minutes are required to achieve this degree of understanding. But he agrees that it is not *habituel* for a book to be *communiqué* for so long.

I ask, in yet more painful and halting sentences, if he could *please* confirm for me that the book is, indeed, with another reader. As I had been desperately hoping, he decides that it will be quicker and easier simply to make a physical check, rather than engage in any more exhausting attempts to communicate advice and/or instruction. Taking my form with its needful catalogue number, he disappears. I wait.

At last he reappears, wearing a worried frown. The book, he tells me, is not there. The *fantôme* on the shelf bears, not today's date – but a date several months in the past. The book has been stolen. Moreover, it appears to have been stolen by one of my *compatriotes*. How does he know this I ask? The name on the *fantôme* is recognisably English, he tells me. Can he give me the name? Well, of course, he shouldn't. But my sterling efforts to speak to him in his own language have, he thinks, earned me a tiny bending of the rules. He gives me the name. And now I *know* that the rat I had smelled all those months ago is still alive and lurking in the wainscote. The name he has so kindly provided is that of my friend who had also been given the *communiqué* story. Why? And why has her *fantôme* been left on the shelf? What game is being played? And by whom? I thank the kindly official for his assistance 'beyond the line of duty' and return to England more than puzzled by the inaccessibility of Antony Hermit's opus.

I decide, however, not to let the matter lie. Through my local library in England, I eventually make contact with an official of our library service who concerns himself with international loans. I explain the curious story to him and he agrees to write on my behalf to the Director of the Bibliothèque Nationale. To my total astonishment, barely a week later, *Un Trésor mérovingien à Rennes-le-Château* by Antoine L'Ermite drops through my letter-box. It proves to be a tiny pamphlet, just a few pages long. I have been sent a photocopy, with the instruction that it should be returned to the Bibliothèque Nationale as soon as I have read it. The matter is growing 'curiouser and curiouser'. A photocopy, after all, is just so much waste-paper, hardly worth the return postage. I duly – and immediately – photocopy the photocopy and send it back to Paris. But this is not the most bizarre aspect of this bizarre saga. As I scan the pages of my hard-won copy of *Un Trésor mérovingien*, I realise that I have read it before. It is the chapter dealing with Rennes-le-Château in a recently published book by Robert Charroux: *Treasures of the world*. But not simply photocopied from the book. The pages are completely differently set and there are very tiny alterations in the text. (E.g. *mettre au jour* is changed to *mettre à jour*; *C'est alors* is changed to

C'est à cette époque.) Why should anyone wish to go to all this trouble to publish a copy of a sketchy, incomplete and garbled account of a story which is already in print? And why make it so difficult for me to lay my hands on it? There is never to be an explanation of this additional mystery. Perhaps somebody is testing my persistence?

Chapter Six

THE PRIEST, THE PAINTER
AND THE DEVIL

FASCINATING THOUGH THE Rennes-le-Château investigation is proving to be, it is becoming a drastic drain on my resources. I still have a living to earn and a growing family to support. The opportunity for a paid sabbatical from my researches comes when I am asked to write the English language version of a French film and to act as dialogue director during the shooting. This will take me to Belgrade for three months – (not, in those long-gone Tito days, an especially enticing prospect). But the Jugoslavian filming will be followed by three months work in the studios in Paris. This is certainly a huge temptation in itself. I love Paris, and my working base there will make a holiday home for the family during the school vacation. Equally tempting is the thought that I will certainly be able to find the odd free day for more delving into the treasures of the Bibliothèque Nationale. My decision becomes inevitable, however, when I discover that the movie is to be directed by Georges Franju – one of the truly great names of French film. The opportunity to work with such a legend of the cinema is not to be missed. I pack my bags and fly off to Belgrade. Rennes-le-Château slips into the recesses of my mind as the enjoyable process of working with a French/Italian/ German/Jugoslav film crew takes over my waking hours.

For days on end, I hear no word of English and the slightly crazy, but highly entertaining world of volatile continental actors and technicians soon swamps any thought of Saunière and his strange story.

Belgrade passes in a blur of *shashlik* and hysteria. The bootless badgering of Jugoslavian actors in fruitless attempts to get their tongues around English dialogue leaves us all helpless with laughter. Especially the wonderful Franju, who, in any case, has not one word of English and is totally dependent upon me for indications of where we may be in the script. '*Je ne comprends rien*,' he says to me one day as we rehearse some actors. '*Ils sont magnifiques . . . mais je ne comprends rien.*' I tell him that, without the script, I wouldn't be able to understand their English, either. Which, strangely, matters not the slightest. We require only the correct lip movements, as all the dialogue will be dubbed later by English actors. *Olzdoza lok tin ball tit* stays in my mind as a typical example of the wilder utterances of a Serbian small-part player who tells me that he 'has a genius for foreign languages'. (He is trying to articulate the phrase: 'All the doors are locked and bolted.') Sanity – of a sort – returns when director, crew and principal actors move on to Paris.

Communism – even of the 'westernised' Tito-sort – can weigh heavily upon the spirit. After the drabness of Belgrade, the sudden contrast makes Paris sparkle like champagne – or rather, like *Blanquette de Limoux*. Her temptations are seductive and almost immediately, I succumb to the charms of Madame l'Ogresse. Her siren call – or is it Rennes-le-Château's? – proves irresistible. On my second morning back, with a free day before me, I seek her out at the Bibliothèque Nationale.

PARISIAN SUMMER

The problem now presented by the research is one of choice. I have an 'embarrassment of riches'. The previous work has indicated numerous lines of enquiry. Which will be the most profitable? Which will prove dead ends? It is impossible to tell. There is no alternative but to slog doggedly through the seemingly numberless tomes which may provide some sort of illumination. Or even some sort of relevance. High on my list of priorities for research is the mediaeval Order of warrior monks, the Knights Templar. I know nothing of them, beyond a faint memory from my childhood of the villainous Brian de Bois Guilbert in Scott's *Ivanhoe*. Lobineau's *Dossiers Secrets*, however, has hinted at something curious in their history as well as a possible link with Rennes-le-Château.

I must also learn what I can of the Cathares, the Albigensian heretics, in whose heartland the village lies. Poussin ... Teniers ... Templars ... Cathares and Dualism ... Visigoths ... Dagobert II and the Merovingians ...

alchemy ... secret societies ... code-making ... The list seems endless and my ignorance profound. There is much to do. And – though I am not yet aware of it – there are stirrings on the BBC's Rennes-le-Château front.

As the weeks pass, Franju needs me less and less. The film's dialogue scenes are all but completed, the sequences which remain are mostly 'action'. My researches at the Bibliothèque Nationale can proceed almost uninterrupted. School holidays arrive. A Paris apartment has few attractions for active youngsters – but the family has a great desire to see Rennes-le-Château. I rent a cottage at the entrance to the village where the children are delighted to see that the famous 'Fouilles Interdites' (Digging Prohibited) notice is on their front wall. The family settles in to become Rennois for the long summer break. From time to time I can take the Paris-Carcassonne train to spend a long weekend en famille. The village begins to seem less like a working location and more a familiar neighbourhood. It is becoming 'home'.

On a hot Saturday morning, I am trapped alone in Paris. Summer is sliding towards its close. The family are back in England and it will be not too long before I join them. Although I have enjoyed the making of the film, I shall be glad to be back with the rumbustiousness of a house full of children. The solitary bachelor life, I have found, does not suit. I leave my flat for the normal weekend chore of a trip to the local Supermarché. As I amble the quiet pavement, a man falls into step beside me. 'Bon jour,' he says. I look at him. The face is familiar – but only just. Where have I seen him before? Perhaps he's another resident in my apartment block? We stroll along, making idle and impersonal chat for a few minutes. Then, suddenly: 'How are the researches going?' Researches? This can't be merely a neighbour. Could he be a fellow reader at the Bibliothèque Nationale? I make a non-committal reply.

'I have some friends who might be able to help you,' he says.

'I don't think that I exactly need help,' I say cautiously. 'It's just a straightforward learning process for the moment.'

'They may have material you won't get anywhere else.'

I am becoming interested – but not tempted. Who is this man? And what is he after? Again I am non-committal. 'Really,' I say, flatly.

'They're having a meeting tomorrow evening. You're invited. If you care to come.'

'I'm not sure about tomorrow evening,' I say, carefully. 'Where's the meeting?'

'Not far. I'll take you. Pick you up in the bar opposite your flat. 7.30.'

I don't like this. 'Cloak-and-daggery' is not my style. But we have reached the *Supermarché*. 'I'll think about it.' And I turn into the store.

'Don't worry if you can't make it,' he calls after me. 'There's always another time.'

I might think about it. But, unknown at that moment to either of us, there is to be no 'other time'. Rennes-le-Château is, yet again, about to dictate its own timetable.

An hour or so later, the shopping is done and I am cooling off in the shower. The telephone rings. 'Hello. Roy Davies here. *Chronicle*.' Roy Davies is one of Paul Johnstone's small 'stable' of directors, all of whom are now well known to me. He tells me that Andrew Maxwell-Hyslop has left *Chronicle* for another BBC department. Paul has decided to make a follow-up Rennes-le-Château film and has assigned Davies to direct it. Can he come to Paris to talk to me about it? As the work on my present film is all but finished, I am more than pleased to have another project 'in the pipeline'. I am surprised to find, however, that Davies wishes to come to see me immediately. There is, apparently, some urgency. With a long and empty weekend stretching ahead, I am happy to agree. He will fly over tomorrow, in time to meet me for Sunday lunch. In the eighteen months or so since *Lost Treasure*, I have gathered a great deal of new and interesting material and have already begun to assemble in my head a rough storyline. The opportunity to discuss it with a director is very welcome. But I am to discover that the projected film is not quite what I have envisaged.

In a restaurant on the Quai Voltaire, I learn the reason for the urgency. Some while ago, a viewer of the first film – (I will call him Mr A) – had contacted *Chronicle*, claiming to have solved the mystery. He has located Saunière's treasure. Will the BBC be interested in filming the excavating of it? This is, of course, a most exciting prospect. Where is it – and what has led him to it? But Mr A is not willing to divulge any details, either of his unravelling of the clues or of the exact location. 'Within sight of Rennes-le-Château' seems as far as he is prepared to go. He will reveal no more until he makes his statement to camera, on location at the village. Moreover, he insists, Henry Lincoln is to be kept out of it. This is Mr A's triumph and he is not prepared to take any risks.

Convinced by the claims, and with a contract drawn, Roy Davies has opened negotiations with Rennes-le-Château for the necessary permissions and access. As far as the village is concerned, however, he is a total stranger.

Chronicle and the BBC mean less than nothing in the Pyreneean foothills. In addition the villagers know that I have been continuing my researches into the story. They are puzzled and concerned by my apparent non-participation. For them, the issue is a simple one. No Lincoln – no filming. While this may be flattering to me – it's an accursed nuisance for the BBC. But the village is adamant. Will I, Davies asks, come down to Rennes-le-Château and help to sort things out? And, of course, in some way become involved in the making of the film? Everything is of an extreme immediacy. If I agree, then we must leave Paris at once. The crew is already on stand-by and the filming date is fast approaching.

But how can we make a film without a script, I wish to know? I haven't begun to shape it yet. The shooting, Davies explains, will be of an immediate 'news-reportage' type. A record of the digging-up of the treasure. We don't need a script. That can be written when we see what we've got. The situation seems to me to be a far from satisfactory one. But I am intrigued, if not totally convinced, by Davies' certainty that the treasure has been found. And I know that 'news-reportage' or not, a script will eventually be necessary.

I agree to help. Sunday afternoon it may be, but I know that Franju is filming a chase in a cemetery in a seedy suburb of Paris. I call the production office and explain my (or rather the BBC's) problem. My release from the film is quickly and easily arranged. I've already rehearsed the actors in what few dialogue scenes remain – and, in any case, the producer will be happy for his budget to be spared another week or so of my expenses. I hurl my possessions into bags and cases, make a shamefully perfunctory attempt to tidy the flat, and leave.

By 7.30 on Sunday evening, while my mysterious pavement acquaintance is waiting to collect me in the bar, I have already left Paris. In a few years time, I shall wonder if I have missed my first opportunity to make the acquaintance of the mysterious 'secret society', the Priory of Sion.

SECOND FILM

The flying visit to Rennes-le-Château is little more than a series of hugs from all my village friends; enquiries for news of the family (particularly one of my sons, who seems to have made quite an impression on the *jeunes filles* of the locality); and a brief and jocular meeting with the mayor, M. Lambège, which unblocks the impasse. Doors are once more open and arrangements are made for our filming. There will inevitably be a larger BBC contingent, which will overstrain Henri Buthion's limited accommodation. I arrange to move back into Mme Fons' house at the entrance to the village which has been my summer 'home away from home'. Here, at least, I can slip back into some sort of familiarity of domestic routine – and be assured of a modicum of peace and quiet for what, I suspect, may be a hectic trip. With a relieved Roy Davies, I return, at last, to England.

Time is short before our return to 'dig up the treasure'. An archaeologist is organised to oversee the discovery and I fret at the total lack of information concerning the background to the discovery which, it seems to me, I will need to script however exciting the 'actuality filming' may prove to be. But Mr A remains mute. He has now accepted my presence on the team but is adamant in his refusal to impart any information. My natural scepticism is compounded by a building irritation. What is he afraid of? I am hardly likely to rush down, dig up the gold and disappear with it. However, it seems that this is precisely what he fears. This paranoia, added to the few faint whiffs which I am beginning to get of his approach to the problem, increases my building conviction that there is less certainty to this 'discovery' than I have been led to believe. I become more insistent, stressing my need to prepare, at least, an introduction to the eventual film. At last, Mr A agrees to meet with me in order to 'reveal all'. This meeting, however, will not take place until thirty-six hours before our scheduled departure for filming which will leave, Mr A calculates, not enough time for anyone to purloin the prize. Clutching my tape-recorder, I cross London for the appointed rendezvous, and prepare for the revelation.

As I have feared, Mr A's recording is made up of a farrago of misconceptions, wishful thinking, and a few impossibilities. For instance, the formation of the landscape creates a shape which, with a little imaginative squinting, matches the forearm and pointing finger of the right-hand shepherd in Poussin's painting. The finger is indicating 'the spot' which proves to be on the flank of *Roque Fumade* (which is, felicitously, the site of Rennes-le-Château's municipal rubbish tip). The 'arm' and 'pointing finger' are visible in aerial photographs. I express my serious doubts that Poussin would ever have had a clear view of the site from the air from which to draw his inspiration. But Mr A's discovery has been confirmed *in situ* by the twitchings of a hazel-twig. Let me here immediately state that I do not deny the efficacy (in certain circumstances) of dowsing. But, as I listen to the detailed explanation of how Mr A has 'found' the treasure, I know that I would most certainly *not* embark upon a costly filming trip with the sort of evidence that I have now been shown.

Having left Mr A with the clear idea that I am not convinced by his reasoning, I make directly for the *Chronicle* offices, where Roy Davies is standing by for the news. I tell him that I prefer not to begin with a verbal report, lest my attitude colour the account. Instead, I play for him the recording of my conversation with Mr A. He listens intently and in silence. When the tape ends, there is a long pause as I wait for his reaction. But, though I can sense that he is concerned, he seems to remain steadfast in his confidence in the conclusions of Mr A. I am not very worried by the tenuousness of the material. I know that I have a film already partly structured in my head and ample additional material to complete it. And, in any case, we are committed. In a day and a half, we shall be filming the 'unearthing of the treasure of Bérenger Saunière'.

DIGGING FOR TREASURE

And so, once more back to Rennes-le-Château, where excitement is again in the air as we assemble on Saunière's *belvédère* for the first morning's shoot. Try as I might (and I confess to not trying very hard), I find it difficult to share the thrill of impending discovery. The weather is clear and bright, the panorama breath-taking in its crystal-sharpness. From the *belvédère* there is an unobstructed view of the site of Mr A's intended excavation. With this as background, the first sequence is to be of the treasure-hunter describing what he anticipates to be awaiting us. Mr A tells the camera that, when we go down on to the flank of *Roque Fumade*, he is 'expecting to find a large rock, beneath which will be a descending tunnel, leading to a cave chamber, inside which we will find Saunière's treasure.'

But I can be pedantic – and am always careful in my choice of words – especially when talking 'to camera'. 'Can we shoot that again?' I ask.

'Why?' I explain that Mr A's expressed 'expectation that we will find a rock' will appear to have been confirmed when the rock is actually 'found'. But we already *know* that the rock is there. Mr A has told us that he has visited the spot where he has found a rock which, he supposes, conceals his tunnel.

For 'Take Two' he tells us that the spot is marked by a rock. When we raise it, he 'expects to find a descending tunnel, leading to a cave chamber, inside which we will find Saunière's treasure.' With this minor, but important, correction, I am satisfied.

Will I now stand in front of the camera and state what I am expecting to find? My response is brief.

'I have no expectations. There is no evidence that we will find anything. Apart that is from the rock, already identified by Mr A.'

'You must say more than that,' I am told. But this is as far as I am willing to go. Indeed, it is as far as I can go.

And now the 'moment of truth' has arrived. Camera, tripod, recording machine and microphones, lighting equipment, film stock, reflectors … everything is gathered up and we make our way down Rennes-le-Château's mountain to *Roque Fumade*. I am fascinated, too, to see the amount of tackle which has been transported for the task of excavation. Picks, shovels – even 'hard hats' in case the tunnel's roof should prove unsafe. Thus burdened, we follow Mr A on a brambled scramble along a deep-sided gulley at the foot of the *Roque*. 'Over hill, over dale, thorough bush, thorough brier' … and at last we arrive at The Rock which covers The Tunnel. Overgrown with thorny scrub, it is embedded in a steep slope. And it is enormous. It looks as though it will take at least half-a-dozen brawny men to shift it. For me, this is the last decaying straw. Mr A has told us that Saunière would have removed and replaced the stone at each of his clandestine visits to the 'treasure cave'. This – without the assistance of a team of helpers, as well as a considerable amount of time and some heavy lifting-gear – is an obvious impossibility.

I clamber up the slope to the top of the rock and stand looking down at the feverish activity below me. Davies has selected his camera position and all is being prepared for a shot of Mr A beginning the clearance of the bramble from around the rock. To one side is Mr A, macheté in hand, awaiting the director's call to 'Action'. I decide that, as far as I am concerned, the moment for action has already arrived. I call down to the busy knot of people waist-deep in gorse.

'I'd like to say something. And I'd like to say it now – before you touch so much as a twig. I have no doubts about what I am saying, and I don't wish to be accused later of merely speaking with hindsight. You're wasting your time. There is nothing here. Nor is there any valid evidence to suggest that there might be. I'm going back up to the village, where I will imbibe liquid refreshment until you decide that you have had enough and come up to join me.'

As I move away down the slope, Davies calls after me: 'You'll be the one with egg on your face when we bring out the treasure.'

'I'll take that chance,' I reply and set off happily up the road. I've got work to do. There's a script to be written.

Back in the little garden of Mme Fons' comfortable house, I begin the task of shuffling order into my notes for the film which I have been intending to write. Down on the hillside, the slashing, sweating and filming continue unabated. At the end of the day, I watch the hot, scratched and exhausted procession passing my window on its way up to the cooling showers of the Villa Bethania – and the cooling draughts of Henri Buthion's beer and wine cellar. 'No question,' I think, as I contemplate the weary hunters' return from the hill and take another sip from my iced *panaché*, 'I made the right decision.'

For two more days, I write peacefully either in my house, or in Saunière's shady garden, enjoying the beauty and tranquillity of an empty Rennes-le-Château. Meanwhile, down below, on the baking hillside, treasure-fever is abating. Hope is disappearing, realism is taking over and tempers are growing shorter. On the third evening, I am summoned to a meeting beneath the shade trees.

'It's hopeless. There's nothing there,' Davies tells me. 'What are we going to do?' he adds, more appositely.

'Make a film,' I respond, with what must seem a smug and infuriating cheerfulness. 'I suggest that you and the crew spend the evening getting drunk. I'll go back to my house and do some scribbling. At breakfast tomorrow, I'll give you script for the day's shoot.'

If ever a situation merited the cliché line: 'I told you so', this was it. I consider it to be to my eternal credit that I did not utter it.

At breakfast on the following morning, Mr A's place at table is vacant.

A search finds his room to be empty. With his dreams of treasure and his hazel-twig, he has faded silently away into the night.*

A REAL FIND

By now, I have shuffled together enough shooting script to keep the crew more than occupied while I continue with my solitary labours *chez* Mme Fons. As I work quietly in my garden, Mme Fons herself appears, to share a customary quiet coffee and to bring the latest gossip about village affairs. But this time, she has brought something else. As we sit in the tiny garden, she drops onto my heap of papers a tattered brown envelope.

'These are for you,' she says. 'They've been at the back of my parents' wardrobe for fifty years. I'd like you to have them. Perhaps you can use them in your film.'

I pick up the envelope and slide out the contents – a handful of scratched and slightly faded sepia photographs. I cannot believe my eyes. Here are pictures of Saunière which I have never before seen. Saunière, in crocheted finery, posing proudly in the porch of his church. Another, beside the famous altar pillar in which, supposedly, he found the parchments. Yet more, with friends, in a festive scene outside his presbytery, arms folded, proprietorial, beside a table laden with glasses and bottles of wine. More still, posed by the gates to the village cemetery. Unselfconscious snapshots of the real Bérenger Saunière; quite unlike the formal, posed, studio portraits of him which have been, until now, my sole, stiff, visual images of the man. There is, though, one new and formal likeness – a disturbing and unexpected death-bed photograph. I am surprised by a curious anomaly in this picture. On the table beside the bed is a bishop's mitre. Can we be sure that this is Saunière? But the likeness is undeniable and, as Mme Fons points out, there is no reason for her parents to have cherished the death photograph of any other priest, bishop or not.

Here, at last, a small, real and, for me, quite wonderful treasure has surfaced. Mme Fons has inherited them from her parents and they have

---

* Later came a Mr C, who also convinced the BBC that he had found the treasure. I did not, however, learn of this dramatic new discovery until after yet another abortive gold-hunting trip had been made. H.L.

Saunière with friends in the church garden.

lain, all but forgotten among their effects. I feel privileged and honoured to have been given such a precious gift. Here, indeed, is wonderful new material for the film. But the photographs are a priceless addition to the village archive and I promise that, when I have taken copies, I will return them to their rightful home.* Later in the day I show my prize to Henri Buthion. He is stunned. Like everyone else in the village, he has thought that all such material has long been identified. Perhaps there are more such treasures still to be found. Roy Davies, too, is thrilled, when he returns from the day's filming, to see the marvellous new visuals which have surfaced and we plan for their incorporation into the script.

He has since told me that he has often 'dined out' on the story of how I 'knocked up' his successful film *The Priest, the Painter and the Devil*, in the couple of days after Mr A's departure – as if I were beginning from a *tabula rasa* when his desperate call came. It is true that my early experience as a writer of 'soap opera' trained me in the valuable art of writing fast to meet an impossible deadline. But not even *Emergency – Ward 10* could have taught me *that* degree of speed. Even so, three valuable shooting days (as well as a quantity of film), have been wasted. The allotted filming time is coming to an end. There is no hope that the remaining necessary Rennes-le-Château sequences can be completed on this trip. We will have to return to England, shape the programme carefully and return. Mid-October seems a likely date. By then, I am sure, I can produce a definitive script.

BELGIAN APPARITIONS

Mid-October duly arrives and the shooting script is ready. Henri Buthion is telephoned to forewarn him of our arrival. The date chosen is the thirteenth. By October, the tourist season is over. The little hotel in Saunière's Villa Bethania is usually closed down. Our out-of-season trade is a welcome addition to the annual 'quiet time'. But Henri has a small surprise in store. He is fully booked for the night of our arrival. Embarrassed, he tells us that we will have to find other accommodation. He will be able to feed us in his restaurant, of course. But unprecedentedly – and for the

* Mme Fons has since died. Although she gave them to me and I returned them, I presume that, as she indicated to me that she would, she passed them over to the ownership of the village. H.L.

one night only – he has a group booking. His rooms are full. We can move in on the fourteenth. This is no more than a minor annoyance and appropriate alternative arrangements are easily made.

And so, yet again, the team assembles. We settle provisionally into our temporary base and make our way up to Rennes-le-Château for the evening. Henri has told me that he thinks his unexpected party are Belgians. More interestingly, they have advised him that they intend to make an excursion in the late evening. They will leave the hotel after dinner and will return in the small hours. Henri thinks it all seems a little odd. So do we. But the restaurant provides us with a splendidly innocent cover. Perhaps, discreetly, we may be able to find out what, if anything, is going on.

The members of the mysterious group seem ordinary enough. There are, in fact, many more diners in the restaurant than can be accommodated in the hotel's bedrooms. Some are evidently, like us, sleeping elsewhere. The dining room is packed and buzzing with animated chatter. The Buthion family is under pressure, both in the kitchen and in serving the multitude. The BBC team are as entertained as they are intrigued. We have been used to having the place almost entirely to ourselves. Both hotel and village take on a different air when overrun by holiday-makers. Though we are, of course, uncertain if 'holiday-makers' is the correct description of our fellow guests.

During the course of the evening, one or other of us manages to contrive an opportunity to initiate brief conversations with various members of the party. When we compare notes, we find that two distinctly different stories are being told. According to some, they are here to witness the arrival of a flying saucer. It seems that we are dealing with cranky, but harmless, UFO-logists. But others say that they anticipate witnessing an apparition of the Knights Templar. We find it difficult to decide which of these alternatives is the more likely – or the more cranky. One detail, however, is common to both stories. Whichever event is to take place, flying saucer or Templars will materialise on the crest of Bézu. This is a very visible mountain, four miles across the plain to the south of Rennes-le-Château. Here, it seems, once stood a Templar commandery. It is the intention of the visitors to climb the mountain, in order to be in place on the summit for the witching hour of midnight, when the apparition, or apparitions, are scheduled to appear.

The BBC squad goes into a huddled conference. Each of us seems to have reached the same conclusion. This is far too good an opportunity to miss. Bearing camera and recording equipment, we shall follow the ghostly saucer-hunters. The event (or even non-event) seems to merit capturing on film. (Having climbed Bézu many times in the intervening years, I now pale at the thought of this incredibly foolhardy venture. To climb Bézu, in daylight, when the tortuous track is at least visible, is arduous and difficult enough. To scale the precipitous flank of the mountain for the first time, on a direct and thorny line, in midnight blackness, and burdened with valuable gear, is very silly.) However, ready for adventure, we load our car and wait for action.

Dinner ends and as eleven o'clock approaches, the milling throng begin to don coats and climbing boots and prepare for departure. And suddenly, they are gone. A twisting snake of a dozen or more sets of headlights careers down from Rennes-le-Château to Couiza in the depths of the valley below. The BBC team, like a contingent of 'Keystone Cops', hurls itself in pursuit after the last of the disappearing tail-lights. Bézu may be only four miles away – but that is 'as the crow flies'. Our quarry are not crows, however, they are Belgians. And, even with Belgians at the wheel, the convoy must follow the road. From Couiza to Campagne-les-Bains, then left off the main road to the village of Granès, then the tiny hamlet of Le Bézu. At least a dozen miles of winding, twisting mountain roads are traversed at *Grand Prix* speed. But at Le Bézu, the road becomes a rather more bumpy track. We slowly gain on the procession of car headlights which is twining onwards across open country. Our map shows nothing ahead of us but the farmstead of *les Tipliés*. But now we can see the dark bulk of Bézu mountain rearing against the star-bright sky.

In the distance, the convoy is drawing to a halt. We watch as the car-lights flick out, to be replaced by a string of torches and lanterns which straggle on down into the valley ahead where, we presume, the farmhouse is nestling at Bézu's foot. We park the car and prepare to follow. There must be at least half-a-mile of track yet to come – and then there will be the daunting mountain still to climb. But we are still in a cheerful post-prandial mood. Shouldering our equipment, we set off in pursuit of the fire-fly gleaming of the tortuously winding line of torches. Maintaining a discreet distance from our quarry, we at last reach *les Tipliés*. The house is dark and empty-seeming – though the farmyard shows evidence of occupation. Perhaps the inhabitants are asleep – or, wisely perhaps, choosing not to show themselves to their unwonted nocturnal visitors. As we cross the farmyard, we can see the line of twinkling lights already high above us. We find the tiny track which heads up the tree- and scrub-clad mountainside. But, within minutes, we lose it in the blackness. With only the torch-light will o'the wisp glinting to follow, we have no alternative but to scramble, as best we may, in pursuit. It is not easy. Neither is it enjoyable. Our jokey whispered conversation fades away. We share the realisation that we must be crazy to have embarked on this schoolboy adventure. But having come thus far, we feel committed. Oh well – it makes 'a night out'.

Sweaty, scratched and cursing, we at last arrive on Bézu's crest. The Belgians are not pleased to see us. And who can blame them? Bedraggled and tattered as we are, we are no substitutes, as we emerge from the darkness, for the expected aliens and/or ghostly knights. Bonfires have been lit, but whether as 'homing beacons' for the approaching spacecraft, or simply for warmth, we cannot tell. (We decide that any phantom Templars hovering in the vicinity will have no need of illumination. Though we are open to correction.) Slumped against the tiny remaining vestige of what once was castle wall, we regain our breath and watch the action. There isn't any. People stand around in quiet murmuring groups, silhouetted against the orange-yellow heaps of flickering flame. A pretty sight, we decide – but fairly boring. Certainly not worth the effort of the climb. We consider joining the Belgians in their hope for other-worldly arrivals. We feel the need of some sort of compensation. We get it in the form of a heartening swig from a hip-flask of brandy thoughtfully transported by our sound recordist.

'I wanted to be sure,' he tells us, 'that we made contact with some sort of spirit tonight.'

Midnight – but nothing else – comes and goes. A morose Belgian wanders over and tells us that the non-materialisation is almost certainly our fault. Our 'aura of scepticism' is a negative influence. By 12.30, a more positive influence is felt in the form of a general desire among the BBC team to 'call it a night' and seek out the warmth of our beds. As we gather up our gear, our sound-man calls us over to listen to something odd. He has been idly swinging a directional microphone and listening to nothing in particular. But unexpectedly, he has picked up a signal. It is below us and seems to be emanating from a couple of miles away to the north. We take it in turns to listen through his earphones, but no one can make anything of the low thrumming sound. It *might*, he thinks, be a generator; though it doesn't sound quite right to his experienced ear. At least *something* unexplained has occurred.* We decide to settle for this and, leaving the Belgians to their hopeful – or hopeless – vigil, we set off on the scramble back down the mountainside.

As we drive home, we light-heartedly debate the sanity – or naïveté – of the Belgians. Can they possibly be serious? Or is it just an excuse for a jolly midnight ramble? What conceivable *real* reason can they have for their curious expedition? And this is the question which provides the unexpected, but bizarre answer. This has been the night of 13 October. It was on 13 October, in the year 1307, that the Knights Templar were arrested. The midnight expedition to the Templar commandery must have been in celebration of the anniversary. But why this particular anniversary? The significance suddenly cries out. We are in 1973. The mental arithmetic provides a fitting end-piece to the grotesque game. This has been a very special anniversary. Its number is the Apocalyptic Number of the Beast in the Book of Revelation. '*Here is Wisdom. Let him that hath understanding count the number of the beast; for it is the number of a man, and his number is six hundred, three score and six.*'

The realisation colours one's attitude. Perhaps the gathering on Bézu is weirder – and less innocent than we have imagined.

MONTSEGUR

While it is true that the strange midnight conclave on Bézu and the treasure fantasies of Mr A would make splendid material for a highly entertaining film, it is not the sort of film that *Chronicle* exists to make. Our brief is more serious and the material which I am slowly uncovering is remarkable enough. Vital to the new film are the stories of the Knights Templar and of the Albigensian heretics, the Cathares, who are figuring more largely in the background. Both these new elements in my researches are well known in France, where their dramatic histories are part of every child's education. For an English television audience, however, *The Priest, the Painter and the Devil* is opening new doors. The history of the murderous crusade led by the Church against the Albigensians sheds an extraordinary

---

* When checked on the map, the location seemed to be in the vicinity of a hill labelled *La Pique*. This was – much later – to prove an interesting coincidence. H.L.

light on the Middle Ages and is far too little known outside the French-speaking world. Here is an opportunity to explore – in an exciting and dramatic context – a fascinating aspect of our past which, until now, has been of interest only to specialist historians.

Saunière's treasure is a wonderful peg upon which to hang these stories of blood, faith, fire and the sword, which were played out in this very landscape. The stories of Templars and Cathares interweave and each involves treasure, of one sort or another. Again, I can tell a tale to make the 'dream and greed muscles' twitch.

The treasure of the Templars was one of the prime elements in their downfall. For the King of France, Philippe le Bel, the Templars posed a political threat. They were an immensely wealthy, powerful and well-organised fighting force. They were established in castles and commanderies throughout his kingdom – and they owed him no allegiance, being answerable only to the Pope. And Philippe was in debt to the Templars. When he plotted their downfall, he hoped to lay hands on their fabled wealth. But when, in a surprise action, the knights were arrested at dawn on Friday 13 October 1307, no trace of their treasure was found. Nor has it ever come to light. Perhaps this was the source of Saunière's riches?

One of the more disturbing aspects of the destruction of the Templars is that, Christian fighting monks though they were, who had laid down their lives in the service of Christ and his Church, yet they were accused of denying Christ and spitting and trampling on the Cross. This denial of Christ Crucified was a charge also levelled at the Cathares. Both Templars and Cathares are wreathed in the sulphurous smoke of heresy. And, like the Templars, the Cathares, too, were said to possess a treasure – though theirs seems to have been more spiritual in nature. It has even been suggested that the treasure of the Cathares was the Holy Grail. As visual background to the telling of their story, we travel the thirty or so miles from Rennes-le-Château to film at the Château of Montségur.

This castle on its incredible and towering *Pog* is one of the truly great and special sites of human history. Like Masada in Israel, this mountain saw the final desperate and tragic stand of a beleaguered faith. Here, on a spring morning in 1244, the last besieged Cathare garrison faced their ultimate and agonising choice. For those who would renounce their faith and embrace the Church of Rome, there was the offer of life and freedom. As they looked down from their towering walls, they could see the alternative which awaited the obstinate. Brushwood, piled within a palisade. The torment of martyrdom in the cleansing fires of the Inquisition.

Even today, as one walks the rocky pathway, it is impossible not to sense the presence of those two hundred brave souls who made the bitter choice. For them, the hideous torture of the flames was less painful than abjuring their beliefs. Hand in hand and singing, they walked that fearsome road into Eternity. Each time I tread those stones, I am aware that I am filling the space of a certainty and a strength of faith which is all but incomprehensible in our more 'enlightened' age. But across the centuries, the flame still burns at Montségur and the martyrs have not been forgotten.

My researches into this tragic story of faith and suffering lead me, inevitably, to the man known as 'The Pope of the Cathares'. Déodat Roché is well into his nineties when I first visit him at his home in the village of Arques. He is steeped in the history and the faith of his ancestors and he has agreed to talk to me about the rituals of his 'heretical' church. He greets me in his spare, almost stark, living room, beautiful in its monastic simplicity. The only adornment is a large wooden bowl, containing three wizened apples, which rests on the long, bare, seemingly centuries-old table at which he sits, upright in a tall-backed carved chair. He has a saintly and ascetic air, his gaunt head and fragile-looking hands seem clothed in an almost transparent and paper-thin skin. All but motionless, he talks in a quiet, clear voice, explaining rituals and prayers; patiently and with gentle courtesy, answering my many questions.

A year later, I call on him again. I find him still seated, in the same pose, in the same chair. It is as if he has not moved. Nothing in the room has altered – save in the wooden bowl, where twelve months before had lain the three shrunken apples. Now there are only two. Somehow, it doesn't seem impossible that the one missing apple may have provided his twelve-months' sustenance.

Chapter Seven

THE POUSSIN GEOMETRY
APPEARS

THE STORY of the Cathares is powerful and moving. Set against it, the venality of treasure-hunting seems almost sacrilegious. But important steps have been taken in the unravelling of the mystery of Rennes-le-Château and they need to be included in the film.

My visit to the Louvre to examine the x-ray of the *Shepherds of Arcadia* has left a 'dangling loose end'. There is an unexplained apparent anomaly in the painting of the right-hand shepherd's staff.* Time and again, I have returned unavailing to this problem. But I am learning 'not only to look, but to *see*'. I am also learning to ask the simple question. If one sets out on a hunt for complexities, then those very complexities may obscure a simplicity which is crying out for attention. As I work on the script, I turn yet again to the question. This time, I ask myself: 'What is the simplest thing I can say about this staff?' The answer is: 'It is cut in two by the shepherd's arm.' I find my dividers and set the distance from the base of the staff to the line of the shepherd's arm. From this point to the top of the staff proves to be *precisely* the same. The stick is not *simply* cut in two – it is *exactly* cut in two. I measure the distance from the top of the staff to the tip of the shepherd's pointing finger. Again, the distance is *precisely* the same. Already the scent of discovery is in my nostrils. Why should such rigid exactitude have mattered to Poussin? Did it, in fact, matter? Or have I simply stumbled upon another of Blunt's 'extraordinary coincidences'?

I test the left-hand shepherd's staff. From the top to that point where it is cut by the kneeling shepherd's back is, again, the same fixed measure.

---

* See p. 71. H.L.

From that mid-point to the base – yet again. This can hardly be coincidence. I embark upon a careful, inch by inch study of the painting. In half-an-hour, I have identified a score of repetitions of the half-staff measure. I am as baffled as I am overawed. Even at first sight, the painting is clearly a work of genius. But now I am discerning another layer of virtuosity. Poussin has presented us with a fluid, relaxed, harmonious idyll of calm serenity. And yet he has achieved this against a rigid and formal geometric framework. Is such rigorous and inflexible control a usual method in his work? Not for the first time in the Rennes-le-Château saga, I find myself sliding out of my depth. This study requires a knowledge and an expertise which I do not possess.

Professor Christopher Cornford of the Royal College of Art has made a special study of the geometric construction of paintings. He agrees to undertake an analysis of the *Shepherds of Arcadia.** In order not, in any way, to influence his thinking, he is, at the outset, told nothing of my detection of the half-staff measure. He approaches the problem with no preconceptions of any kind. And he makes a stunning discovery. In the words of his written report:

> Most old master paintings (in fact every single one that I've so far investigated) seem to be composed, whether loosely or rigorously, in conformity with a system of directional lines, orthogonal and diagonal, based on one or other of half a dozen or so fairly straightforward geometric and/or arithmetic subdivisions of the rectangular format – all of which can be readily constructed with ruler, compasses, dividers, T-square and set square.
>
> The systems used fall into two basic classes: those using geometric construction primarily, and resulting in the determination of sequences of magnitudes that are geometric progressions ... and, on the other hand, those based on ratios between small whole numbers, e.g. 2:3, 3:4, 3:5 etc. This latter system is based on the account of the creation given in Plato's *Timaeus* and was published by Alberti in his *Ten Books on Architecture* (Florence 1485). It proceeds by calculation as much as by construction using instruments, and it had great appeal in the High Renaissance and its aftermath, since it both dissociated art and architecture from the old manual masonic tradition of mediaeval times, and associated them with humanist scholarship. Moreover, the number system used was a kind of invocation of the divine,

* Professor Cornford made no analysis of the Teniers' *St Antony*, as only the Shugborough copy was available and it was impossible to tell how accurate it might be. It was after Christopher Cornford's death that the original was at last tracked down. H.L.

inasmuch as the building or painting became a microcosmic rehearsal of the primal act of creation.

The masonic-geometric system is incomparably the older of the two. Indeed, it seems to have been known to the ancient Egyptians and to our own megalithic culture. It survived, often surrounded by an atmosphere of craft (if not cult) secrecy, until Alberti's time and subsequently went into eclipse ...

Thus, since the *Bergers d'Arcadie* was painted about 1640, one would expect it to have an Albertian-Timaean substructure rather than a masonic-geometric one ...

Nevertheless, to his complete surprise, Professor Cornford finds that Poussin has resurrected this long-outdated system for the construction of the *Shepherds of Arcadia*. It is based with precision upon the pentagon, the five-sided figure whose chords form the five-pointed star, or pentagram. He goes on to say:

What convinces me in this case that there is pentagonal geometry present is the actual format of the painting ... The dimensions are ... 120cm × 87cm = 1 : 1.3793 – a discrepancy of only . 0033% ... from the rectangle 1:1.376, which has a very particular and strong relationship with the regular pentagon ...

The pentagon (and) pentagram ... have enjoyed immense prestige and excited nothing short of reverence among geometers, architects, and masons since very ancient times. For the Pythagoreans (6th century BC onwards) the pentagram was a symbol of life, eternity and health ... The use of the pentagram in later magical practice as a protection against uninvited spiritual agencies is, presumably a reminiscence of, or direct inheritance from, the Pythagorean tradition.

At the end of his careful and scholarly analysis, Professor Cornford makes this interesting statement:

If Poussin is saying *anything* ... he seems to be saying that pentagons and pentagrams and their constituent angles are very much involved.

As I read through the Professor's report, this sentence seems to leap from the page. Poussin has taken enormous pains both to conceal – and at the same time to hint at – the presence of this very particular geometric form. I find myself experiencing a clear sense of *déjà vu*. The parchments have

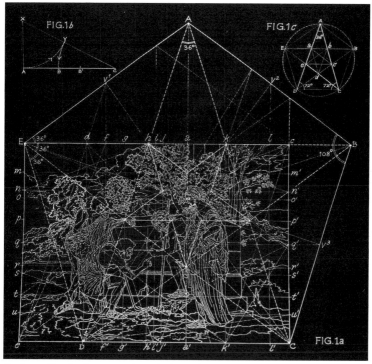

Professor Cornford's geometric analysis.

already shown me exactly this same subtle hinting at concealed geometry. Moreover, the hidden geometric form is, in both cases, pentagonal. Can this – yet again – be coincidence? Add to the equation the statement in the 'Fouquet letter' that: 'Poussin had a secret which kings would have pains to draw from him.' The Blunt-esque refusal of certain academics even to *consider* a possible validity in the newly-opening avenues of research, seems not simply wilful. It is unscholarly.

IMAGERY AND THE DEVIL

Inevitably, Professor Cornford's work makes me turn my attention to the possible significance of the five-pointed star. In what way could this elegant geometric form help us to understand the mystery of Rennes-le-Château? For the unexpected nature of its double appearance in the investigation makes its relevance beyond question. Until now, I have been aware of the pentagram in one context only. Magic. I remember seeing a production of Marlowe's *Dr Faustus*, in which Faustus raises up Mephistopheles by conjuring within the protection of the 'magic pentacle'. I remember, too, the novels of Dennis Wheatley, in which he describes the use of the pentacle in terrifying 'Satanic Rites'. Even Professor Cornford has made reference to 'the use of the pentagram in magical practice'. But, for all its strange and heretical elements, the Saunière story, in all the complexity of its details, seems to need something more to explain it. This is no mere smokescreen around the activities of dabblers in the 'black arts'. Something is still missing.

As I ponder upon the problem, I become aware that the cause for its apparent intransigence may lie in my own twentieth-century attitude.

This has already come home to me with moving power in the story of the Cathares. Clearly, their view of the world was quite different from ours. Perhaps my world-view is distorting the image? This story has its roots in a distant past. If we are to understand it, then should we not try to avoid imposing our preconceptions upon the beliefs and actions of our ancestors? At the mention of the words 'magic', 'occult', 'devil-worship', we react with 'enlightened' scorn. Rubbish! Mumbo-jumbo! Only 'cranks' take such things seriously.

But this truth is *our* truth. And our forefathers were *not* cranks. They inhabited a different world. And they believed, with a power and an intensity which we cannot comprehend, in the reality of such mystic 'nonsense'. How many innocents screamed out their last breaths in the agony of the fire? How many devout and righteous men racked and flayed and tortured in the name of Jesus Christ? To understand, we must try – however faintly – to see the world with their eyes. Most people today, if they think of the Inquisition at all, think of it as being made up of sadistic and perverted monsters. But the Inquisitors, in their own eyes – and in the eyes of the majority of the society they inhabited – were good and godly men. They acted out of compassion for the souls that they were trying to save. As the executioners set their torches, they sang *Veni Creator Spirituus*. Can we honestly claim to understand their world? It is too easy to condemn. Much more difficult is it to strip away our own preconceptions. And the attempt must be made if we wish to comprehend. To look at the past through modern eyes is to see only the images produced by a distorting mirror.

Such thoughts lead me to reconsider some of the elements of the story. I begin to wonder how much the beliefs of the past might have filtered down through the centuries. The story of the Cathares, for instance, ends with the tragedy of Montségur in March 1244. Montségur may, indeed, be the last page in the book – but is it truly 'the end'? The faith, the belief and the society which bred it, did not switch off with the abruptness of an electric light. There must have been many villages and hamlets, untouched by the calamity, where life and the Cathare church continued, if only clandestinely. Laurie's book on *Montaillou* bears witness to this simple fact.

Both Cathares and Templars had been accused of worshipping the Devil. But, in both cases, the accusation is an over-simplification. As Dr Hugh Schonfield established in his book, *The Essene Odyssey*, the supposed devil-figure of the Templars, Baphomet, was, in fact Sophia, the (female) Wisdom Principle. For the Cathares, it is true, all matter was the creation of *Rex Mundi*, King of the Earth, the God of Evil who stood in opposition to the God of Good. But to acknowledge the power of evil is not by any means the same as to worship it. To acknowledge the power of Nazism does not make one a Nazi.

As I play with these ideas, I am reminded that Saunière had placed a statue of the Devil in his church. In this new context, it seems a strange thing for a priest to do at the beginning of the twentieth century. On a hot afternoon of filming *The Priest, the Painter and the Devil* I seek out the coolness of the church and stand contemplating the ugly and deformed little monster. Saunière has made him the support for the Holy Water stoup. Yet again it is necessary to look beyond the surface statement and to *see* the true meaning – if meaning there be. In this case, the key lies in the insignificant and apparently decorative details which Saunière has added to his statuary group.

Rex Mundi, Lord of the Earth, supports the Holy Water. Above are the figures of four angels who, with the gestures of their right hands, are marking out the Sign of the Cross. But between the water and the angels are two

The alchemical statuary group.

irrelevant and unreal decorative beasts. As I gaze at Saunière's florid embellishments, I realise that all the elements of the group make sense – with the apparent exception of these creatures. But decoration for decoration's sake is not Saunière's way – at least as I am coming to understand it. His work is too careful, too thought out, too purposeful. Too easily, the eye slides over them; but the beasts are there because they have a meaning to convey. For the first time I take the trouble to look at them. And I see that they are salamanders.

The mythical salamander is born out of fire. It is a creature of fire. Here is the hidden, yet open, statement which gives another and startling sense to the sculptured group. At the base is *Rex Mundi* – Lord of the EARTH. Above his head is the sculpted shell which holds the Holy WATER. Then come the salamanders – FIRE. And standing above them, are the angels, who are creatures of pure spirit – or AIR. Saunière's statement is now as clear as it is apparently anachronistic. Here are the Four Elements of Hermetic thought. Earth ... Water ... Fire ... Air.

Any attempt to interpret Saunière's meaning is bound to stray into the dangerously subjective realm of speculation. Nevertheless, the message is undeniably there and it is undeniably intended. We are being given an extraordinary glimpse of a mode of thinking which belongs to a much earlier age. Whatever it is, the statement is not one which chimes harmoniously with modern thought. It does chime, though, with other strange and relatively modern elements which have surfaced.

In Lobineau's *Dossiers Secrets* I have unearthed a list of the alleged Grand Masters of a 'secret society' – the Priory of Sion.* The story which is beginning to unfold suggests that this society may well have been, in Saunière's time, made up of such 'dabblers in the occult'. *Fin de siècle* Paris, like London, was home to many such organisations. Even so, our priest's involvement with such dubious practices would not suffice to explain all the many, centuries-old threads of the mystery. The Rennes-le-Château research is developing the nature of a strange and tantalising fishing expedition. As a line is reeled in, the catch proves to be not 'the answer' but rather two more questions. Two more hooks to be reeled in, to double yet again new possibilities, new insights, new questions. The horizons of this world into which I have stumbled, are ever-expanding.

But I cannot ignore the other world which I inhabit. A demanding world

* For details of this organisation, see *The Holy Blood & The Holy Grail* and *The Messianic Legacy*. H.L.

of studios, production schedules and deadlines. The new film cannot await the indeterminate outcome of uncertain research. In any case, with only the brief confines of a television documentary programme at my disposal, I already have more than enough material for a fascinating further exploration of the story. The programme must be finished. Its slot on the air-waves is already allotted. While I am immersed in the routine work of preparation for the broadcast, yet another Rennes-le-Château *pétard* explodes.

TREASURE FOR SALE

Quite without warning, Gérard de Sède re-surfaces. Having been unable either to placate, or explain to him, the reasons for his omission from the first film, I have not expected to hear anything further from him. But, in mid-April 1973, the following letter arrives:

Paris, 13 April 1973

Dear Mr Lincoln,

Having passed through Rennes-le-Château, I have learned that you have just shot a second film there.

It is for this reason that I think you will be interested to learn that one of my colleagues and myself have found the treasure discovered by Bérenger Saunière, that it is indeed a royal visigothic treasure including the famous missorium, and that we are in possession of colour photographs of it.

If this is of interest to you, we are prepared to provide the 7 colour photos of the 7 pieces of treasure to the BBC on the basis of a precise contract.

As there are other propositions, I would beg you to let me have a rapid response.

Yours sincerely,

He also appends a telephone number for use 'at the end of the morning or after 7 p.m.' – presumably to facilitate the rapidity of my response.

Here, indeed, is a bombshell. No doubtful expectations *à la* Mr A. Here is a bald certainty – with visual evidence already in support. Here is something concrete. Here is a 'hot news' story which is demanding to be grabbed with both hands – the climax of the Saunière treasure mystery. *N'est-ce pas?*

Paris,le 13 avril 1973

Cher Mr Lincoln

Etant passé à Rennes-le-Château,j'ai appris que vous veniez d'y tourner un second film.

C'est pourquoi je pense que vous serez intéressé d' apprendre qu'un de mes confrères et moi-même avons trouvé le trésor découvert par Bérenger Saunière, qu'il s'agit bien d'un trésor des rois wisigoths comprenant le fameux missorium,et que nous en pos- sédons les photographies en couleurs.

Si cela vous intéresse,nous sommes prêts à fournir les 7 photos couleurs des 7 pièces du trésor à la B.B.C sur la base d'un contrat précis.

Comme il y a d'autres propositions,je vous prie de bien vouloir me faire connaitre rapidement vo- tre réponse.

Sincérement vôtre

Gérard de SEDE

Paris — France.

Phone :   fin de ma- tinée ou après 19 heures.

De Sède, presumably, waits beside his telephone at the appointed times. But it does not ring. A week later, my brief response flutters on to his doormat.

Thank you for your interesting letter. Tell me more.

With no undue impatience, but with a certain degree of interest, I wait. Another ten days pass and I receive his reply:

Paris, 25 April 1973

Dear Mr Lincoln,
I have received your letter of 17 April.
My proposition is very simple. I had first thought that I could sell the eight photographs of the treasure to the BBC, at the same time as an interview relating the circumstances of the discovery. But in this case, there would be the possibility that the interview would be cut at the last moment, as in your earlier programme. So, as we say in France, 'a scalded cat fears even cold water'.
I propose therefore to sell to the BBC a ten minute sound film in which I recount the circumstances of the discovery and I present the eight pieces of treasure; the missorium, the golden throne encrusted with rubies and emeralds, etc. In colour naturally. The film will be available at the beginning of June. Before buying it, the BBC will, naturally, be able to view it in Paris.
Yours sincerely,

But this exciting missive does not receive the response which M. de Sède evidently expects. The 'golden royal treasure, encrusted with rubies and emeralds', I decide, is not worth the postage stamp. Having read his enticing offer, I send no reply, but file it and return to my work. Why am I not tempted? Why do I not fall upon this dazzling prize with yelps of delight and joy? My reasoning is quite simple. De Sède's mistake has been his assumption that I am treasure-obsessed and naïf. His 'treasure' is obviously a fraud.

Reading his first letter, a phrase remembered from my schooldays has floated into my head: *Timeo Danaos et dona ferentes – I fear the Greeks, even when bearing gifts*. Why is de Sède making such a generous offer? To say that he has found a lost royal Visigothic treasure is like saying: 'I have found a lost Titian'. The world – and the world's press – would beat a path to his door were he to make such an announcement. He certainly would not need the pittance which, he knows, is all the BBC could afford to pay for his photographs – even 'on the basis of a precise contract'. But he must have *something* to show me. Has he forgotten that it is my habit to check and double-check everything which comes my way and that, as an amateur, I always seek the advice of experts? If his photographs are *not* of a genuine hoard, then, he should know, I will quickly discover the fact. Yet all artifacts which might be classed as 'Visigothic treasure' are well known. He can't simply be offering me photographs of something sitting in the Louvre or the British Museum. It follows, therefore, that he must be offering photographs of genuine artifacts – but which are normally inaccessible. How can this be? I can guess at only one answer to this conundrum. We are still firmly enmeshed in the era of the Cold War. Can it be that, behind the Iron Curtain, and thus not well known to western scholars, there is a treasure hoard of the appropriate period?

His second letter, with its increase in the treasure pieces from seven to eight, indicates to me, yet again, that he may well not be the prime source of his 'discovery'. Yet again, I sense that de Sède is being used as an intermediary. Certainly, too, his revised offer of 'sound film' rather than photographs demonstrates his ignorance of the techniques of film-making. It would be just as easy to remove him from the one as from the other. However, the fact that he is offering to expose himself, on film, in the perpetration of a fraud, suggests to me that he may be an innocent victim, dazzled by treasure and being used to entrap me into a like gullibility.

My failure to rise to his bait leaves de Sède with some photographs on his hands. Surely he can find a market somewhere? In the autumn edition of a quarterly magazine entitled *Charivari*, the pictures duly appear.* It is de Sède's 'colleague', one Jean-Luc Chaumeil, who provides the accompanying article: *The Treasure exists – we have seen it*. The dramatic account relates how the intrepid treasure-hunters were taken to a secret villa beside Lake Leman, where they were privileged to see the magnificent hoard unearthed at Rennes-le-Château by Bérenger Saunière.

My hunch concerning a possible Eastern European provenance for the photographs is immediately and felicitously confirmed when I am coincidentally asked to script the English-language version of a documentary film on the 'Treasure of Petroassa' in Roumania. And here, not in Switzerland, but in Bucharest, is de Sède's gold. Even *Charivari* is worried by the resemblance. But, the magazine tells us, the contributors of their article are

* *Charivari*, No. 18, Paris, Oct.–Dec. 1973.

'categorical'. The pictures are similar but not 'identical'. This is certainly true. De Sède's photographs show the Petroassa treasure – but printed in reverse.

There is to be a disgraceful coda to this already discreditable story, some fifteen years later. In 1988, de Sède publishes a new book on 'the impostures and fantasies' of Rennes-le-Château.* In it he tells us that 'a pseudo-journalist – one Jean-Luc Chaumeil – went beyond a joke' in publishing an article in *Charivari* relating the supposed discovery of Saunière's treasure in Switzerland. De Sède condemns Chaumeil as an 'ignorant mystificator' and fulminates in righteous and superior fashion about the fantasy. A fantasy of which, he conveniently omits to inform his readers, he was himself co-instigator.

TRIANGLE OF CASTLES

However, de Sède's unsuccessful – if amusing – trap has been no more than a minor distraction. I have much more interesting and important leads to follow. Professor Cornford, in concluding his report on the Poussin painting, has made an unexpected and original suggestion. 'Would it,' he asks, 'be worthwhile testing the map for the presence of pentagonal vectors and angles?'

Such an idea has not previously occurred to me and I am, at first, at a loss to know how to begin the pursuit of such a complicated hunt. But Professor Cornford's cool and objective view of the puzzle is not to be underestimated. With the completion of *The Priest, the Painter and the Devil*, I have time to devote to this new and intriguing idea. I spread out the map and, daunted by the mass of detail, seek some sort of inspiration. In my ever-hopeful search for a means of avoiding complexities, I pray for a simple approach to present itself. But how to simplify a pentagon? I draw out the five-sided shape on a piece of paper, then join the internal points to produce the pentagram. The realisation comes that the five-pointed star is made up of five overlapping triangles. Each triangle has one short side (the outer face of the pentagon), and two longer but equal sides. The internal angles are 36°–72°–72°.

* *Rennes-le-Château – le dossier, les impostures, les phantasmes, les hypotheses.* Paris 1988.

Plate 1. Rennes-le-Château with Esperaza beyond.

Plate 2. The church at Rennes-le-Château. Saunière's Devil.

Cardou

Blanchfort

Rennes-le-Château

Plates 3 and 4. 'The Arcadian Shepherds' by Nicolas Poussin (the 1640 version) with the matching landscape.

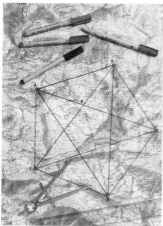

Plate 5. The Star Pentagram within the Pentagon of mountains with the triangle of castles.
A = Rennes-le-Château;
B = Blanchefort Castle;
D = Bézu Castle.

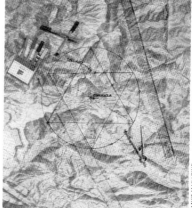

Plate 6. The Esperaza Star of David or Seal of Solomon.

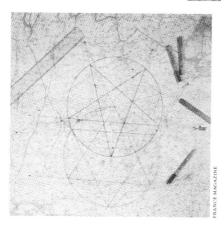

Plate 7. Patricia Hawkshaw's Brittany discovery of the linked Pentagram and Hexagram.

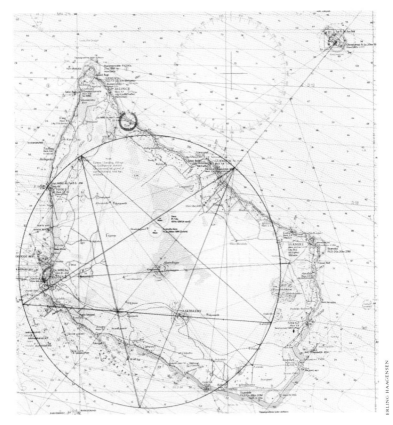

Plate 8. The basic geometry of the Danish island of Bornholm in the Baltic Sea.

Plate 9.
Østerlars Church.

A triangle seems to be a more readily identifiable shape. But how, on a map, to find even a triangle? I need three places. Three noticeable – and in some way related – locations. And here is the obvious and simple starting point.

Rennes-le-Château ... Rennes-the-Castle ... seems an obvious beginning and there are two other mountaintop castles in the immediate vicinity which are linked with the mystery. One, clearly visible across the plain to the south, is Bézu, a mere four miles away, scene of our midnight 'Templar -ghost' expedition. To the east – and even closer, some two-and-a-half miles – is Blanchefort, also with a Templar connection (Bertrand de Blanchefort was a Templar Grand Master). This tiny trace of a watchtower is on the recognisable mountain which Poussin has incorporated in his view of the landscape in *The Shepherds of Arcadia*. Each mountain can be seen from the other and each castle site is indicated on the map. Three castles – forming a triangle. I draw in the connecting lines. Immediately, the familiar scent of discovery is in the air.

One would expect a random placing of castles upon convenient mountaintops to produce an irregular triangle. But what I have drawn is anything but irregular. This triangle is isosceles – with two equal faces. The distance from Rennes-le-Château to Bézu is the same as the distance from Bézu to Blanchefort. I measure the internal angles. They are 36°–72°–72°. Professor Cornford is right – I have found a 'pentagonal' triangle. Here is another 'extraordinary coincidence'. But, with Rennes-le-Château, is every new discovery to remain merely in the realm of coincidence? Or is it time to be considering some other explanation?

LEY-LINES – MAGIC – AND THE OCCULT?

I am, at first, cautious about reading any undue significance into lines drawn across a landscape. This is drifting towards the uncertain area of 'ley-lines' which dowsers claim to have traced, but which, to my knowledge, cannot be objectively proven to exist. Any line, when projected far enough, will inevitably pass through more than one point of interest. But where does coincidence end and purposeful intent begin? The lines of the Rennes-le-Château triangle are short. The points are visible, one from the other. They are, therefore, in some sense 'practical'. They can be used for sighting, for communicating, or perhaps – it occurs to me – for indicating other points.

So far, I have three locations which mark three out of five angles of a perfect pentagon. The inevitable next step is to seek out the other two points in order to complete the figure. There are no more conveniently placed castles and so there appears to be no further marking of the landscape (if, indeed, this is what has occurred). In order merely to tidy up this stage of the investigation, I draw in the other two points that form the regular star-pattern. And now 'coincidence' ceases to be, in any sense, a likely explanation for what I have found. The three castles crown three mountain peaks. The two new points are, astonishingly, already marked upon the map by the cartographers of the *Institut Géographique*. In precisely the required places there are 'spot heights' – the map-makers' indication of the highest point in the immediate area. To the west, the spot height of 559 metres is marked at the height of a crest – the Serre de Lauzet. To the east, 587 metres on la Soulane. Each point is, again, a mountain. Here are five natural mountain peaks lying in perfect pentagonal symmetry to one another.

This phenomenon can only be of an unbelievable rarity. How often can one expect to find natural topographical features so placed as to form a complex and regular geometric pattern? And, moreover, a pattern which our forefathers have endowed with such powerful meaning. A pattern which, since very ancient times, again in Professor Cornford's words: '... enjoyed immense prestige and excited nothing short of reverence.'

I cannot emphasise too strongly the futility of adopting a 'modern' approach to such a phenomenon. I have encountered far too many people who still insist, with an 'enlightened' superiority, that it is foolish, time-wasting and unscientific to take such matters seriously. I repeat – this is *our* truth. How are we to understand the actions of our ancestors if we insist that their 'foolish' beliefs have no relevance? We do not need to share those beliefs – but we do need to acknowledge them.

With the discovery of the Pentagon of Mountains, I realise that, again, I have strayed into a realm which lies beyond my expertise. Believe it or not ... accept it or not ... decry or condemn ... disapprove or treat as a joke ... I have stumbled upon something which, for some people in the past – and still for some people today – is mystical, magical – and therefore of religious significance. To say that the shape is meaningless is to ignore the meaning that others may attach to it. And one of those meanings, as

I am uncomfortably aware, is Satanic – or, at least, occult. Such words colour our attitude. Today, the word 'occult' is used only in the rather dubious context of magic and witchcraft. But the word simply means 'hidden'. In that sense, we are certainly confronting knowledge which was hidden from the uninitiated.

Over the centuries, the influence of the occult has waxed and waned. At the end of the nineteenth century – Saunière's time – as again now at the end of the twentieth, the power of magic is for some minds a potent, attractive force which they try to harness. And 'magicians' have always used the five-pointed star for conjuration, for 'raising spirits' – even for the raising of the Devil himself. For them, the 'pentacle' is their girdle of protection as well as their focus of power.

The appearance of the idea of magic into the affair of Bérenger Saunière, does not instantly transform it into a matter worthy only of 'the lunatic fringe'. The Rennes-le-Château Pentacle of Mountains undeniably exists. Those 'rational' people who would dismiss its 'magical' implications as unworthy of serious consideration must remember that, whether they are right or wrong, there are still very many people who, even today, will disagree with them. And who will act accordingly.

VICARAGE TEA-PARTY

This discovery is made just before the scheduled date for the transmission of *The Priest, the Painter and the Devil*. It is too late to incorporate it into the programme. Furthermore, it sheds a disturbing and, in some sense unwelcome, new light on the Saunière mystery. I am reluctant to become involved in revelations that may prove to be of a 'sensationalist' nature. I need advice and must devote considerably more thought to these possibilities before I can risk exploring them publicly. Fortunately, I have a friend to whom I can turn for informed and down-to-earth guidance in such matters.

John is the vicar of a rural parish. He is a priest of much wisdom, learning and humanity, with an open and enquiring mind. I know that he will listen carefully to what I have to say and that his advice will be calm, sensible and valuable. I arrange to call on him at his vicarage in the peaceful

Oxfordshire countryside. As I drive out of London on the very twentieth-century motorway, I am struck by the incongruity of the almost mediaeval subject-matter contained in the bundle of papers and maps which lie on the back seat of my car. I find myself half hoping that John will pour cold water on my apprehensions and with a 'good talking-to', send me back home with an admonition against allowing an over-active imagination to run away with me.

We sit in his sunny vicarage, drinking tea and exchanging the gossipy personal news that is inevitable when two friends are meeting again after a lapse of months. Again the incongruous nature of what I am about to tell him seems emphasised by the utterly tranquil normality of our surroundings. What have heresy, devil-worship and conjuration to do with tea and biscuits and sunshine pouring down upon a pretty English garden? As tea finishes, I get up and stare through the window at the neat lawn, the flowers, the trees and the busy cluster of birds pecking at seeds in the shade. Where is the Devil's place in all this? How am I to begin? John waits quietly. There is something on my mind – and he knows it.

'John … what makes a place holy?'

We begin to talk. Slowly, piece by piece, I lay my evidence before him. There is no pouring of cold water on my fears. John listens and I can see that, for him too, the matter is a serious one. He is struck by the uniqueness and significance of the Rennes-le-Château pentagram. Such a place, he feels, would have been (perhaps still is), of awesome import to all practitioners of the 'art of magick' who have come to learn of it. He stresses that I should not consider the place to be stamped by evil. The pentacle, itself, is inert – neither 'white' nor 'black' magic. It is the use to which it is put that gives the symbol its effect.

When the dabbler in the 'black art' wishes to summon up the spirits, he will draw out his pentacle upon the floor of his 'temple'. He may then make a sacrifice – a black cat, or a cock, perhaps – to infuse and animate his focus of power with its blood. What sort of sacrifice, John wonders, might be deemed suitable to animate a pentacle of some twenty miles in circumference? Here is a very practical danger that may be inherent in my discovery. Even though we dismiss the implications as rubbish … even though they *be* rubbish … there may well be one criminal lunatic who might be tempted to go down to the centre of that five-pointed star and 'try it out'.

This is not a discovery which can be blithely broadcast as television entertainment. How many times have I wondered about the nature of the supposed mystery of Rennes-le-Château? What sort of secret can be kept inviolate over centuries? If I am now approaching a reality, then here, indeed, the admonition 'Publish and be Damned' may have a grain of literal truth.

However, I am talking to a good and wise man and he tells me that, on this occasion, he finds it hard to give simple advice. Such a discovery should not be suppressed. Perhaps the glare of publicity will inhibit the misuse of the place? Our conversation has brought a chill into the vicarage. As I prepare to leave John says:

'Henry, please do something for me.'

'Certainly – if I can.'

'I suspect that you may not take this as seriously as I do. But ... will you kneel down. I wish to pray.'

Slightly self-conscious, I do as he asks. As I listen to his words, again the bright and sunlit garden outside the window seems a strange backdrop against which to play this almost theatrically unreal, but awe-inspiring scene. Let anyone who has heard his own name spoken in sonorous phrases invoking aid against 'the dark powers of His Satanic Majesty' say that I have over-dramatised. For me, though, the principal memory of this episode is one of golden sunlight. Perhaps something may be read into that?

SAUNIERE THE PRIEST

As I head for home, thoughts of the Devil and his possible modern worshippers are appropriately driven away by the necessity to cope with the hellish rush-hour traffic at the end of the motorway. But John's words have given me a new perspective from which to view the Saunière mystery, and as I drive, the kaleidoscope of unconnected images begins to be shaken into a new pattern. Some strange tales which I have heard seem suddenly to have acquired an unlooked-for sense. Even, I am startled to realise, the glint of gold may be explained. Saunière, we have been told, spent huge sums of money and therefore must have found a treasure. The new thoughts of 'the occult', as well as other anecdotes which I have garnered in my questioning of the locals, enable me to create an unexpected hypothesis. Perhaps there *was* no treasure?

I have already made reference to the obscure and possibly occult interests of the Priory of Sion, the 'secret society' which has been glimpsed lurking in the shadows, and with which Saunière may have been involved. Two curious stories seem to be hinting at some such questionable activity. I encounter the first when I am endeavouring to check de Sède's claim that, when the Bishop of Carcassonne came to bless Saunière's extravagant redecoration of the village church, he was so disturbed by what he saw that he removed Rennes-le-Château from his list of Visitations. The bishop, de Sède tells us, never returned. My own enquiries suggest that de Sède's account is probably untrue. It is possibly a confusion of the attitudes of two different bishops.

During the last years of Saunière's life, his bishop was unquestionably opposed to him; perhaps did not visit the village; and certainly attempted to have Saunière removed and replaced. Saunière, nonetheless, refused to budge. 'My interests keep me here,' he is reported as saying. Certainly, too, his parishioners did not wish to part with him. However, the previous bishop, who occupied the See of Carcassonne at the time of the dedication of the new church decorations, seems to have had a quite different attitude. From an aged villager, I hear an anecdote which seems so odd and is so meaningless as an invention, that I am inclined to believe that it is giving us a glimpse of the truth.

According to this account, the bishop was far from being shocked by Saunière's activities. After the Dedication Service, the two of them were seen strolling in the church garden, deep in conversation, their arms around each others' shoulders ... and *they had exchanged hats*. So bizarre and pointless a story may well contain a germ of fact. Especially when put together with the strange detail of the bishop's mitre lying on the table beside Saunière's death bed.[*]

An old lady, who claims to have been present, tells me an even more bizarre story of Saunière's funeral in 1917. Before the burial, she says, the body was taken up onto the terrace beside the Tour Magdala. There it was seated in a chair and draped in a tasselled, crimson robe. The mourners then filed past, each cutting off a tassel *en souvenir*. A curious homage to pay to a humble parish priest.

---

[*] I must note that I still set a question mark beside this strange photograph. With Henri Buthion, I made a careful examination of Saunière's villa and presbytery. We could not find a room which exactly matched the image. The likeness to Saunière is striking; the provenance of the picture impeccable. And yet ...? H.L.

Saunière in life … and death?

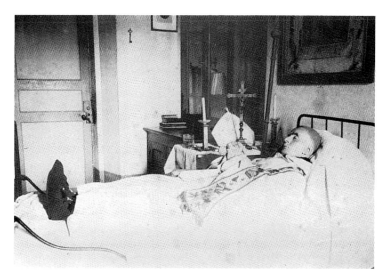

These stories, I must again emphasise, are hearsay and thus unreliable. But, in the context of the Saunière legend, they are creating a shadowy picture. Moreover, this picture may help to explain Saunière's huge expenditure, without the tantalising (and distracting) necessity for him to have discovered a treasure. At this stage, I can sketch out a tentative hypothesis to fit the facts, as they are understood in 1974.

Chapter Eight
HYPOTHESIS

SAUNIÈRE, BORN AND brought up within sight of Rennes-le-Château, would have been steeped in the history and legends of the area. He would have heard stories of the 'devil-worshipping' Cathares and their connection with the Holy Grail. He therefore knows his region has links with something both occult and powerful. In 1891, he discovers something in his church (the parchments?) which, perhaps, reveal to him the existence of the pentagram of mountains.

Unfrocked priests are much valued by occult groups for the performance of their rituals. If, for them, there is still a power in a man once ordained, how much better – or stronger – would be the power of a man still in holy orders? Saunière is a priest and he is inhabiting 'the Temple'. His reported trip to Paris for the 'decipherment of the parchments' is just as likely to have been made in order to contact the people who would show most interest in what he has found. His supposed 'liaison' with the world-famous opera singer, Emma Calvé, becomes more understandable in this light. Calvé, too, is a friend of the composer Claude Debussy, who is listed in the *Dossiers Secrets* as Grand Master of the Priory of Sion. And both are known to have contacts with figures in the 'occult' world of Paris. The Rennes-le-Château murmurs also speak of a Habsburg Archduke who visits the village in Saunière's time. Wealthy and influential people are being drawn into the net of possibilities. And Saunière has something immensely attractive, immensely valuable, occult and unique to offer them.

Back home from his trip to Paris, we are told, he took to wandering the hillsides – collecting stones, he said, when anybody asked. Could he, in fact, have been verifying the angles and positions of the five points? Was he in some way marking them – or marking the surrounding circle? Fire, or light, is placed at the corners of a pentagram when it is used for conjuration. Most significantly, this is when his days of poverty come to an end and he begins to spend large sums of money.

In 1891, Rennes-le-Château is a decaying, isolated and impoverished peasant hamlet, remote and difficult of access with no modern amenities. Saunière buys the plot of land beside his presbytery and builds a handsome villa. For Rennes-le-Château, it is impressive. Transfer it to the outskirts of Carcassonne, or even Limoux, and it ceases to impress. It is simply a comfortable, bourgeois family house. He builds a water tower – and every house in the village now has running water. A generous gesture – but running water is a simple amenity of civilised living. Much more money is spent in modernising the dirt track which leads up from the valley. But even this munificent gesture does not, in those days of cheap labour, require a Croesus for its funding. And for all this creation of a comfortable setting in the village, we are told that he never inhabits his newly-built villa. He continues to live in the rather more humble presbytery. The Villa Bethania is reserved for his guests.

A group of cultured and wealthy Parisians, with their own good reasons to wish to visit this secluded backwater and even better reasons to wish to keep Saunière *in situ*, provide sufficient money to ensure their own comforts and the priest's accessibility. In the terms of such a group, the sums expended are by no means extravagant. Did Saunière necessarily find a treasure? Or was he simply provided with the generous means to establish and maintain an appropriate *milieu* for his new and wealthy friends?

This hypothesis could also explain the strange story that the priest who heard his deathbed confession refused to administer the Last Rites. Had Saunière confessed to performing magical or, at best, heretical rituals? The story grows darker and less comfortable. I have lifted the corner of an alarming and intimidating veil. Like it or not, I must follow this trail a little further in order to be sure that it is real. I will be happier to find that it will simply peter out.

THE 'X' ON THE TREASURE MAP ?

The pentacle and its magical significance occupies my thoughts. Although some such meaning may be inferred in the parchment's use of the design,

I find it hard to impose any like significance to Poussin's use of it in his *Shepherds of Arcadia*. Christopher Cornford has pointed out that one of the most impressive confirmations of Poussin's conscious manipulation of the geometrical structure of the painting lies in the significant placing of the centre of the controlling pentagram. It lies, with precision, upon the forehead of the shepherdess. He makes the comment that 'It suggests ... that the whole scene is somehow emanating from her meditative consciousness, or pivoting round it ... It is her mood of gentle sadness that dominates the picture.' Now that the pentagonal structure has been found in the Rennes-le-Château landscape, the identifying of the central point is both logical and inevitable. It is also very easy to do. The attempt releases a new torrent of possibilities.

As I draw in the lines which fix the centre of the star, I realise that here is an admirable place to hide something. Have I, perhaps, pinpointed the 'X' upon a treasure map? With the knowledge of the shape hidden in the surrounding mountains, this location can always be precisely identified. Without that knowledge, the site is lost without trace. But such an uniquely significant site is too impressive, too important to serve simply as the hiding place for gold and jewels. 'Treasure' ... wealth ... is, after all, in essence too mundane to deserve such a setting. Even if the place has indeed been used for such a purpose, this can only be of secondary importance to anyone aware of what is here.

Such thoughts are, of course, uncertain. While it is necessary to remain open to any possibility, it is important that we should not impose any wishful-thinking, nor take a likelihood to be a certainty. The defining of the centre of the star, however, produces still one more startling and concrete fact. The location is marked by yet another mountain. It is called la Pique. Yet another – and amazing – coincidence. This time, though, the highest point does not lie with exactitude upon the geometric intersection. It is some 250 yards to the south east. A first reaction is one of disappointment. But then, I must ask, should one expect a miracle? The phenomenon of the five peaks is already dazzling enough. These 'structures' have not been planned and built to conform to a pattern. They are natural landscape features. To find yet another dominating hilltop, even approximately placed, in such a significant spot, is breath-taking.

Yet another piece of the jigsaw also falls into place. A clue provided in de Sède's book has been a curious carving on a stone known as *La Dalle de Coumesourde*. This stone, de Sède tells us, was found 'somewhere near to

Coumesourde'. At the foot of the central mountain is an ancient farmhouse. It is called Coumesourde and also lies a couple of hundred yards from the geometric centre. I wonder if this stone might once have marked that significant spot? But then, if knowledge of the place is a jealously guarded secret, why draw attention to it by marking it in such an obvious way? Such questions float to the surface from the muddy depths which are being plumbed. But they cannot be answered with any feeling of certainty – and I am disinclined to speculate. The accumulating facts are already problematic enough without compounding them with doubtful conclusions.

The question of the purpose and exact location of the *Dalle de Coumesourde* leads me to a consideration of how this stupendous Pentacle might be used by somebody intent on conjuration. The necessary 'protection' afforded by the centre of the star shape does not mean that only the *exact* centre is suitable. The precise centre proves to lie, in fact, on a steep scree slope on the northern face of la Pique. It might be difficult to hold one's footing here, still less perform any elaborate rites. But, with so large a shape, the central area is, itself, very extensive. Perhaps I should look for the

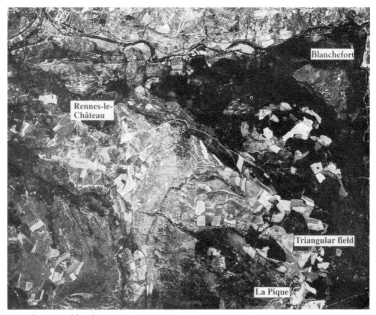

Aerial view of landscape.

(132)

nearest, level and practically usable piece of land? For this hunt, I decide that I should gather as much information as I can before returning to the area to examine the place 'on the ground'. But I need to know more than a map can tell me. Aerial photographs seem an effective means of exploring the landscape and are readily available from the French Geographical Institute. They quickly present a possibility.

Close to the farm of Coumesourde – and in the 'horns' of the small pentagram which fits inside the pentagon at the heart of the larger design – is a triangular field.

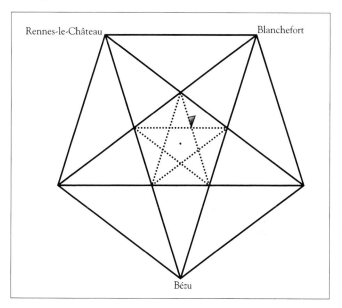

The field catches my eye as it is large and flat and is the only one in the vicinity which is recognisably 'geometric' in shape. Moreover, and more interesting still, the field shows a curious design of crop markings. These are caused by alterations in the vegetation growing over disturbances which have been made in the ground – old field outlines, for instance, or trackways or even the foundations of long-gone buildings. Certainly, such markings are not visible on the ground and, in any case, the 'design' can only be my subjective reading of the marks. But, I am uncomfortably aware that, subjective or not, like it or not, I can 'see' the shape of a huge winged figure laid out upon the field.

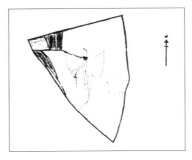

Later aerial close-up reveals the dot to be a copse of trees.

The crop markings, the design and the winged figure may all be the products of my imagination, but this is certainly the nearest level and usable piece of ground to the centre of the star. And the photograph shows something more tangible than my imaginary outline. In the centre of the field, at the point which might be called the 'head' of my subjectively seen figure, there is a solid black 'dot'.

The picture is too small to show what this feature may be, but it is certainly not a building. I decide that it is far too easy to embroider fantasies upon this oddity which may, indeed – and for once – be no more than coincidental. It must be left out of my thinking until a trip can be arranged to examine the terrain with care. But I know that it is too tantalising to be left for long. In the gloom of late January 1975, it is not too difficult to persuade a few friends to climb into my car and accompany me on a trip to the Pyrenees.

THE BLACK SPOT

After several days of rain and howling winds, the weather is cold, but bright and quiet as we set off from Rennes-le-Château to drive south across the plain in search of the triangular field with its strange dark 'something' in the centre. Were this a fictional story, then almost anything could be imagined to be awaiting the little team of investigators. An altar? An Aladdin's cave of riches? A Satanic Temple? A group of mad magicians, watching us in their scrying glass as, innocent of our fate, we walk into their trap? In fact, the reality is – not surprisingly – much more ordinary. It also proves to be much more perplexing.

As we know from the aerial photographs, the field is skirted by the narrow track which runs past the few isolated farmhouses which dot the plain. As we pass the farm of La Maurine, we know that the next curve in the road will reveal our goal. I am driving very slowly and already we think we have identified the 'black dot'. It is a copse of trees, whose tops we can see beyond the rise in the ground.

As we reach the corner of the field, the suspicion is confirmed. I pull the car off the road and we look about us. The huge plain is beautiful in its empty wildness. No human figure is to be seen. It seems that we, alone, inhabit the landscape. To the right, the ground rises sharply to the great rocks crowning the central hill, la Pique. To the left, the empty expanse of the triangular field is bordered in the distance by a wood. The field itself is featureless, save for the tiny copse which, from where we stand, seems quite unremarkable. Nothing about this clump of trees would cause the rare passerby to wish to cross the field to examine it more closely. A tangle of scrub and bramble enmeshes the trunks of a few small trees set in a circle. Evenly spaced around the circumference are four much taller trees, their slender tops barely moving in the still morning air. One of my friends, knowledgeable in such matters, remarks that the trees seem more or less of an age, planted perhaps a century ago. 'About Saunière's time,' he comments. A tiny rivulet snakes from between the trees and crosses the field towards us, to empty itself into the ditch which runs beside the road.

We set off across the field, following the course of the trickle of water. As we approach the trees, we can see that the scrub at their feet creates a dense and impenetrable wall. The line of the rivulet is the only gap providing access to the space between the trees. We squeeze through the narrow entrance and find ourselves in an open circular area, some twenty or so feet in diameter. Once through, we are enclosed and hidden, screened from the outside world, as it is screened from us. The space between the trees is not empty. The little stream is seeping through a square-cut notch in the wall of a deep and sunken stone basin.

The sight is as unexpected as it is undramatic. It is also puzzling. The basin is obviously man-made. It is rectangular, some fifteen feet in length, by eight or nine feet wide. Smooth and vertical, the walls rise several inches above the level of the water, which is about three feet deep. Another notch at the far side of the pool allows the water to enter. (We are to find that its source is a spring at the far side of the field, which seeps from the ground and forms the streamlet which runs into the hidden basin.) The two notches at the rim of the stone walls ensure the maintenance of a constant water level. But – what is it for? There is, after all, no need to seek anything other than the most mundane of explanations. We debate the possibilities.

'Perhaps it's just for watering cattle?'

'Unlikely. It's too deep.'

'And it's sheer-sided. If a cow or a sheep were to fall in, you'd have hell's own job getting it out again.'

'The trees are too close, anyway. Almost as if they were planted to make a barrier for straying livestock.'

'How about a reservoir for crop watering?'

'Doesn't seem very practical. How d'you get it out? With a bucket?'

'Perhaps siphon action with a hose-pipe?'

'Not much use even so. One light sprinkling, at most, is all you'd get for a field this size. And then what? It's a long hot summer down here and the land gets baked dry.'

HYPOTHESIS

Innocent-seeming though it is, we can think of no obvious purpose for the little pool. Its very isolation makes it unlikely to be a simple amenity for the nearest farmhouse which is a good few hundred yards away. The stream, after all, could have been channelled much closer to the house if it were to serve simply as a convenient water storage tank. In any case, the map shows a tapped spring immediately adjacent to the farm.* Although I have no desire to attach anything other than an ordinary explanation to what we have found, it is impossible to forget the curious conjunction of evidence which has led us to it. As we stand in contemplation of this minor mystery, another oddity presents itself. The pool is clean.

Superficially, this may not seem worthy of notice, but I know, from the pond in my own garden, that such small basins of water very quickly accumulate a thick bed of mud. Indeed, soil *is* being carried in through the inlet notch of this pool, beneath which there is a deposit of mud sufficient, perhaps, to cover a large soup plate. Apart from this tiny trace, the smooth stone base of the pool is clearly visible. Moreover, as we now notice, after days of blustery weather, hardly a leaf or twig is floating on the surface of the water. It is impossible to draw from this evidence any other conclusion than that the pool has been very recently cleaned. We cast about around the clearing to find any sign of spoil which may have been removed from the basin, but there is no trace. This compounds the mystery. I know of no farmer who would take such pains over an isolated water reservoir. Again we remind ourselves of what has brought us here – and again a faint hypothesis presents itself.

Could we be contemplating the activities, not of a peasant farmer, but of the mysterious and mystic 'secret society' which seems to be dogging my footsteps? We are in the first days of February. The Priory of Sion documents which I have seen, stress the importance of a particular date – 17 January – barely two weeks ago. If they – (or someone) – do, indeed, find a significance and a purpose for this singular construction at the heart of the pentagon, then perhaps it may have been tidied for use in a rite of some kind on what is, for them, a significant day in the year? But what sort of ceremony requires pure, clean, natural, running water? An obvious answer is ritual purification

---

* My archive contains a recorded discussion in which Roy Davies reports that he was told that local women used the pool for washing clothes, with which explanation he was satisfied. I, however, remain uncertain. As each of the adjacent farmhouses has its own spring and water trough, one must wonder why the local ladies would wish to trail half a mile or more to do their laundry in an inconveniently sited, vertically walled pool, in the middle of a field, across which there is no trace of any sort of path which might indicate habitual use. H.L.

and certainly, the pool could serve admirably for a ceremony of total immersion baptism. But baths of ritual purification have more than baptismal uses. I have seen them in the Middle East, outside mosques, where the faithful purify themselves before entering the holy place.

This fresh thought helps us to notice another strange and disconcerting addition to our growing mass of indicative 'coincidences'. Just a few hundred yards to the south, the map shows la Valdieu – the Valley of God. Try as I may to avoid an over-dramatisation of what I am uncovering, the extraordinary conjunctions of hints and possibilities which confront me at every turn, cannot be denied. The developing picture may be pushing us toward 'lunatic fringe' territory, but this is no reason for turning one's back. Without *solid evidence*, it is as much an act of faith to say 'I don't believe it', as it is to say 'I believe'; to say 'This must be rubbish', as to say 'This must be the truth'. It is not for us to decide what may, or may not, have significance and importance for other people. We must keep an open mind and remain prepared to confront any likelihood. Fantasy or not ... it is certainly not unreasonable to postulate that whoever gave to a place the resonant name 'Valley of God', may have seen in it something denoting holiness. Such a person may well have wished to purify themselves in the face of whatever divinity they may have imagined to inhabit the spot.

We are unable to come to any conclusions concerning this strange water basin, but an interesting, if uncertain, possibility presents itself in relation to the nearby la Pique, the pentagon's central hill. As we drive southwards, away from the pool and towards la Valdieu, we notice that the configuration of the hilltop changes. Viewed from the south, it appears not as a hill, but as an ascending slope, crowned by large slabs of stone. It bears a striking resemblance to the central crag in the *Shepherds of Arcadia*. The shape of the rock behind the painted tomb is reasonably matched and, as in the painting, the hill descends gently to the left. Is this, perhaps, an explanation for the anomalous change in Poussin's otherwise accurate rendering of the landscape? Has he incorporated two locations into the one scene? His right-hand painted landscape certainly presents an accurate view from the tomb. Does the central portion show the view from la Valdieu?

Again, it is essential to bear in mind that any such visual interpretation is purely subjective. This similarity of landscape features at la Valdieu, unlike the precision of the view from the tomb, is no more than a suggestion. Before any conclusions, or even hypotheses, can be constructed, there is the need for much more concretely objective proof of Poussin's intention.

La Pique.

En passant, with regard to the water basin, I should record a subsequent and rather bizarre incident. When, a couple of years later, I am making the third BBC film, *The Shadow of the Templars*, I return to the pool with the director, Roy Davies. As we approach the tiny entrance way between the trees, we can see that something is hanging from one of the branches to the right of the gap. It proves to be the headless and half-charred carcass of a goat. The burnt skull, complete with horns, is lying within the clearing, beside the pool. Have we stumbled upon the evidence of some diabolic rite? I am inclined to think that this is less likely than the possibility that one of our habitual and invisible watchers has left us the unsavoury clue in order to make us think so. Even so, it seems that someone is aware of the unpleasant potentialities of the site.

FORTUITOUS ENCOUNTER

The pentacle of mountains with its accompanying new lines of enquiry has been found too late for inclusion in *The Priest, the Painter and the Devil*. A third programme is now inevitable. Not only do I have an amazing and unprecedented discovery to climax a new film. The background, peopled as it is with Cathares, Templars, magicians, alchemists and secret societies, is becoming richer and more colourful. The public's appetite, too, is growing, as my ever-increasing mail-bag testifies. The workload is daunting and, fascinating though the never-ending research may be, it is rapidly draining my resources. Rennes-le-Château risks becoming an expensive luxury. It is also demanding. It cannot easily be picked up and then casually dropped to make way for a normal script commission.

In August 1975, I carry these working worries with me as I set out on another ordinary bread-winning chore. I have been invited to give a course of lectures on writing at a summer school. The setting is magnificent. A wonderful, centuries old manor house, lost in the depths of the English countryside. As lecturers and students gather for the first evening meal, I encounter the unforeseen fly in this otherwise delectable ointment. The establishment is strictly vegetarian. As an unregenerate carnivore, I can yet acknowledge that some vegetarian meals can be delicious. Unfortunately, such dishes are not to be found on this menu. The cuisine is utterly atrocious. The injury is compounded by the inevitable insult. Water is the only liquid available as accompaniment to the singularly unsavoury repast. As I toy with my platter of dry lettuce leaves *avec garniture de vieux fromage sec*, I notice that the same game is being played across the table by a long-haired and saturnine individual whose expression of distaste is in no way masked by the dark glasses he is wearing. He looks up as I push the almost untouched plate aside. 'You, too?' I nod. 'Worse still,' he says, 'I have an excess of blood in my alcohol stream. Why don't we get out of here and see what the nearest town has to offer?'

Thus, over a pleasant restaurant meal, is my workload suddenly diminished. We find common ground in our interest in the history of the Middle Ages. Better still, Richard Leigh has spent a considerable time in researching the history of the Knights Templar. He has already pursued many of the lines of enquiry upon which I am about to embark. During the remaining days of the summer school, we fill the free time between our lectures in a mutual exchange of information. Richard is able to fill in many of the blanks in my knowledge of the mediaeval orders of fighting monks and he becomes aware of the importance of some of the curious apparent anomalies which I am beginning to unearth. We decide to join forces in an undertaking which has, by now, become too extensive and time-consuming for one man. Richard brings in additional support when he meets Michael Baigent, a New Zealand photo-journalist who has abandoned his calling in order to research the history of the Templars. With a team of three, the work progresses apace. By the end of the year, the shape of a possible third film begins to emerge.

It is at this time that an unexpected but, in its way, valuable hiatus occurs in my concentration on the Rennes-le-Château story. I am asked to write the screenplay of *The Silent Witness*, a documentary film on the Shroud of Turin. This subject, with its links with the Templars, mediaeval relics and the history of early Christianity, is very much within my sphere of interest. The subject is stimulating; the producer, David Rolfe, is professional, committed and likeable. The project is, for me, an enjoyable, if hectic, 'holiday' which occupies a large part of 1976. I am able to return to the Saunière saga reinvigorated and with fresh enthusiasm.

THE MEROVINGIANS – AND FISH

With the commitment of *Chronicle* to the production of a third Rennes-le-Château programme, *The Shadow of the Templars* begins to take shape. It is during a day-long script conference in the Cotswold cottage to which I have now removed, that a startling leap forward occurs in the story which is slowly beginning to emerge. Richard Leigh and Michael Baigent have come down to the quiet of the country in order to work in detail on the rapidly growing mass of research material. Roy Davies, who will again direct the film, joins us for a day of concentrated work on the proposed script. We become deeply engaged in a speculative discussion about the nature of the supposed 'secret of Rennes-le-Château'. The Priory of Sion documents have laid great stress on the importance of the Merovingian dynasty of French kings. This bloodline is the one which apparently came to an end with the assassination of Dagobert II in 679 AD. Moreover, he is the king referred to in the coded parchments: 'This treasure belongs to Dagobert II King and to Sion and he is there dead.' What, Roy Davies asks, is so special about the Merovingians?

Our researches have produced a number of curious answers to this question. Merovée, founder of the line, is said to have had two fathers, his pregnant mother being re-impregnated, while swimming, by a Quinotaur – some sort of fabulous sea-creature. Like Samson, the Merovingian kings were forbidden to cut their hair in which, it was said, their power resided. Most significantly, they were recognised as kings 'by right of their blood' – and not by sanction of the anointing of the church.

As we play with these ideas, one of us makes the tiny 'joke' that 'the Quinotaur business sounds distinctly fishy'. Sometimes such a flippant, or even a silly, remark can trigger an unexpected flash of illumination. A silence falls as we are momentarily distracted from the confusing fragments of history and legend which we are contemplating. Suddenly I catch Richard's eye. We gaze at each other questioningly for a moment more – and I hear the proverbial penny drop with a resounding clang. 'Are you thinking what I'm thinking?' Richard asks. 'I think I am,' I reply. An astounding idea has trundled out of the miasma of maybes. 'I think we've got to talk this through,' I say. Excusing ourselves, Richard and I leave the others in my study and, for ten minutes, perambulate around my overgrown garden and tease a startling, but totally coherent proposition out of a rapidly coalescing conglomeration of clues and suggestions. A sea creature ... *a fish* ... one of the earliest of symbols to represent Christ. Could this be a hint that the Merovingian kings, by right of their blood, claimed descent from Jesus? Here is our first glimpse of the hypothesis that will create such a stir in *The Holy Blood & The Holy Grail*, though it is to be several years before the idea becomes tangible enough to present in a book.*

AS ABOVE – SO BELOW

None of this, of course, has any effect upon the work we are doing in preparation for the making of *The Shadow of the Templars*. Since the first

* I must here, parenthetically, refer to the often misunderstood thesis of *The Holy Blood & The Holy Grail*. I have more than once seen it written – and, indeed, have frequently been told that: 'You claim that Jesus was married and fathered a blood-line', as if our book professes to have established this as a *fact*. There is, of course, no way that such a proposition could ever be proven. The book presents an *hypothesis* which is certainly concordant with all the evidence which we had gathered. That hypothesis still remains valid. Even were it established not to be so, that would not alter the fact that some people in the past appear to have believed it to be true and that the belief affected their actions. H.L.

awareness that the Saunière story contains contentious and difficult material, one of the constant objectives of the research has been the hunt for evidence which would *tend to contradict* any emerging hypothesis. But an undeniable and, at times, alarming realisation has been growing. Every new fragment, every new hint, every new discovery – has *tended to confirm* the strange and growing picture. It is becoming clear that Rennes-le-Château is the focus of a much greater mystery than the mere provenance and content of a buried treasure. The 'treasure story' seems more and more to be a smoke-screen which is concealing something else. And that 'something' appears to be, in some sense, religious and/or mystic.

As I struggle to clarify the relevance as well as the reality of the Pentagon of Mountains, yet more hints appear which *tend to confirm*. One such hint surfaces out of an attempt to answer a seemingly simple question. Is there any significance in the fact that the church of Rennes-le-Château is dedicated to St Mary Magdelene? Saunière's new church decoration included the placing of a bas-relief of the saint on the front of the altar. I have been drawn to this peripheral enquiry because I have been told that Saunière himself painted the background details of this altar-piece, which shows Mary kneeling in a cave. Early in the investigation, this has been part of the assemblage of potential treasure clues. But now I am looking for other possibilities.

There is considerable debate about the exact identity of Mary Magdelene, who was present at the Crucifixion. She has been identified with Mary of Bethany, who anointed Jesus' feet with precious oils, and also with the reformed harlot. In the early seventh century, Pope Gregory I proclaimed these women to be one and the same and in the Middle Ages, her cult was widespread. Still today, at the village of Les Saintes Maries de la Mer, there is an annual festival to celebrate her arrival in France, 'bearing the True Cross and the Grail'. Rennes-le-Château church has two statues of her, in both of which she is carrying the Cross and the Grail and in the east window she is depicted in the act of anointing the feet of Jesus. Many theologians today regard the three women as being separate personalities but, as usual, the conclusions of present-day experts should not colour our understanding of the beliefs of our ancestors.

The most illuminating of the mediaeval beliefs concerning Mary Magdelene relates to her role in the story of the Crucifixion and Resurrection of Jesus. According to the Bible accounts, she was the first to see the Risen Christ. As such, she was looked upon by the Gnostics and by the mystics of the Middle Ages as the Medium of Secret Revelation. This resonant appellation catches my attention.

Again, I need informed advice and I am fascinated to learn that those mystics had accorded her a symbol in the Heavens. That symbol was the planet Venus. Once more I am being drawn down a trail which seems to be leading me toward irrelevancies. It would be too easy to turn away. To say 'This has nothing to do with the present enquiry'. But Rennes-le-Château teaches one to make *no* such assumptions. For the Saint and Venus, her heavenly counterpart, have indeed a 'secret revelation' to impart.

The stars and planets were, of course, of enormous interest and importance to mediaeval scholars. Indeed, such enquiries began in remote antiquity. Babylon, as well as Egypt and ancient China have left us evidence of highly skilled and detailed astronomical studies. The great stone monuments of Carnac in France and Stonehenge in Britain also show that complex astronomical work had been undertaken in megalithic times. Yet again, we must not allow our modern knowledge of the workings of the cosmos to affect our reaction to our ancestors' understanding. For them, the heavens were the home of the gods and became, in Christian times, the holy place where dwelt God and all his saints.

As they turned, the planets were showing us the mysterious workings of God's hand, expressed in the harmonious movements of the spheres. One aspect of that ancient study related to the invisible patterns which the planets draw across the firmament. Each planet, as it revolves in its orbit, reaches positions where Earth, Sun and Planet form a direct alignment. For each planet, every revolution produces a fixed number of alignments. And each planet differs in the number of its alignments and the shape of the pattern it thus produces. The orbit of Mercury, for example, creates three such alignments. When these are plotted, it is possible to draw across the sky an invisible and irregular triangle. Mars, Sun and Earth align four times during each revolution, creating a four-sided figure. Only one of these unseen patterns is regular. Only one planet shows us a perfect geometrical form. The form is pentagonal and the planet is Venus. Creating five equally-spaced alignments over a period of eight years, she draws the perfect, hidden and secret symbol of the five-pointed star in the heavens.

Here is an utterly unexpected and astonishingly meaningful answer to my simple conjecture that the dedication of Rennes-le-Château's church might be relevant. In this very place, not created by man, but fashioned of mountains by the hand of God, is that mighty symbol of the village's patron saint. 'As above . . . so below'. The very landscape bears the invisible sign of the secret revelation in the Heavens. Here, again, is knowledge which would have been accessible 'only to the initiated'. It is impossible to tell how far back in the past this amazing phenomenon was first noticed. But, noticed it undoubtedly was. Here is yet another new fragment which *tends to confirm* that I am on a valid pathway. Rennes-le-Château's Pentacle of Mountains is the mirror on Earth of the wonder in the Heavens. Real, yet invisible – save to the initiated few who share the secret. *Terribilis est locus iste* – This place is awesome. Here, Earth is touched by the secret and heavenly revelation. Here is a sacred place.

All the years of research have been building a complex story of treasure, blood, fire, faith and heresy. But stories can be mis-told, mis-heard, distorted – even invented. I begin to realise that, out of the mass of material, there are very, very few solid and incontrovertible facts, and those few facts have led unswervingly toward this discovery. The parchments certainly contain a hidden five-pointed star. Poussin's painting of the landscape, equally certainly, conceals a five-pointed star. Rennes-le-Château itself is part of the invisible five-pointed star in that landscape. And the village's saint is mirrored in the heavens by the five-pointed star symbol of Venus. Can such a sequence of logical clues be no more than a meaningless accumulation of coincidence? Undoubtedly, there are many people who wish to think so. As I contemplate the remarkable new vista which Rennes-le-Château has opened up before me, I am already satisfied that to cry 'coincidence' is a pointless reaction to a difficult truth which needs to be confronted. It is also lazy. It is saying: 'This is so unlikely and fits so uncomfortably with modern ideas, that it is not worth wasting time in investigating it further.' With this assumption, I am bound to disagree.

Chapter Nine
PLANTARD AND HIS PRIORY

AS WE WORK on the *The Shadow of the Templars*, I find myself wondering who, in the past, may have been aware of what I have found? Are de Sède's shadowy informants aware? Does that mysterious body, the Priory of Sion, still exist and, if so, are *they* aware? This is a path I am longing to follow and, fortunately, the way is about to be found. The BBC has engaged a Paris-based researcher. Jania Macgillivray's brief is to track down the Priory of Sion. And she succeeds. Her success, moreover, establishes the identity of de Sède's informant. I have already (p. 46) noted the mysterious reference to 'Plantard' on the back of photographs sent for the first film. The Grand Master of the Priory of Sion is one Pierre Plantard de St Clair.

Jania Macgillivray is able, without too much apparent difficulty, to persuade the Priory to meet with us. In addition to the looked-for opportunity to ask some pertinent questions, there will also now be the chance to persuade someone to speak for them in the forthcoming film – perhaps M. Plantard himself. A meeting is accordingly arranged, at which the BBC agrees to screen *The Priest, the Painter and the Devil*, to allay any possible fears on the Priory's part that we might be intent on sensationalising the material. This film was, fortunately, made in co-production with a French company and so a French-language version is available. The rendezvous is at a private viewing theatre in the heart of Paris. The meeting is arranged for late morning, so that we may, we hope, continue discussions in the more informal setting of a lunch break. The BBC team duly assembles some ten minutes or so before the appointed time, to be joined by a handful of supposed Priory members. Formal introductions are made. But M. Plantard is not among the assembled group. However, we are assured, he has promised to be present. His followers are unwilling to commence proceedings before his arrival.

We wait, making anodyne conversation in a somewhat stilted and un-comfortable fashion. At precisely the pre-ordained time, the door opens and Pierre Plantard de St Clair enters. He is a tall, gaunt, reserved individual with an air of quiet, if detached, command. The Priory members greet him with every show of deference. Everyone is *enchanté* to make everyone else's acquaintance and with no further social chatter, the group take their places to watch the film.

M. Plantard settles into the centre of a row of seats, his closest colleague, the Marquis Philippe de Chérisey on his right. I carefully position myself in the seat immediately behind them. There is no need for me to watch the screen. I know the material all too well. I am much more interested in watching M. Plantard's reaction to our recital of the story. I find myself remembering that cryptic statement of de Sède at our first meeting – 'We thought it might interest someone like you ...' Here, at last, are the mysterious 'we', though de Sède seems no longer to be of their company. 'Someone like me' is, apparently, someone with access to the media. Why else have they been leaking information into the Bibliothèque Nationale? Why else have they been dribbling additional information my way as I work on the story? But what are they after? If this were a simple 'con' of some sort, then there would be some hint of a way in which somebody might be profiting from the deception. But there is no suggestion of anything of the kind; money is not part of their equation.* M. Plantard and his group have, during all the years of my research, remained discreetly in the background. They have left me to draw my own conclusions from the material which they have filtered through to me, asking nothing in return. If this is a hoax of some kind, then it is subtle, long-lived and incomprehensible. And why, at last, have they decided to show themselves? Presumably they are seeking some sort of exposure. We shall now discover if I have said what they expected. Or perhaps I have said more? Or less? Will the film encourage them to co-operate further? Or will the door, which has just creaked ajar, be slammed in my face?

The Grand Master and his acolytes watch the film with quiet concen-tration. Occasionally Plantard's and de Chérisey's heads incline together as they exchange a whispered comment. It is not until the film has almost reached its end that they show anything other than relaxed interest. But

---

* The 1990s have seen agitated attempts, particularly by the BBC, to establish that the entire *affaire* is a fraud. No attempt, however, is made to explain it. The mere accusation is deemed sufficient to resolve everything, while resolving nothing. H.L.

suddenly the two backs in front of me stiffen and M. Plantard sits upright, bending forward in concentration. But the image on the screen is a fleeting one. As it disappears, the two heads lean together again in a brief and vehement conversation. *Touché*! I have shown them something they weren't expecting. The image, which has no explanatory text, is of the parchment overlaid with the pentacle. Are they unaware of the existence of the geometry? Or are they simply surprised that I have found it?

The film ends and we wait for the reaction of the Priory audience. But the Priory audience is waiting for the reaction of M. Plantard. Evidently no one is prepared to pre-empt the decision of the Grand Master. M. Plantard smiles. The film, he tells us, is an admirable presentation of the story. He will be happy to co-operate with us personally in the making of our third film. He will appoint a member of his entourage to speak on the Priory's behalf. He is willing to discuss in detail the content of the interview which the BBC would like to film and will then brief his representative accordingly. I have not expected this 'secret society' to be so willing to expose itself to the eyes of the world. But, M. Plantard explains, the Priory is not really a secret society – it is rather more a 'discreet' society; essentially 'a family affair'. His ready agreement is, from my point of view, very good news, though I would rather have the Grand Master speak than a mere 'member'. But, at least, we shall now be able to present an embodiment of this questionably 'secret' and/or 'discreet society'. There is, moreover, no need, to hurry my enquiry. M. Plantard is willing to talk. I can play my fish with rather more subtlety than would have been possible, if this were to be my only opportunity. M. Plantard will now be accessible for further meetings. I can proceed more slowly; getting to know him better before posing my more difficult questions. However, to my surprise, M. Plantard jumps in at the deep end. He is bent, it seems, on testing my mettle without further delay.

CONFECTIONS

After a few moments of general conversation and compliments upon the film which they have just seen, Plantard and de Chérisey draw me to one side. The presentation of the hidden codes in the parchments, M. Plantard says, is of an admirable clarity. However, he feels that I should know that the documents are 'confections', concocted by his friend de Chérisey. De Chérisey says nothing. He appears as much amused as discomfited by this abrupt and unexpected revelation. But I have already encountered the suggestion that the parchments were cooked up some years ago for a ten-minute television film. Why, I wonder, does M. Plantard wish to remove one of the major props to his de Sède-given story?

However, I have spoken to a code-breaking expert of British Intelligence, who has told me that they are among 'the most complex ciphers he has ever seen and would have taken months of work to prepare.' I have also discovered the geometry, hidden with brilliant subtlety beneath the written text. No one would undertake such arduous labours for a fleeting present-ation on a television screen. Besides, it is not many minutes since I have watched, with interest, the startled reaction of these two gentlemen to the appearance of the pentagon in the *Chronicle* film.

M. Plantard is waiting for my response to his revelation, with good-humoured, if quizzical geniality. I shake my head. 'No, M. Plantard,' I reply. His smile broadens and he abruptly changes the subject. Much as I would like to pursue this question further, I can see that he has, for the moment, said all that he intends to on this matter. He was after my response – and he has had it. For my part, I know that these will not be our last words on this particular subject.

We leave the cinema and BBC team and Priory members relax over an animated lunch-table discussion. I am fascinated to note that, though M. Plantard accompanies us to the restaurant and sits at the head of our table, the Priory's Grand Master will neither eat nor drink in public. He is, however, urbane and charming in his demeanour, courteously answering – or skilfully evading – any questions put to him. Arrangements are duly made for him to spend some time with us on the day preceding filming, in order to discuss the questions I wish to pose and the answers his spokesman will give, as well as any specific points which he wishes to have made. This private preparatory discussion will, I hope, allow me to explore some of the more 'delicate' areas of enquiry.

To my surprise, the appointed spokesman is to be one Jean-Luc Chaumeil. This is de Sède's 'colleague' in the 1973 'discovery' of Saunière's treasure. So the Priory *was* behind the hoax, after all. Or at least, it would seem so. As de Sède had not named him in his letters, I can only think that Chaumeil has assumed that I do not know of the connection. Or perhaps

Chaumeil was not aware of de Sède's letters to me? Clearly, both these men are being used as mouthpieces, retelling only what they are told. The waters are becoming extremely murky. I must proceed with care. The location for the filming is to be a small art gallery owned by Chaumeil's mother. A drawing by Cocteau (last name on the *Dossiers Secrets* Grand Master List) is to be provided as 'background interest.' It is at the gallery that I am to meet with M. Plantard for the briefing session while Roy Davies, as director, makes his filming arrangements.

Not surprisingly, I approach this meeting with caution. The subject of the authenticity of the parchments is one of my priorities. Again, Philippe de Chérisey is present. I tell them that I cannot accept that such an elaborate and time-consuming task was undertaken solely for a fleeting moment of television exposure. Ancient or modern, fake or genuine – it is possible to say of these documents, with literal truth, 'that there is more to them than meets the eye'. M. Plantard smiles broadly. 'Well,' he says, 'de Chérisey's confections are based upon very good originals.' I express a desire to see them. M. Plantard nods: 'I think you should.' He turns to his companion. 'Bring them tomorrow,' he says, without any elaboration and then turns to other matters.

These are principally concerned with the role of the Priory of Sion as support to the descendants of the Merovingian kings. He is, he tells me, in direct line of descent from the murdered Merovingian king, Dagobert II. 'France', he says, 'would not exist without the Merovingians. The Priory supports us – and we support the Priory.'

These are aspects which he will be happy to see us include in the interview. This begins to sound like a somewhat eccentric claim to the throne of France. Rather akin to a descendant of Queen Boudicca laying claim to the English Crown. Hardly a matter to be taken seriously. But, M. Plantard points out, that his family makes no such claim. 'The king,' he says, 'does not need to reign. Simply, it is enough that he *is*.' For this reason, he wishes to have his young son included in the film somewhere. As the representative of the next generation, the continuity of the bloodline, the son is more important than the father. These and other like matters are explored and the content of the filmed interview is sketched out. On this occasion, however, I decide to make no reference to my interest in the geometrical aspects of the story. Although this is an essential part of my enquiry, his reaction to the geometry in the earlier film has left me uncertain about what would be the best approach to the subject. For the moment it seems better to play for safety and find another opportunity for gentle sounding.

On the day of filming, I meet early with Messrs Plantard and de Chérisey. While Roy Davies is organising the 'establishing shots', I am, at last, to see the parchment 'originals'. They prove, in fact, to be nothing of the kind, though they are instructive – and more than interesting. The documents which de Chérisey produces from his briefcase are black and white photographs – roughly eight by ten inches in size.

The parchments, as reproduced in de Sède's book – and in every other book and film since (including my own) – have many dots, strokes and accents inserted into the spaces between the lines of text. Many researchers have spent much time in attempting to wrest some sort of sense from these marks. The photographs I am shown demonstrate that these are not present in the originals. They have been added in blue ink, clearly visible on the glossy surface of the prints. These are de Chérisey's 'confections'. He tells me that he has also made one other, and very important, alteration. The two documents are no longer in correct scale. In relation to each other, one is larger – or smaller – than it should be. Beyond this, no explanations are forthcoming.

One can only speculate on the significance of de Chérisey's alterations of what M. Plantard has called 'the very good originals'. It is possible that the two texts were originally back to back on the same document and that they may, in some way, interact with each other when held up to the light. Were it possible to reproduce them to the correct size and place them in accurate relationship to each other on the page, it would be interesting to see if the pentagonal design of the one, in some way produced a significant indication upon the other.*

This is not, however, the time for pursuing these problems in detail. Today is the day for filming. Roy Davies has set up for the establishing sequence of M. Plantard crossing one of the bridges of Paris. In accordance with his request, he is filmed walking hand in hand with his son, Thomas. This completed, we move on to Mme Chaumeil's art gallery, where the interview is to be shot. The routine work of setting up lights and camera

---

* The authenticity of these documents is much called into question, as if the entire mystery in some way depends upon them. However, whether these documents are ancient originals or modern 'confections', is merely of academic significance. Whatever their provenance, the content remains unaffected. And they certainly contain a cipher of staggering complexity as well as the significant and magnificently concealed pentagon. H.L.

is quickly completed. Chaumeil has been briefed and is, somewhat embarrassedly, suffering the attentions of his mother, who is brushing his hair preparatory to his appearance before the camera. At what is virtually 'the last moment', M. Plantard suddenly sets the cat among the filming – and the Priory – pigeons. He has decided to speak for himself, he announces. M. Chaumeil can stand down. Chaumeil is mortified. Chaumeil's mother is heartbroken – and very cross. M. Plantard sails urbanely through the upset and takes his place in front of the Cocteau drawing.

I am delighted. Not only will the Grand Master be more authoritative than a mere spokesman, I also realise that I have been given a wonderful opportunity. M. Plantard has already carefully prepared the answers to the questions I will put. He will be relaxed and confident, knowing his ground and feeling in control. At the end of the interview, however, and while the camera is still running, I shall add an unexpected supplementary question. It will be fascinating to capture his genuine and unprepared response to what is, for me, a key question.

The filmed interview proceeds smoothly and, at last, my chance comes. When I ask him about 'the secret of Rennes-le-Château', he replies that the secret is 'not only at Rennes-le-Château – it is also *around* Rennes-le-Château'. Here is my opening. I ask him about the geometry I have found and what significance he sees in the stressing of the pentacle. For the first time in his fluent and well-expressed responses, he hesitates. The pause lengthens. One corner of his mouth curls in the beginnings of an uncertain grin. 'I ...' he says and pauses again. Then, with a small shrug, he says all that he is prepared to say: 'I cannot give you a reply on this subject.' 'Cannot?' or 'Will not?' I wonder. He seems suddenly uncomfortable, even shifty. My unexpected question has produced a more fascinating – and real – reaction even than I have hoped.

CHERISEY

The problem with probing the representative of a 'secret' – or even a 'discreet' – society, is that one simply does not *know* their secrets. It is too easy for them to say: 'Oh, yes – we know all about that', even when they know nothing. Even if he knows nothing of the geometry, there is no need for M. Plantard to admit his ignorance. He would, after all, be diminished were he to say: 'I don't know what you're talking about.'

(Hereafter, and in the years to come, in the course of many interviews, he will always avoid being drawn into a discussion of the geometrical nature of the discovery. Only once is he even to comment, when I produce a drawing of a linked pentagon and hexagon. I ask him what he thinks of it. 'I find it disturbing,' he says – and, as usual, the subject is changed.) Even now, I cannot be sure what M. Plantard and his group may know of any of the discoveries I have made. I cannot even be *sure* that any organisation, such as the Priory of Sion, exists in the form which he has implied. Undoubtedly though, over the years, he has sought assistance from us in the clarifying of certain matters which are of concern to him – including the tracking down of members of his family now resident in England.*

The remainder of our day's shooting proceeds without incident, though in a somewhat strained atmosphere. Chaumeil and his mother, perhaps naturally, feel let down and ill-used by M. Plantard's somewhat high-handed actions.† But then, he *is* Grand Master – as well as *Roi Perdu* – The Lost King. From my point of view, I have, for the moment gone as far as I can with my geometrical enquiries. M. Plantard, it is clear, will not enlarge on his statement that he cannot give me a response to my query. The filming over, he departs at once. He is plainly not prepared to submit to further questioning, nor is he the sort of person to indulge in social intercourse. His friend, de Chérisey, however, is quite a different creature. His work is in the theatre and, like all actors, he is, at least superficially, open, gregarious and entertaining. He is happy to end the working day in relaxing chatter over a coffee. A chance, at least, for me to probe a little further. But it seems that he has been instructed to maintain a careful discretion. Each time I approach a subject which may prove contentious, he skilfully diverts the train of conversation. He is an able raconteur, with a sharp and ready wit and a fund of amusing stories. I find myself as entertained as I am frustrated. I am only too conscious that, in his briefcase, are the parchment photographs. This may be as close as I shall ever be to 'the originals' – perhaps even my last opportunity to get at these '*almost* originals'.

* For an account of our relationship with M. Plantard and his colleagues, see *The Messianic Legacy*. H.L.

† This upset may have been the root-cause of what was to prove a vicious war of words between Chaumeil and his erstwhile brethren. See *The Messianic Legacy* Chapter 19, for an account of the vitriolic correspondence in which Chaumeil is accused of involvement in the Affair of the Stolen Priory Archives. H.L.

The day is ending, but it is fine. De Chérisey expresses a desire to take a stroll and a lengthy perambulation ends on a bench in the Tuileries Gardens. He is still regaling me with well told – and often very funny – anecdotes. But I have more on my mind than entertainment. We are getting on well and the atmosphere is friendly. At last, with time passing and nothing to lose, I decide to put my request baldly. 'Can I take another look at the parchment photographs?' With only minimal hesitation, he opens his briefcase and hands them to me. 'Why add the marks?' I ask. 'To amuse the laity,' he replies. 'But why?' I insist. He shrugs. 'I'm an entertainer.' It is clear that I am to get no straight answers. But – perhaps simply because it was to hand – he adds another fragment. Picking a few sheets from his case, he says: 'I'm writing an explanation of the codes. I'll send you a copy. You'll be amused.' But I am never to see it.* Nor am I ever to get any closer to the 'parchment originals'. Sadly, Philippe de Chérisey died suddenly in July 1985.

---

* There is reason to suspect that this document may have been part of the haul of 'stolen Priory papers' which figured in the Chaumeil imbroglio. H.L.

Chapter Ten

AN INDEPENDENT DISASTER

WITH *The Shadow of the Templars* completed, it is possible to turn with full concentration to the development of the hypothesis which is to be pub-lished in early 1982 as *The Holy Blood & The Holy Grail* and expanded in *The Messianic Legacy* in 1986. But these years contain more than our ongoing research and continued contacts with M. Plantard and his col-leagues. It is during this period that an independent production company appears with a proposal to make a feature-length documentary film on the Rennes-le-Château Mystery. The notion of addressing the subject without the usual sobering constraints of the BBC's more serious documentary approach seems appealing. In the event, freedom from those constraints was to prove the reverse of liberating.

I meet the producer in his office in Wardour Street, the heart of London's film-making quarter. We discuss at length the subject matter and a fresh treatment of the material. At last, it seems, I will have access to a more generous budget. Filming will not be a rushed affair and I will be able to devote more screen time to an exploration of some of the interesting, but so far untold, byways of the story. More time and money can at last be spent in achieving the sort of visual effects that a *Chronicle* budget cannot afford. I have, for instance, long wished to be able to film the village from the air. This would be a superb way to visualise the geometry in the real landscape rather than on a map or, as in the last *Chronicle* film, with a relief model. Now such 'extravagances' will be possible. I begin work on the script with enthusiasm.

With the first draft prepared, there is a second meeting in Wardour Street. I am now ready to consult with the director before developing the script further. Who is he to be – and when may I meet with him? But the producer is busy with other pre-production matters. The director will work with me on the script during the shooting, he tells me. Everyone is happy with things as they are. Everyone, that is, but me. I am, after all, only at 'first draft' stage.

I consider it to be an important part of my job to incorporate the director's ideas into the final shooting script. Filming and editing exigencies will, inevitably, demand later alterations. But, I insist, we should at least begin with a firm and mutually agreed structure. To arrive on location with only a rough-hewn screen-play is, for me, akin to attempting to make an omelette without first breaking the eggs. Much time will be wasted in fishing out any unwanted debris. This is, after all, a complex story which needs careful structuring. It is not a piece of actuality news-reportage, where things are merely shot as they happen. Consultation with the director is an important part of my working process and I repeat my urgent request for a meeting with him before we leave for shooting. My worries, however, are brushed aside. There will be ample time on location, I am told. Problems can be solved as they arise. The director is looking forward to meeting me at Rennes-le-Château. He won't have time for script-conferences in advance. As I prepare for yet another filming trip, I am sunk into a nervous despondency. I am trapped in what seems to me to be a highly unsatisfactory undertaking and the omens are anything but good.

As I wait at the airport for my flight to Toulouse, I am apprehensively aware that we shall be filming in a mere few days and I haven't yet so much as seen my director. More worrying still … he has not yet seen Rennes-le-Château. But I am not even to have a couple of hours with him on the plane. He is driving down and will join us tomorrow.

This time, my pleasure at being back in the village is definitely tempered by discomfort at what seems to me to be a somewhat *laissez-faire* attitude to the project. Not only is the subject-matter complicated. There is also the necessity to maintain good relations with the locals. The villagers have become my friends and I have no desire to see them upset. They are rightly sensitive about the story of their home and their priest and I have always done my best to ensure that they understand and are happy with our plans. Now, even I do not know how my director intends to approach the subject. I also know that some film crews can be tactless and unfeeling, indifferent to the distress which they may leave behind when they move on. I can only pray that my fears are groundless.

I sit in Saunière's garden, waiting for the director's arrival and going over the itinerary of the flying visits we must make to reconnoitre the many locations I have included. There is little more than a day before the arrival of the crew and the commencement of shooting. Before then, I must try to get to know the man who will make the film – and to introduce him to the background of his story. For this task, I have today and tomorrow.

Today begins to trickle away. Henri Buthion keeps me supplied with cooling drinks and pacifying conversation as he senses my increasing disquiet at the waste of the morning. Perhaps he'll be here for lunch? But lunchtime comes and goes. So does most of the afternoon. All my training throughout years of television work has taught me that 'wasted time is wasted budget'. I am simply not used to this rather *insouciant* approach to the task. At last, with half the afternoon gone, I hear the sound of a car. I forsake my table under Saunière's shade-trees and station myself in the car park. A large and gleaming convertible edges its way past the Villa Bethania and purrs to a halt beside the Magdala Tower. A tall and considerably overweight figure squeezes from the driver's seat. 'Hi,' he says, 'You must be Lincoln.' I plead guilty and introductions are effected. I tell him that I have been growing concerned at his late arrival. Lunch in Carcassonne, he tells me, was too good to hurry over. Today is holiday. Tomorrow will be time enough for work. I resign myself to the uncaring Fates – and my apparently equally uncaring director.

At the end of the afternoon, a second car arrives bringing our producer and his personal assistant. From my fleeting acquaintance with her in London, I know that she is likeable and efficient. He, however, seems strangely on edge. He has found the journey from England fatiguing, he says, and is suffering from a blinding headache. He will go and rest for a while. Let's all meet for a consultation before dinner, he suggests. There is nothing for it, I decide, but to enjoy what remains of my enforced vacation day. With a glass of Ricard, thoughtfully provided by Henri, I sit on Saunière's *belvédère* and watch the evening sun glinting on the far-off snow-capped peaks of the Pyrenees. No work-a-day worry can diminish the beauty of this landscape. Tomorrow, I comfort myself, will be another day. Unfortunately, I have forgotten that today isn't yet over.

DIRECTOR'S ANGLE

At dinner, our director appears, reinvigorated – and with 'an angle'. He has just taken a preprandial stroll around the village and he has 'come up with something'. He has been talking to the owner of Rennes-le-Château's ancient and decaying castle, who has told him something that isn't in my script. While I am delighted to learn that the director has, at least, read my rough draft, I am uncertain about the value of what he may have heard from the village *châtelain*.

This is an amiable, if eccentric old character, who seems to have inherited his eccentricity from his father. This latter gentleman spent many years scouring the surrounding countryside and bringing home oddly shaped stones. Each of these stones bears some resemblance to one or other bone in the human body. Thus, over a long and active lifetime, he had found tibia-like rocks, ulna-like rocks, vertebrae-like rocks and even cranial-like rocks. From these he had assembled a complete 'human' skeleton, which he was wont to exhibit to any passing voyager who showed interest, with the claim that this was 'a fossil human being'. A generation later, the skeleton continues to be exhibited, the castle continues to crumble and the eccentricity continues to flourish.

But, I hear with relief, fossil humans are not to figure in our director's ideas. 'These are just nonsenses for the tourists,' he tells me. 'The old boy agreed with me … it's just a heap of old stones. We had a good talk and he admits that he just gives visitors the sort of rubbish he thinks they want to hear.' Our director, however, is convinced that he has been singled out for an unique privilege. For him, the *châtelain's* story is not 'any old rubbish'. For him alone, 'the real truth' has been preserved down the generations.

'And it fits terrifically with all your devil-worship stuff!'

'So what have I missed?'

'It's all pagan sex-magic. Saunière used to have Satanic orgies. He was the High Priest and all the local women had to give in to him. He even put sex images in the church!'

'Where?' I ask, weakly. This is all becoming even more alarming than I could have imagined.

'In the window over the altar.' 'But that is a simple and quite orthodox representation of Mary Magdelene anointing Jesus' feet,' I point out. It's hardly an orgy. But, of course, I should have realised. The imagery is much subtler – and at the same time more blatant. Saunière has apparently had incorporated into the stained glass scene a clear depiction of the female genitals.

'Clear as anything,' the director informs me. 'He showed me a photograph. We'll go and check it out in the church first thing tomorrow.'

'There you are!' he says, pointing at the window bathed in the light of early morning. Mary is kneeling at the feet of Jesus. Where the curving folds of the skirt bend around her knees, I am supposed to see a display of flagrant obscenity. I can't.

'You'd have to have the overheated imagination of a grubby-minded schoolboy to see it,' I insist.

'Oh, no,' he says, cheerfully, 'I can get a really convincing shot.'

John – Chapter XI, verse 35 floats into my head. It may be the shortest verse in the Gospels, but in my present mood, it says all that can be said.* How, I wonder, can I extricate myself from this nightmare?

From here on, chaos swirls around me. The film, I am told, will relate the story of the investigations into a Satanic cult, instituted by Saunière and still continuing.

SEX AND SATANISM

The village church is introduced by a close shot of one of the gargoyles upon the porch, which is made to 'vomit blood'. (Several bottles of Henri Buthion's extremely good house wine are wasted in achieving this effect.)

The abandoned wreck of an old car is conveniently to hand in the corner of the village car park. This will be pushed over the edge of the mountain below the Magdala Tower and set on fire as the depiction of an attempt by the Satanists upon 'The Investigator's' life.

All the 'ladies (and gentlemen) of the night' who can be found in Carcassonne, are rounded up and paid to dance naked around a bonfire near the pool in the centre of the pentagon. One of the ladies is filmed on the roof of the Tower in the role of a naked altar within a five-pointed star. Wreathed in crimson smoke, one of the crew, dressed as a magician

---

* Jesus wept.

Satanic cavortings.

in cloak and pointed hat, 'sacrifices' a (fake) dove over her out-stretched nude body. (More imitation blood!)

Horror is being piled upon horror. Time and again, I ask the producer to release me from this purgatory of which I wish no part and to which I can make no contribution. But he seems unaware of what is happening around him. Often, he disappears from the village for hours at a time upon some errand or other. Not even his personal assistant can enlighten me about what he is doing or planning. In one of the few brief conversations which I manage to have with him, he tells me not to worry. 'The director knows what he's doing. It will all work out fine. By the way,' he continues unexpectedly, 'have you got any cash?' This being a rural area, the nearest banks are only open on a couple of days a week and he has urgent necessary purchases to make. 'How much do you need?' 'As much as you've got. I'll return it the day after tomorrow, when the bank opens.' As I am trapped in the village with no transport of my own and no immediate need of money, I hand over my cash supply. He climbs into his car and departs on his shopping trip. The crew disappears into the countryside to film another directorial sexual fantasy. My services are not required. I have no script to cover unclothed cavortings in Arcadia.

I climb to the roof of the Magdala Tower to brood in quiet solitude. At least, I can enjoy the view. But for the first time, I wish I were anywhere but Rennes-le-Château. I realise that I am trapped. If I simply 'abandon ship', I will be leaving the village to the less than tender mercies of the director. I feel that I must be on hand to pour oil upon any troubled waters which he may stir up. And, without too much hope, I cling to the faint possibility that I may be able to restore a little sanity to the proceedings. Suddenly, Henri Buthion's son appears.

'Thought you'd like to know,' he says, 'de Sède's turned up. He's talking to Papa in the restaurant.'

REUNION

It is now many years since I have seen de Sède. He was, I know, angry at his omission from the first film and has been somewhat impolite to me in his later writings. However, I see no necessity to hide myself. Much has happened in the Rennes-le-Château story since our last encounter. It would be polite, I decide, to go down and say hello. In any case, it will be a relief from my frustrating and depressing inactivity.

Henri is standing in the doorway to his kitchen as I enter the restaurant foyer. De Sède looks up as I come down the stairway into the cool semi-darkness. Beside him is a woman (Mme de Sède?). Another man, also unknown to me, and carrying a professional-looking camera, is stationed by the entrance.

'Hello, Gérard,' I say, holding out my hand, 'Good to see you again.'

He takes my hand with a mumbled greeting, but no introductions are effected to the other players in the scene. As if he has been waiting for the opportunity, and with no further preamble, nor any attempt at social niceties, de Sède challenges me.

'Why did you write to the Louvre claiming that it was not me, but you, who discovered the Poussin Tomb?'

I am puzzled. This is news to me.

'What do you mean?' I ask, 'I've never made any such claim.'

'Yes you have. Your letter's in the Louvre archive.'

'But I've written no such letter,' I protest.

Mme de Sède(?) suddenly intervenes. 'Liar!' she shrieks.

'*Couchez!*' bellows de Sède, gesturing at the carpet. (This is the manner of ordering a dog to 'Lie down, sir!' Although, in English, this would be a fairly silly thing to say, in French it is intended as a – very definite – insult.)

'I assure you that I have not written to the Louvre. Nor have I ever denied that you sent me the information about the tomb.'

De Sède decides to echo the lady.

'Liar!'

'Hit him!' cries Madame.

De Sède needs no further encouragement. His arm swings back and he delivers what is termed, I believe, 'a hay-maker' to the side of my head. I see the proverbial stars as I rock back on my heels. A split-second later, I also see the flash of the other gentleman's camera – too late, unfortunately, to record anything other than the frozen aftermath of the blow. An (almost literally) stunned silence follows. It seems that I am expected to make some sort of response.

'If that has given you any pleasure,' I say, 'then I'm happy for you.'

This seems not to be the desired reaction. De Sède shuffles from one foot to the other, in the uncomfortable pause. Then:

'Come on,' he mumbles, 'Let's go to the church.' And, trailed by his two companions, he makes a somewhat undignified and anti-climactic exit.

Henri Buthion has not moved from the doorway to his kitchen. He looks at me with quiet amusement. '*Henri*,' he says, '*J'admire votre sang-froid britannique.*' We hoot with laughter. This has been my most ludicrous Rennes-le-Château encounter so far. As Henri administers an ice-pack to my rapidly developing black eye, he comments sagely: 'To use violence suggests that one is at the end of one's argument.' The gentleman with the camera, Henri suspects, is a journalist; perhaps on hand to capture an anticipated brawl. Unfortunately, though, he has missed his chance.

Needless to say, there is no letter such as de Sède has described in the Louvre archive. Yet again, it would seem, he is 'acting on information received'. The Louvre records show a note of my visit to examine the x-rays. The note simply records that an English writer, Henry Lincoln, reports that a tomb resembling that of the *Shepherds of Arcadia* has been located. Who convinced de Sède that I have been trying to steal his 'glory'? But I am to be given no opportunity to question him further on the matter. Within minutes we hear the sound of a car bearing the trio away. They have left me with yet another mystery. But, for the moment,

I am indifferent to such problems. I have enough with the Saunière Sex and Satanism Saga.

TAKEAWAY

When the crew returns at the end of the day from who knows what filmic excitements, our director seeks me out. 'I need your help,' he says. I find this hard to believe, but quickly discover that the required assistance is less professional than politic. Tomorrow is the day ordained for the arrival of a helicopter, which is being flown out from England to capture the aerial shots of the village. Will I tell Henri Buthion that we will not require him to provide dinner tomorrow evening?

I have come to realise, over the passing days, that I am not perfectly in tune with the director's thought processes. Now, however, I confess myself completely flummoxed by this particular *non-sequitur*. He expands on his requirements. Can I use my skills to persuade Henri Buthion to allow the director to take over his kitchen tomorrow night? Why? It seems that a special directorial treat has been arranged. He has a favourite Chinese restaurant in London – and the helicopter will be bringing us its finest offerings. As the flight will take most of the day, they will, not unnaturally require re-heating. It takes all my diplomatic arts to persuade Henri that this particular folly is not a calculated insult to his cuisine. It is, rather, a sort of joke. With the arrival of the air-borne oriental offerings, the Director officiously occupies Henri's sanctum. We watch in fascination as the con-gealed repast is given a laborious kiss-of-life. Needless to say, the corpse is beyond recall. It may once have been 'London's Finest Chinese' ... but it's still a ridiculously expensive (and probably world-record distance) takeaway meal. In due course, it is also rejected by the village's discerning dogs. Henri's scraps are less exotic, but infinitely more attractive.

The arrival and landing of the helicopter is, of course, an unprecedented event for Rennes-le-Château. The villagers are briefly entranced by the unusual sight and then return to their quotidian labours. For me, it is the opening of the final page in the dismal story.

The unusual activities of the past days have, naturally, attracted some little attention. Rumours are beginning to circulate concerning the unwonted carryings-on of the strange film crew. At last, a couple of reporters from the local press arrive at Rennes-le-Château and seek me out for an interview. Over the years, this has become a common practice, but this time I am aware that I may have to be somewhat more circumspect than usual in my replies to their questions.

As I sit talking to the journalists on the *belvédère*, the producer suddenly appears. As he can neither speak, nor understand, any French, I wonder why he has chosen to join the discussion. Perhaps there is something he wants me to say? There is – but it has nothing to do with the journalists. He seems even more edgy than usual. His manner is of a barely controlled agitation. 'I've got to leave the village,' he says, 'Straightaway. I've got to get back to London.' There is nothing more for him or for his personal assistant to do on the location and, as I have expressed a desire to return to England, he proposes that I pack my bags instantly. He intends to leave at once. I suggest that it would be politic for me to finish my interview with the journalists, but he will have none of this. 'Immediately!' he repeats. 'Pack now. We're leaving in five minutes.' His perturbation is very real. He obviously means what he says.

I apologise to the bemused journalists, run down to the Villa Bethania and hurl my things into suitcases. I am completely at a loss to understand what has brought about this dramatic turn of events. But, with no time to think, it seems best to grasp the opportunity for escape while it is there. As I come back out onto the road, I find the producer's car is stationed outside the Villa's front door, with the engine running. The producer is standing by the already open boot, into which I hurl my bags. He slams it shut and makes for the driver's seat. 'Wait!' I call out, 'I must tell Henri Buthion that I'm going – and say goodbye to the family.'

'There's no time!' he yells, climbing into the car.

But I cannot accept this degree of discourtesy to my friends. Fortunately, Henri has come out into his garden to discover the cause for the apparent commotion. I explain hurriedly and we embrace as, behind me, I can hear the producer revving the engine of his car. I throw myself into the back seat and, with the door barely closed, we accelerate away. I am breathless, confused and angry. What the hell is going on?

As the producer drives at excessive speed around the hairpin bends of the descent to Couiza, I notice that, beside him, his personal assistant is looking pale and worried. I suspect that it is not merely the wild driving which is giving her cause for concern. She looks back at me from the passenger seat and I raise my eyebrows in silent query. She responds with a tiny shrug of puzzlement. Clearly, she is no more *au fait* with developments than I am.

The car tears through Couiza and then, to my surprise, takes the right turn towards Rennes-les-Bains. 'It's the left turn for Carcassonne and the westbound motorway to Toulouse,' I yell. But I am being taken to Perpignan Airport, I discover. As we drive eastwards at breakneck speed, I try to explain the new predicament which this decision creates. One – I do not know if there is a suitable flight from Perpignan today. Two – I do not know if there will be an available seat, even should there be a flight from Perpignan. Three – my return ticket to London is valid only from Toulouse. Four – assuming that there *is* a flight with an available seat from Perpignan, there will, presumably be a supplement to pay on my ticket. And five – and most drastic – I have not a penny in my pocket. The producer has still not returned my cash, of which he had had such urgent need some days before. (It should be noted that this is happening in a time before today's more general use of credit cards.) 'You'll have to sort it out,' he tells me and, hunched over the wheel, he speeds the car onwards down the road.

For the remainder of the hair-raising journey, I endeavour, with desperation, to convince him of the fact that I will have some difficulty in 'sorting things out', if I am simply abandoned at the airport with no ticket – possibly no flight – and certainly no money. I am more than a little worried. Not simply for myself, but for his personal assistant, who must accompany him on what promises to be a terrifying drive back to England. The man is behaving in an altogether incomprehensible and frightening manner.

Perpignan Airport is tiny, with a parking area in front of the terminal building. The producer pulls to a halt before the entrance, leaps from the car, extracts my cases from the boot and drops them to the ground. I insist that he accompany me into the building to discover exactly what problems I may be confronting. His PA joins in my persuasions and, with agitated reluctance, he agrees.

We sprint to the enquiry desk, where I am able rapidly to discover that – happily – flight and seat are both available. I translate. 'Good', he says and turns for the exit.

'Wait!' I yelp, 'There's a supplement to pay.'

'How much?' he snarls, producing a cheque book.

I enquire, I translate and he begins to write the cheque. The girl at the enquiry desk points out that she cannot deal with the payment, which he must make at the bookings desk across the hall. I translate. He yells enraged and profane imprecations, which I do *not* translate. He runs across to bookings and scrawls the cheque, flinging it across the counter and, with no further pause, rushes for the way out. I gallop after him.

'Can you *please*,' I implore, 'leave me at least a few francs? I haven't the cost of a cup of coffee. And I've still to get myself home in England.' He ignores me and throws himself back into the car, turns the key and, with a cloud of burnt rubber, accelerates away. But his PA has heard my shouted plea. As they zoom from the car park, I see her arm waving from the passenger window – and she releases a handful of banknotes into the car's slipstream. The cloud of cash flutters high in the air as the car disappears. Breathless, I watch them go; then, with relief, begin my absurd paper chase. At least I can now indulge in the extravagance of the desperately called for, and calming, cup of coffee.

This extraordinary, burlesque experience is not farce, however. It is the enactment of a very real tragedy. The producer's apparently insane performance is, in fact, exactly that. The headaches and the irrational behaviour are the effects of an unsuspected brain tumour. Within days of his return to England, the poor man is dead.

Much as I have been praying for a way out of my predicament, I would never have wished for so dreadful a means of salvation. However, the producer's death is followed by the collapse of his company and the abandonment of the film. From my point of view, at least, this is a tattered silver lining to an otherwise appalling cloud of disasters. But, disturbing and infuriating though this whole episode has been, it serves to demonstrate that bizarre interpretations are easily heaped upon the few facts which have emerged over the years of research into an already bizarre story.

Chapter Eleven
INTERPRETATIONS

INEVITABLY Rennes-le-Château is no longer the tiny, lost and sleepy hamlet which I had first encountered in 1971. Tourism has now arrived, with its summer throngs of visitors who require information, guidance, picture postcards, maps, books, souvenirs – as well as a coach park, food, drink, ice-cream, toilet facilities and the seemingly innumerable rubbish bins which now line the village streets. I have contributed my own share to the visiting hordes. In 1979, the French Government Tourist Agency decided that more tourism should be attracted to the Languedoc. Having brought Rennes-le-Château to the notice of the outside world, I was asked to guide groups of Saunière seekers around the relevant sites. I have continued to do so, on and off, over the years and thus have been able to watch the development of the worldwide fascination with the story.

In an isolated castle perched upon a giddy mountaintop, I have encountered a group of Americans, listening to their guide as he read aloud passages from my work. On the wooded slopes of Blanchefort, I have met an earnest Dutch party who were carefully following the *Holy Place* alignments. And in Rennes-le-Château, I have been fervently and tearfully embraced by a Latvian lady, clutching a (pirated) Russian edition of *The Holy Blood & The Holy Grail*.

At each visit, I have climbed la Pique, the central mountain of the Pentacle. From there one can still enjoy, in solitude, the matchless panorama, with the awareness that, here, one is at the heart of the mystery. But below, where once the enigmatic pool lay isolated in a sweep of open and deserted countryside, now its screen of scrub has been stripped away and a large house stands beside it. At the very foot of la Pique, a rash of wooden holiday chalets has appeared.

More regrettable are the drastic lengths to which some people have been driven by the fantasies bred in their deluded imaginations. Thus, in 1988, the lunatic 'treasure-hunter's' attack with explosives upon the Poussin Tomb and its consequent, tragic destruction. Even more disgraceful, in 1996, the head of Saunière's devil statue was struck off and stolen. This deplorable desecration of Rennes-le-Château's church was apparently a misguided and futile attempt to 'defuse' malign influences.

Inevitably, every visitor brings a personal view of the story. Many come to realise that the peace and beauty of the landscape are recompense enough for their journey. But some are still obsessively on the hunt for treasure and/or seek to commune with the shade of Saunière for guidance. Psychics and 'New-Age' enthusiasts (particularly of the Anglo-Saxon variety), are drawn as to a mystic honey-pot and many have bought properties in the area. In my brushes with these earnest folk, I have been puzzled by their conviction that I share their views of the story. Having interpreted what I have written in their own curious ways, they seem unable to accept that I do not seek to substantiate, let alone share, their paranormal preoccupations.

One such enlightenment-seeker sent me a copy of a book which she had written. 'Here is the truth,' she informed me in her accompanying letter. 'You know it – but you haven't the courage to say it.' This 'truth' is apparently that extra-terrestrials arrived on Earth and created the human race. I fear, however, that I 'know' no such thing.

Another writer informed me that her book had 'put me in great danger' as it revealed that I was among the few who knew 'the truth' which, again, I had not dared write, but at which I had only hinted. This 'truth' differed from the first. According to this author, I 'know' that the Earth is hollow and that a subterranean Master Race is controlling the world from beneath our feet.

Other writers 'solve' the riddle by mind-bending contortions based upon arbitrary and excruciating anagrams. E.g.: Saunière's Tour Magdala is battlemented – which when defined as 'a crenel'(?), renders the anagram *le crâne* (the skull) and thus is a reference to the skull of St Dagobert (!). I note *en passant* that the letters will also provide *élancer* – to hurl forth ... or to chuck out. Which seems a useful indication of what should be done with such meaningful insights.

A recent and much-hyped publication devoted some 500 pages to an exploration of the Rennes-le-Château geometry. The appearance of this book was surrounded by the not-unfamiliar aura of paranoia which, in my experience, always signals nonsense. This was in the form of a (very permeable) security blanket, apparently spread to augment the pre-publication excitement. However, as well as preventing authors and publisher from showing the normal professional courtesy of asking for permission to reproduce copyright material, it also led them into some grievous foolishness.

Having pillaged *The Holy Place* for both prose and geometry, the book reproduces, several times, one of my diagrams which, the authors tell us, 'proves' that my conclusions are wrong. The diagram, they insist, was 'clearly intended' to indicate a symmetry which I had not noticed and which helps to substantiate their own conclusions. But, I can assure them, there was no such intention to indicate symmetry. I can be quite definitive about this. The hand which drew the diagram was mine. When, at the beginning of their book, their argument compels them to accuse me of error, the qualification of this statement is reserved for some 450 pages later where, in a footnote, they confess that they 'had to decide' what was acceptable!

What conclusion did their highly questionable geometry reach? The identification of a location on the flank of Cardou, the mountain opposite to Blanchefort. But David Wood, Erling Haagensen, Patricia Hawkshaw, myself and others, have indicated innumerable such locations, as I shall explain in Part Two. However, one spot on a hillside hardly merits hype. The reading public cannot be expected to wax overly excited about it. So Cardou is now blessed with a tomb of Jesus. Why not? With a sufficiently fertile imagination, anything can be proposed and accepted on faith and wishful thinking alone.

I am as amused as I am amazed by the claim of each new publication to have at last reached 'the solution to the mystery'. How can the creation of the human race by Venusians explain Saunière's wealth? How can an anagram interpret an alignment of churches? How can a tomb of Jesus solve the problem of a fixed measure? Each solver of the puzzle seems bound to ignore the findings of the others. Why? With each new publication, I hope for fresh and genuine insights. Authors around the world have sent me their ideas, their findings – even their manuscripts. Those with provable data receive all the assistance I can give. Having, over the years, made my position clear, I fortunately hear less from those on the lunatic fringe. These are more inclined to wrap themselves in their dubious shrouds of secrecy and apparent fear of the hidden magi, who may try to influence, undermine or threaten them.

When the discoverers of Jesus' tomb found that I had got something 'right' in my geometry but did not arrive at the same conclusion as themselves, they said:

> There are three possibilities: the deductions are fallacious; they were a lucky guess and are correct; Henry Lincoln was told what to do.

Who are these mysterious entities who go around 'telling people what to do'? The Government? Well ... perhaps. The Church? Unlikely. My publisher? Hmm. I certainly do what J, 'my better half', tells me to do. (Sometimes.) But, not only does she have no knowledge of geometry, she has less interest. I am bound to conclude that the authors are wrong when they specify only three possibilities. But, as 'conspiracy fantasists', they would find too banal and boring the fourth possibility – namely, the truth ... which is, as my files, recordings, correspondence and notebooks amply demonstrate, that I thought it through myself. There is also, of course, a fifth possibility. My ideas might have come gift-wrapped from Santa Claus ...

Part Two

THE DISCOVERY

Chapter Twelve

THE PATHWAY OF
DISCOVERY

OVER ALMOST THIRTY YEARS, I have pursued the ghost of a nineteenth-century priest who has led me down a long pathway into the past. Others are now tramping down that same road – some with more purpose and more intelligence than others. In this book I have retraced my own steps. In the pages which follow I will attempt, as simply as possible, to show the reader the view which I see ahead.

Thus far, I have recounted the story of the many years of activities, distractions, lunacies and sheer hard work which have brought me to a point where the Mystery of Rennes-le-Château has changed from the small, localised puzzle of *The Accursed Treasure*, to a reappraisal of the history and beliefs of the last two thousand years. With my two co-authors, I was staggered by the strength of the worldwide reaction to the publication of *The Holy Blood & The Holy Grail* in 1982. With hindsight, it is now easier to see that what came to be known as 'the Jesus material' of that book, was bound to elicit vehement protests; especially among those who had not actually read it. We were accused of having made wild and unproven attacks upon Christianity when, in fact, we had simply presented an hypothesis. However, it is not my intention in this present book to reiterate, nor to expand upon that hypothesis.

What follows is an exploration, not of hypotheses, nor of further adventures along the Rennes-le-Château road.

Rather is it the statement of a series of *facts* and a brief exposition of how those facts crystallised out of the confusions.

My investigation of the Mystery of Rennes-le-Château has led me to the conclusion that Rennes-le-Château is *itself* a mystery. The purpose of the second part of this book is to confront the unexpected with no preconceptions, no 'attitude', no theorising and certainly no sensationalist claims. What, then, am I setting out to demonstrate?

The simple answer which will, for the moment, indicate the pathway of discovery, is that the layout of certain man-made structures in the Rennes-le-Château area is so placed that they create coherent and precise geometric patterns. They seem to show evidence of a 'structured landscape'. That is, the placing of these structures appears to have been carefully and skilfully measured and demonstrates a highly sophisticated knowledge of mathematics, geometry and the techniques of land-surveying. History teaches us, however, that such knowledge and such techniques were not available to the society which existed at the time this work was done, which must, of course, be earlier than the known origins of the structures.

The most obvious of these buildings are ancient churches, some of which date back at least a thousand years. Again, we are told that such complexity of mathematics was not available in the tenth century either. Furthermore, it is well known that the Church usurped existing – and much more ancient – sacred sites. A newly Christianised population would thus continue to frequent its habitual places of worship, where their pagan rites would now be replaced by the sacraments of the Church.

Naturally, not every pagan sacred site became a church, but it is interesting to note that a seventh-century bishop was imploring his flock to cease practising rites at 'sacred stones, rocks, springs and *places where three trackways meet.*' The French countryside is dotted with innumerable wayside crosses. These *Calvaires* stand, almost invariably, at '*places where three trackways meet*'. Thus they, too, may be preserving the memory of significant sites. The few prehistoric Standing Stones in the area seem to be incorporated into the Rennes-le-Château geometry. This would appear to indicate that the original lay-out had been created in megalithic times and was marked out by stones now, for the large part, replaced by churches and wayside crosses. In attempting to eradicate the pagan worship, the Church has inadvertently preserved what it wished to destroy.

Reactions to such an unexpected discovery are predictable. At one extreme there are the hostile rationalists who insist that the findings are 'impossible'. The blinkers of scholarly superiority are donned and the facts are ignored.

The other extreme is represented by the New-Age, mystic, 'seekers-after-truth', who leap upon the bald facts as 'proof' of some hidden, or supernatural, or extra-terrestrial activity. I confess to being as puzzled by the one reaction as I am by the other. Such 'proof' requires an enormous leap of faith. The willingness to accept guesses as facts and wishful thinking as reality. Many people willingly swallow whole the claims of encounters with aliens. Indeed, even Rennes-le-Château has its own flying saucer, apparently buried beneath a field below the village. But claims are not proofs. Belief – as well as the rationalist's non-belief – *without proof*, is evidence of nothing.

I will embrace, wholeheartedly, *objective proof* of the activities of super-intelligences, extra-terrestrials, gods or even of hidden magi lurking upon inaccessible Himalayan peaks. I will *not*, however, accept anybody's mere assertions of these notions. Such pronouncements are evidence of nothing more than a desire to believe that which has been asserted.

For this reason I do not wish the reader to *believe* what follows. Simply, I ask that the facts be checked and verified. Certainly, the evidence which I shall present seems to run counter to our previously accepted under-standing of the past. That does *not* mean, however, that it is impossible. Some people may find the facts which follow to be unpalatable. Their aversion does not invalidate the data. I do not doubt – indeed, I hope – that errors in the data will be noted and corrected. But the overall picture which emerges is beyond dispute.

Rennes-le-Château has opened the door onto a fresh understanding of some of the skills and activities of our ancestors. I can see no reason to assume that the creators of what I shall describe were anything other than normal – and normally intelligent – human beings. That their skills were lost seems evident. That they possessed those skills is equally evident.

Chapter Thirteen
BASIC FACTS

WITH THE APPEARANCE in 1986 of *The Messianic Legacy*, I felt that I had come to the end of my struggles to understand the mystery of Rennes-le-Château. As I looked back at the films I had made throughout the seventies, I found it fascinating to see how the story had changed and developed over the years as the evidence slowly accumulated. Throughout, I had been gnawing at the 'givens' of the story. Trying to take nothing 'on faith'. Trying to prove this or disprove that 'fact'. Things which had been straightforwardly accepted: that the priest had found a treasure; that the Templars had worked the local silver mines; that the Priory of Sion was an age-old and genuine 'secret society' became less and less solidly factual. These 'facts' are merely hearsay reports. After almost two decades I had come to realise the extent of my own ignorance. Almost everything in the story was fished from a quagmire of questions. The undeniable *facts* were remarkably few. Even those few facts were open to interpretation and thus, again, to uncertainty.

Before once and for all turning my back on the story, I thought that it would be interesting, as well as salutary, to sum up the certainties which were the fruit of all those years of work. The result was illuminating.

FACT I   Two 'parchments' were published by de Sède. (Provenance uncertain; date uncertain; authorship uncertain.) Ancient or modern – fake or genuine – valid or fraudulent ... they demonstrably and self-evidently exist.

FACT 2   The 'parchments' conceal a geometric design which is pentagonal. (Demonstrable.)

FACT 3   Nicolas Poussin's *Shepherds of Arcadia* depicts a landscape near to Rennes-le-Château. (Demonstrable.)

FACT 4   Nicolas Poussin's *Shepherds of Arcadia* conceals a geometric design which is pentagonal. (Demonstrable.)

FACT 5   The landscape near to Rennes-le-Château conceals a geometric configuration of mountains which is pentagonal. (Demonstrable.)

FACT 6   Rennes-le-Château's patron saint is St Mary Magdelene – whose celestial representation was the planet Venus, whose orbital alignments form a geometric design which is pentagonal. (Demonstrable.)

With this summing up of the accumulated *solid* evidence, I was suddenly made aware that, struggle as I might, I could find nothing else in the story that was thus unassailable. The above facts do not depend upon unreliable hearsay evidence. They do not depend upon documents which might be falsified. They do not depend upon hypotheses which, by their very nature, are non-proven. They do not depend upon faith, belief or wishful thinking. They are verifiable facts.

The story had begun as the local mystery of a nineteenth-century village priest and a possible treasure. Research and the creation of an explanatory hypothesis had unexpectedly widened the horizons of the story. But now, the filtering of fact from theory had once again narrowed the field. The mystery had again become local. Each one of the tangible facts on my list, related directly to Rennes-le-Château itself – and linked with pentagonal geometry. The years spent in pursuit of the Priory of Sion and the Merovingian Connection had produced two books. Wide-ranging though the work had been, I was always aware that I was, necessarily, leaving aside one tangible discovery. The geometry of the Pentacle of Mountains remained firm, inexplicable and – for the time – seemingly irrelevant.

But one other element had been introduced into this aspect of the story which demanded my attention. The demonstration of the geometry of the mountains in *The Shadow of the Templars*, had caught the attention of a skilled cartographer. David Wood began his own concentrated work on the landscape configurations and made an astonishing leap forward.

THE SECOND PENTACLE

Over the years, I had received very many letters from viewers and readers who claimed to have 'solved the mystery'. The solutions ranged from the ludicrous to the incomprehensibly convoluted. Most were obsessively fixated upon a hiding place for a treasure, or a mummified body of Jesus, or some other such similar fantasy, and demonstrated varying degrees of paranoia. One letter (sent via a solicitor), spoke of 'vital information' and charged me to meet with the writer in the rear entrance to a certain public library, bringing with me some evidence to prove that I was not an imposter.

Another was written upon paper which had been baked in order to render it brittle, so that it disintegrated as I read it.

The desire to communicate the good news of the 'solution' was coloured by the fear that I would steal the credit for the discovery, if not the gold and jewels themselves, from under the noses of the 'solver'. 'We have carefully considered whether we should make contact with you,' said one missive, 'as we have no intention of in any way surrendering our rights or copyrights . . . We insist on guarantees and security.' Why, I wondered, if they think I am so dangerously dishonest, have they bothered to write at all?

David Wood's communication, however, was of a different order. Here, for the first time, were findings which fell squarely into the necessary category of 'the demonstrable and provable'. More exciting still, the new discovery was geometric and pentagonal. His cartographic skill had enabled him to move the investigation into a new dimension. It was now clear that my discovery of the Pentacle of Mountains was but the first glimpse of something much more complex. Here was proof that there had been a conscious and highly skilled geometric plan, which governed the placing of certain structures in the Rennes-le-Château landscape.

I was happy to write a Foreword to his book *Genisis*, which was published in 1985, even though I was bound to say that I could not accept his conclusions, which were that the extraordinary ingenuity of the work implied an intelligence that was, in some sense, 'superhuman'. These conclusions worried me, as they moved from the certain to the subjective and I could not follow him down this path.

His mathematics and geometry, however, were impressive and seemed to be a logical extension of the pathway upon which I had already stumbled. To my six demonstrable and provable facts, I could now add a seventh. David Wood had identified pentagonal geometry associated with a circle of churches and castles.

But his work lay beyond my expertise. I had no more knowledge of cartography, geometry or mathematics than I had carried away with me at the end of my schooldays, almost forty years before. For a while, the new development lay dormant. But, much as I wished to turn my back on the story, letters from readers continued to arrive which required responses and which kept Rennes-le-Château on the edges of my consciousness. Some asked for my opinion and comments upon David Wood's discovery. It was inevitable that I should look again at his work. And a simple and obvious question immediately presented itself.

His book explored in fascinating detail the construction of the geometry he had identified at Rennes-le-Château – and yet it ignored the original Pentacle of Mountains which had led him to the discovery. His preoccupation was solely with the strange irregular pentagon he had found and with its numerological and sexual significance, which he equated with the gods of Ancient Egypt. But, although his pentagon included more than one of the five peaks which I had identified, he made no reference to them, nor to any possible significance which the 'original' shape might hold. I could only assume that this was because he could find no links with the number system which he was developing.

But if both Pentacle of Mountains and Pentacle of Churches were valid – and the evidence suggested that they were – then it would be truly extraordinary if no link existed between them. I decided to look for it. And the simple act of superimposing the one design upon the other immediately showed their brilliant inter-relationship (see diagram overleaf).*

Apart from the obvious sharing of Rennes-le-Château as the north-west corner and the positioning of the eastern point of the original pentacle on the face of the new one, it can also be seen how elegantly the two star shapes are aligned in relation to each other. The dotted lines show how precisely placed are the bisections of the angles.

The realisation that David Wood's discovery was not, as he seemed to think, the 'solution' to the mystery, but only part thereof, led me to undertake a further investigation of my own. This, in its turn, led to the

* See *The Holy Place* for a more detailed description. H.L.

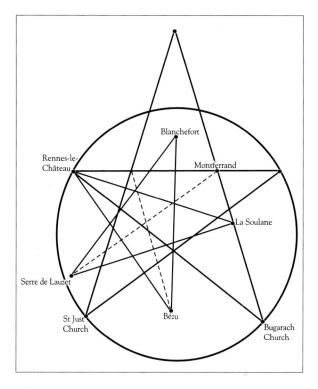

discovery that the geometric 'structuring' of the Rennes-le-Château land-scape was incredibly much more extensive than either he, or I, had realised. An astonishing masterpiece of ancient land-surveying was revealed.

In 1994 David Wood published *Geneset*, a further exploration of the pentacle which he had discovered. But, to my astonishment, although he was able to indicate flaws in my account of the extension to his discovery, he continued completely to ignore the new findings. However, his Circle of Churches is not the only Circle of Churches in the Rennes-le-Château area. His accurate alignments are not the only accurate alignments. One cannot but regret that, with his unquestioned mathematical expertise, he has chosen to turn his back on anything other than his own – admittedly beautiful – fragment of the geometry. Were he to bring his skills (which I lack) to the greater mystery, I am convinced that he could extend the boundaries of our knowledge yet further. Though I suspect that I may still find it difficult to accept his interpretations of the data.

BORNHOLM

In *The Holy Place*, I pointed out that I was uncertain of the extent of the geometric phenomenon which had been uncovered. The structured landscape which I had identified, presented no clearly defined limit and certainly extended beyond the boundaries of the maps upon which I had been able to find its traces. Although the horizons of the Mystery had narrowed once more to the Rennes-le-Château area, it seemed possible that they were not quite as limited as had at first appeared. What I had seen as the 'Temple' constructed to enclose the Pentacle of Mountains, seemed to lack 'outer walls'. With clearly defined alignments which were as much as twenty miles long, the hunt for a perimeter seemed a daunting one. Even so, I was not prepared for the vast new vista which was to appear.

In early 1991, I was contacted by a Danish television director. Erling Haagensen, however, was not thinking about making a film. He knew only that I was interested in landscape geometry, and that I had discussed it in a TV programme called *The Shadow of the Templars*. At this stage, he knew nothing of David Wood's discovery, nor of the recent publication of *The Holy Place*. Simply, he had some data which he wished to discuss with someone who was aware of such matters and he thought I might be able to comment usefully on what he had found.

Erling was born on the Danish island of Bornholm, in the Baltic Sea, where his family had been established for many generations. As he grew up, he became more and more interested in Bornholm's past and particularly in the ancient churches which are scattered across the island. These fifteen churches, of which four are circular, are unique in Scandinavia and date from about the time of the Templars.

Furthermore, he had discovered that the churches appeared to be laid out in conformity with an elegant geometric pattern. Perhaps I might be able to shed some light upon the extraordinary evidence which he had assembled?

In a brief telephone conversation, it became clear that Erling's work was careful, meticulous and seemed to be producing results which had a curiously familiar ring. He had been thinking that the geometry dated from the time of the construction of the churches – that is, *circa* thirteenth century (Knights Templar time). I told him that I had reason to believe that the

Rennes-le-Château patterns might originally have been laid out much earlier. Perhaps in the period which saw the construction of such great megalithic monuments as Stonehenge. Were there any such traces on Bornholm? He confirmed that there were, indeed, traces of megalithic construction all over the island and that many of the churches were associated with Standing Stones. Some churches even enclosed them, having them embedded in the walls. Already the picture was growing more interesting. But when he told me that the geometry he had identified was pentagonal, we knew that we were each uncovering a different portion of the same mystery. And was it simply a coincidence – albeit a delightful one – that Bornholm's principal town is called Rønne?

It was obvious – and imperative – that Erling and I should spend some time together in making a careful comparative study of our findings. As we expected, the two geometric systems interlocked. We were looking at the evidence for a sophisticated knowledge of measure, mathematics and land-surveying which was being widely employed throughout Europe at an indeterminate time in the past. That time could not be more recent than the thirteenth century, when the Bornholm churches were built. Given that those churches were associated with megaliths, the dating could well be as much as two millennia further back.

How could it be that no record seems to have survived of this extraordinary skill and wisdom? Experts in the study of ancient systems of measure had noted that certain evidence seemed to imply an unexpected degree of competence in startling feats of measurement. A serious work on the subject had even posed the question: 'Was the Earth measured in remote antiquity?'[*] It seemed that, at Rennes-le-Château and on Bornholm, we were, for the first time, confronting 'demonstrable and provable' evidence of those very skills at work.

The fruit of my collaboration with Erling Haagensen was a series of documentary films which we made for *TV2 DANMARK* in 1993 and entitled *The Secret*.[†] Erling has also written, in Danish, a skilful and scientific exposition of the Bornholm findings.[‡] The information was beginning

---

[*] *Historical Metrology* by A. E. Berriman, Dent, 1953.

[†] This series has been transmitted widely throughout the Continent and North America. It has also been shown many times on the European satellite TV channels. (Meanwhile, in the UK, the BBC now pursues the curious path of attempting to prove that the Rennes-le-Château phenomenon does not exist.) H.L.

[‡] *Bornholms Mysterium* by Erling Haagensen, Bogans Forlag, Denmark, 1993.

to become more widely disseminated. More people were picking up, and adding to, our data. The geometric configurations have now been identified in other locations, both in France and in Scandinavia. They will doubtless be found elsewhere.

OPENING THE DOOR

For those who wish to join in the search for the hidden traces of our ancestors, the simple first key to the sacred pattern is readily to hand. The door is easily opened. Further investigation is slightly more difficult, but not dauntingly so. It is not my purpose in this book to enter deeply into the complexities of the discovery, which have already been detailed in *The Holy Place*. I intend to explore, as simply as possible, those elements of the landscape geometry which are most readily accessible to the general reader and to demonstrate the solid ground upon which the work stands.

What follows is an exercise in observation. Most importantly, that observation contains no element of desire to prove anything other than the plain, unvarnished – one might almost say arid – facts. I did not begin with a desire to prove the existence of 'a structured landscape'. Nor do I wish the reader to begin with that desire. From my point of view, it is better to begin with a wish to *disprove* it.

Most of the details which follow have been identified upon the carefully detailed maps of the relevant areas. For France, these are produced by the *Institut Géographique Nationale*. The maps to be used are those of the scale 1:25000, upon which individual buildings may readily be identified. Such a scale is adequate to establish whether or not the configurations are present. Before the Scandinavian discoveries, it was difficult to decide upon the tolerances within which the builders were working. If one is measuring from one church to another, is it sufficient, for instance, for the point to lie *anywhere* within the church? Or should we demand that the measure should run from, say, altar to altar?

On Bornholm, the four principal churches are round and so one can measure to the centre of the circular building. Fortunately, for all the Bornholm churches, exact co-ordinates are available, which makes for a more precisely defined exactitude. On this matter Erling Haagensen says:

The geometry is extremely precise. The system is established with angles of an accuracy of less than 0.2 degrees from absolute precision.* Often there is *no* measurable inaccuracy ... With the co-ordinates – which have been provided by the Danish Government Bureau of Land Surveying – anyone with a pocket·calculator and a knowledge of simple Pythagorean Geometry can confirm the exactitude of the calculations ... But – as a comfort to those readers who find such exercises either daunting or too abstruse – there is no need for a Master's Degree in Mathematics to appreciate the beauty of the geometry – any more than it is necessary to understand the science of Harmonics in order to enjoy a good tune!
(*Bornholms Mysterium*, p. 10)

GROUNDWORK: THE KEY

My last book, *The Holy Place*, with Erling Haagensen's *Bornholms Mysterium* and David Wood's *Genisis* and *Geneset* are presently the only published works dealing with the identification of the landscape geometry. Each, in his own way, has attempted to explain the mathematical proofs of the undeniable configurations which have been identified. This, unfortunately, has made for difficult reading for those not equipped with the necessary expertise. But, as Erling Haagensen has noted, a total understanding of the scientific proofs is not essential in order to grasp the basic facts of the discovery. It is my intention, therefore, to present those facts as simply as possible. I make no apology for allowing a minute degree of tolerance in this exposition, as this will not affect the conclusions, but will enable the general reader to grasp more readily the extraordinary nature of the phenomenon which has been uncovered. Mathematically skilled readers will, I hope, pursue and augment the proofs for themselves – and with greater precision.

This book is called *Key to the Sacred Pattern*. That key is a simple one. It is defined at the side of the following page by a line. That line is 188 mm in length. Although this is not, by a tiny fraction of a millimetre, the perfect representation of the key measure, it is close enough for all practical

---

* To understand the significance of this, one needs simply to hold out a matchstick at arm's length. Very little of a distant horizon is blocked out by that 2mm width. But this is *more* than 0.2 degrees. All the Bornholm geometry is more accurate than this. E.H.

purposes. The naked eye will not detect any additional precision – and we are working on a scale of 1:25000, at which 10 metres on the ground is equivalent to less than half a millimetre on the map.

Plate 5 of this book shows the original discovery of the Pentagon of Mountains.

Point A is fixed upon Saunière's Tour Magdala at Rennes-le-Château.

Point B is the small ruin of the watchtower which crowns the mountain of Blanchefort.

Point D marks the high rocks on the summit of the mountain of Bézu, marked on the map as *Château Templier Ruines*.

The above three points form the triangle of castles which were the first step in the discovery.

Points C and E are the spot heights indicated by the map-makers of the *Institut Géographique Nationale* on the *Serre de Lauzet* and the mountain of la Soulane as the highest positions in each locality.

These five points are clearly visible mountain features.

Plate 5 also shows a dotted line which links Point D (Bézu) with Point F.

Point F does not indicate a visible structure. It is simply the intersection of the lines A–C and B–E. The point is fixed by the geometry of the mountains, as, obviously, is the distance D–F.

This distance – from one point of the Star to the opposite intersection of the pentagonal design – is the origin of the basic measure used by the ancient creators of the structured landscape. As I shall later explain, it seems possible that a 'rough' rule-of-thumb measure used as an *aide-memoire* by the builders was 2 miles, 1618 yards. (I shall also explain why I have defined this distance in terms of the English Statute Mile.) On the scale of the 1:25000 maps we are using, 2 miles, 1618 yards is equal to 187.9274 mm – thus, our key of 188 mm. (I shall, in a later section, discuss the several methods which have been employed to define the precise distance used.)

COINCIDENCES?

With the key distance thus defined, I must now show, as simply as possible, the available evidence that this measure is indeed being used. (The facts are easily verified on the appropriate map: IGN Map 2347 OT Quillan.)

The first indicators are related to churches, for which French map-makers use the conventional symbol ŏ. The space occupied by the building is thus not precisely designated. (Unlike Danish maps, where the shape and position of a structure are clearly defined.) Nevertheless, even allowing for the imprecision of the cartographers' symbol, very few churches are less than 25 metres in length (1mm on the map). It will be seen that such a degree of tolerance is unnecessary.

1.   On the map, the distance from the church of Rennes-le-Château eastwards to the sister church of Rennes-les-Bains is 188 mm.

Thus, there is a point within the structure of one church which lies at a distance of 2 miles, 1618 yards from a point within the other church.

The fact that this is the same as the distance D–F which was defined by the Pentacle of Mountains could, of course, be coincidence.

2.   On the map, the distance from the church of Rennes-le-Château westwards to the church of Campagne-sur-Aude is also 188 mm.

Thus, there is a point within the structure of one church which lies at a distance of 2 miles, 1618 yards from a point within the other church.

This repetition could, of course, also be coincidence.

3.   Northwest of Rennes-le-Château are the churches of Antugnac and Roquetaillade. The distance between the two church symbols is 188 mm.

Thus, there is a point within the structure of one church which lies at a distance of 2 miles, 1618 yards from a point within the other church.

This repetition could, of course, be yet another coincidence.

4.   A mile to the west of Antugnac is the church of Croux. The map shows it to be 188 mm southeast of the church of Bouriège.

Thus, there is a point within the structure of one church which lies at a distance of 2 miles, 1618 yards from a point within the other church.

While this fourth repetition could, of course, be nothing more than yet another coincidence, one cannot but begin to grow, at the least, mildly surprised by this extraordinary continued chance repetition of the same meaningful measure.

5.   Five miles or so to the northeast of Rennes-le-Château is the church of Terroles. It lies, on the map, 188 mm southeast of the church of St Salvayre and 188 mm northeast of the church of Arques.

Thus, there is a point within Terroles Church which lies at a distance of 2 miles, 1618 yards from a point within each of these other two churches.

Already it can be seen that, even were one to allow generous imprecisions, these numerous buildings are showing a remarkable consistency in their placing relative to one another.

I have been told that 'a map does not represent any sort of reality on the ground.' While I find this statement puzzling, I take it to mean that because there is a fixed measure upon the map, this does not necessarily imply that there is a fixed measure in the real landscape. This seems simply to mean that the map is not accurate (!). But even were this strange statement to reflect a profound truth, I am still confronted by the remarkable fact that an 'inaccurate representation' is yet producing an astonishing regularity in the (inaccurate?) placing of its symbols.

All the churches which I have listed above lie within a very small area. I have not hunted throughout thousands of square miles to find fortuitous echoes of a measure which, I have decided, has significance. None of these churches is further than six miles from Rennes-le-Château and the Pentacle of Mountains which has defined the measure. Nor is this list exhausted.

Esperaza Church is two miles to the west of Rennes-le-Château. The churches of Les Sauzils, St Ferriol, Granès and Coustaussa are all precisely equidistant from Esperaza Church. The distance of separation is the now familiar 2 miles, 1618 yards. Esperaza Church is therefore the centre of a circle which is 2 miles, 1618 yards in radius. The four churches of Les Sauzils, St Ferriol, Granès and Coustaussa lie upon the circumference.

To add one further touch to this string of 'coincidences', David Wood has defined a circle upon whose circumference lie the churches of Rennes-le-Château, St Just, and Bugarach, as well as the castle of Serres. With good reason, he defines the radius of this circle as being 2 miles, 1630 yards and some 10 inches. For the moment, there is a discrepancy of 12 yards and 10 inches between the two radii we are considering. On the map, this is represented by 0.449 mm. It is just about visible and, as I have said, I am, for the moment, using a 'rough rule-of-thumb *aide-memoire*'. Whichever of the two measures is used, the distance will be defined by points which lie within the confines of the church structures.

On Bornholm, Erling Haagensen has been defining his measurements, of course, in the metric system. His equivalent indication of a significant distance has proved to be 4700.4913 metres. This is equal to 2 miles, 1620 yards and some 18 inches, which differs from David Wood's measure by a little more than 29 feet and from my 'rule-of-thumb' measure by 7 feet and

6 inches which, on the map, is 'roughly' represented by an invisible 7 hundredths of a millimetre.

Three researchers, each pursuing his own pathway of discovery, have found evidence for pentagonal geometry. Coincidence? Each has found evidence of a controlling measure which, with a few yards in variation, is just under 3 miles in length. Coincidence?

FIRST PATTERN

The churches, however, preserve more than this echo of the use of a fixed measure. Their placing relative to each other is not arbitrary. Simply observed upon a map, they are scattered, as one would expect, in a seemingly haphazard way.

If, upon this diagram, one were to set a pair of compasses on Esperaza Church and, taking the radius to Les Sauzils Church, draw a circle, the

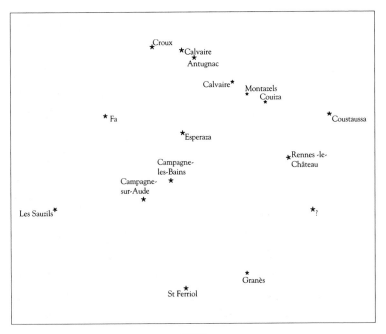

churches of St Ferriol, Granès and Coustaussa will lie, as noted above, upon the circumference.

A diameter drawn from Les Sauzils Church through Esperaza will prove to pass directly through the church of Montazels. (Where this diameter eventually reaches the circumference of the circle, I will name Point X.)

A diameter drawn from St Ferriol Church through Esperaza will prove to pass through a *Calvaire* which stands upon a trackway junction, close to the village of Antugnac. (Where this diameter reaches the circumference, I will name Point Y.)

A chord drawn from Les Sauzils Church through the church in the village of Fa will meet the circle circumference to the north at Point Y.

A chord drawn from Point Y, to pass through Montazels Church will reach the circumference in the southeast at a point which has been marked on the above diagram with a '?'. At precisely this place upon the map is the indication of a small building of some kind. It is, in fact, an insignificant and ancient crumbling heap of stones.

This is not one among many specks upon the map. It is the *only* building in the area.

A line drawn from this point to Les Sauzils Church will complete an equilateral triangle.

A chord drawn from Point X to pass through Antugnac Church will reach the circumference at Point Z.

Chords drawn from St Ferriol Church to Points X and Z will produce another equilateral triangle.

The completed design is well known and, even today, retains significance. It is the six-pointed Seal of Solomon – or Star of David (see Plate 6).

FANTASY OR REALITY?

The question must be posed: is this meaningful piece of geometry the result of a conscious and laboriously undertaken exercise in marking the landscape? Or is it the fruit of my fantasy?

Readers who choose to follow the above steps on a piece of tracing paper laid over the diagram on p. 188, will easily grasp the simplicity, elegance and precision of the design. But it is necessary to realise that this simplicity, produced upon a flat piece of paper, is the reflection of the layout of structures upon a terrain which is anything but flat. Rennes-le-Château, for instance, crowns a mountain some 250 metres above the level of Esperaza, which lies on a valley floor. Yet the horizontal distances have been precisely calculated. The skills which have, necessarily, been employed are astonishingly sophisticated. There is no evidence for such skills being available at the time of the creation of the structures which define it. Still less is there any evidence for those skills even earlier in history if the churches do, indeed, preserve the placings of yet more ancient sacred sites.

This lack of evidence leads to attempts to 'explain away' the findings as the result of my subjective search for them. It has been suggested, for instance, that I have, in some way, *chosen* the structures which conform to my wished for design and ignored those which do not.

> Instead of detecting geometry concealed in the landscape, Lincoln has imposed abstract designs on it. Like those of any ley-hunter, his figures contain only one or two points of genuine archaeological or historical importance. (*Dr Paul Bahn*)*

* *Times Literary Supplement*, 12 April 1991.

But the Seal of Solomon is marked out, not by 'one or two points', but by *six* churches (with two more churches lying on the circumference of its enclosing circle), one *Calvaire* and an ancient ruin. Ten points. Why pretend otherwise? Moreover, there is an undeniable elegance in the relationships of, for instance, Montazels Church and the churches of les Sauzils and Esperaza. The three are in perfect alignment, with the distance between Esperaza and Montazels being exactly half the distance between Esperaza and les Sauzils (the circle radius). This placing ensures that Montazels lies on the midpoint of the face of the equilateral triangle. This is not haphazard coincidence. Had Esperaza Church been placed anywhere else – even by so much as a few yards – then this coherent design could not exist. Nor could it be 'imposed' upon the landscape, as Bahn claims.

Dr Bahn also informs us that 'statisticians have found that complex geometric structures can easily arise on maps by chance'. This is undeniably true. But such patterns are isolated phenomena. They do not generate coherent, interlinked and measurable data which can then be reproduced in other locations. The statistical analysis necessary to determine a probability for the church layouts falls into the highly specialised area of Geometric Combinatorial Statistical Theory. The scientists, statisticians and mathematicians who have examined the evidence, agree that the Rennes-le-Château findings deserve further serious analysis. Indeed, as I write, a project has been initiated with the object of providing the confirmation of the non-random positioning of the structures.

It seems that we are confronting one of two propositions. Either there is, at Rennes-le-Château, some natural force which causes human beings haphazardly to construct churches in geometric relationship and with a constant separation distance of 2 miles, 1618 yards. Or the sites were selected by people skilled in geodesy. Of these possibilities, the second seems, to me and to my scientific contacts, to be the more likely. Dr Paul Bahn, however, appears to prefer the first option and accuses me of 'turning to geomancy' – the magical 'art' of divination by means of signs derived from the earth.

I am at a loss to see what is magical or divinatory about the bald fact that, in an area of barely 7 miles square, some fifteen churches are placed at 2 miles and 1618 yards from each other. Is the likelihood of ancient and previously undetected skills so abhorrent that it cannot be considered?

There seems to be a sad division of attitude when History is confronted by Science. The former adopts too quickly a defensive and closed-mind approach, as if the past and our understanding of it are immutably fixed. The latter, however, works in a world of change, and is not intimidated by it. Dr Vanessa Hill is a scientist. Her professional life is spent in the world of Biochemistry and Molecular Biology – though she has a working knowledge of statistics. When she came upon the Rennes-le-Château material, she was attracted to it as a stimulating fresh insight upon the past. She has commented:

> I feel somewhat disillusioned by certain members of Academia who have made statements about (the church separation distance) being random when it is obvious that they lack the appropriate qualifications ... They have not looked at the data, nor applied the necessary scientific procedures ... (The work) must, at all times, be carried out in a totally unbiassed manner, even when the conclusions do not fit in with the investigator's own views, theories and outlooks. If a member of Academia cannot do this, then Silence would be more advisable in order that others, more suitably qualified, should not be put off by false summations. It should also be remembered that a statement claiming randomness must also be backed by a confirming statistical analysis. In such matters, opinion will not do!

STAR PATTERNS

But I have not yet finished with my 'imposition' of designs upon the Esperaza Circle. Two points of the six-pointed star are fixed by les Sauzils and St Ferriol Churches. They are therefore so placed as to define one sixth of the circle's circumference. But what of Granès and Coustaussa, the other two churches which lie on that circumference? They are not part of the hexagonal design. They are, however, so placed that the distance between them also divides the circle evenly. Their distance of separation fits five times into the circle and thus creates a pentagon. Moreover, their placing relative to the hexagon is such that the two designs are interlinked by the sharing of a third point. Point Z, as defined above, is common to both; as is the beautifully precise positioning of the church of Fa.

The chord from Granès through Fa Church reaches the circumference at Point Z.

The chord from Coustaussa through Couiza Church also reaches the circumference at Point Z.

The chord from Coustaussa through the church of Campagne-sur-Aude reaches the circumference at a point which I shall designate P.

The chord from Point P which passes through the *Calvaire* NW of Antugnac, reaches the circumference at a point which I shall designate Q.

The chord from Granès Church to Point Q passes through a *Calvaire* NW of Montazels.

The Esperaza Circle has four churches upon its circumference and encloses nine other churches. Of these thirteen churches, ten contribute to the hexagonal and pentagonal designs. The other three are Croux, Campagne-les-Bains and Rennes-le-Château. But we are merely at the beginning of our examination. Rennes-le-Château has already been seen to be an essential part of the original pentagonal structure. Croux has demonstrated

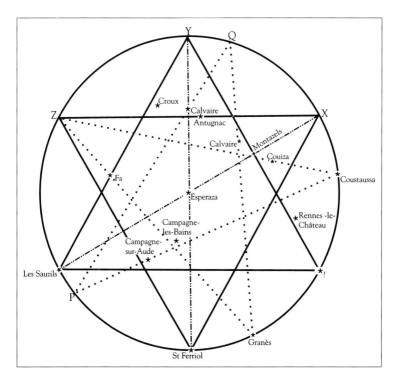

a link through its 2 miles, 1618 yards separation from Bourège. Thus only *one* church in the designated area has not yet shown evidence of planned positioning. (It will certainly do so when further layers of the geometry are examined.) But, for the moment, twelve out of a total of thirteen churches are involved.

I have neither chosen structures to fit my design, nor ignored those which do not. The landscape shows clear evidence of conscious method and planning. Geomancy is not involved. Nor is magic. Nor is wishful thinking. Clever design, knowledge, purpose and motivation are evident. I am delighted to discover that my ancestors were more ingenious than I thought.

LEY-LINES?

These lines upon the landscape inevitably invite comparison with ley-lines. Indeed, Bahn equates my methods with those of the 'ley-hunter' – which simply demonstrates that he has chosen not to examine the evidence. To my knowledge, ley-lines have never been shown to exist in any objectively observable manner. They are generally detected by dowsing and while this art has certainly produced enough successful results to demand serious consideration, it is not a scientifically observable or measurable technique. Ley-lines are generally extremely long. Any line, projected from a given base-point, will eventually pass through other 'interesting' or 'significant' points. But there seems to be no method which might be employed, which will remove the possibility of coincidence. Which of the points on a given line are there by pure chance – and which are demonstrably intentional?

It is in this aspect of the investigation that the Rennes-le-Château phenomenon differs from the attempts to define ley-lines. Those lines which we have so far considered are all short-distance and, for the most part, inter-visible. At night, a beacon lit upon Rennes-le-Château will be clearly visible from, for instance, Bézu, Esperaza, Fa, St Ferriol and even from as far away as St Salvayre, six miles to the north. The alignments can be considered to be, in some sense, 'practical' as sightings may be taken along them.

Much more important than the inter-visibility, however, is the evident use of fixed measure. Structures which are both aligned and which conform to a measure-system are less likely to be in arbitrary or coincidental relationship than are those which merely 'line-up'.

That a measure-system is being employed at Rennes-le-Château, is undeniable. The repeated stress upon the distance of 2 miles, 1618 yards cannot arise through mere coincidence. The definition of the system in use, however, raises other, and even more thorny problems. Before addressing those problems, it is necessary to demonstrate that the patterns stemming from the Pentacle of Mountains are part of a carefully and rationally devised plan.

EXTENDING LINES

One of the first steps made by David Wood along his pathway of discovery, was to notice an extension to the original Pentacle of Mountains. In *The Shadow of the Templars*, I showed that the northern face of the five-sided figure ran from Rennes-le-Château to the Château of Blanchefort. At the time this was part of what I had identified as 'a triangle of castles'. But Rennes-le-Château's church is adjacent to its castle and both lie on this same alignment. David Wood saw that this line continued. Extended to the east, it ran directly to the church at Arques.

Although this fact may, yet again, seem to fall into the rather mundane area of simple coincidence, it is rather more interesting than may superficially appear. A check on any map showing a similar open landscape of scattered villages will quickly confirm that it is not easy to find three major structures (in this case, churches and a castle) in perfect alignment over so short a distance. This unexpected chance led David Wood to his circle of churches and to his extended pentagonal figure. But, just as I had been unable to see past my own original and startling discovery, so was his new breakthrough blinding him to what lay beyond. His line from Rennes-le-Château to Blanchefort runs eastward to the church at Arques. He did not notice that it also runs westward to the church at Campagne-sur-Aude.

Having identified the Arques–Rennes-le-Château line, Wood's work thereafter virtually ignores it in favour of his concentration upon other

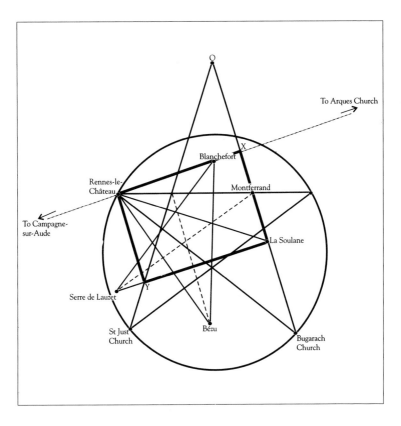

aspects of his geometry. But this line provides yet more clear and readily understandable indications of a purposeful surveying of the area.

In order properly to appreciate the ingenuity which has been employed, it is necessary to understand the very special and remarkable properties of the regular five-pointed star. Pentagonal geometry has, in Professor Cornford's words, 'enjoyed immense prestige and excited nothing short of reverence among geometers, architects, and masons since very ancient times'. Why? Its most remarkable property is its embodiment of what has become known as the Golden Section or Golden Proportion. It has also, more portentously, been labelled The Divine Proportion. In *The Holy Place*, I explained it thus:

> In simple terms, the Golden Section is the division of a line in the most

economical way possible, so that the lesser part is to the greater as the greater is to the whole. Thus, in the diagram below, the line AC is divided at B in such a manner that AB is to BC as BC is to AC. The proportion expressed mathematically is 1 : 1.618.

A   B   C

The pentagon with its star-pentagram or pentacle, is a Golden Section figure.

In the following diagram, the ratio of the sides (for example AB) and the chords (for example AC) is as 1 : 1.618. Moreover, the chords intersect each other in the same ratio; for example, AC is cut at F by EB so that AF is to FC as 1 is to 1.618. The same ratio repeats itself many times within the pentagon. In fact, the ratio can be repeated infinitely by producing further pentagrams within the pentagons created by the intersections of the chords, as indicated by the dotted figure. These figures also diminish in Golden Section progression.

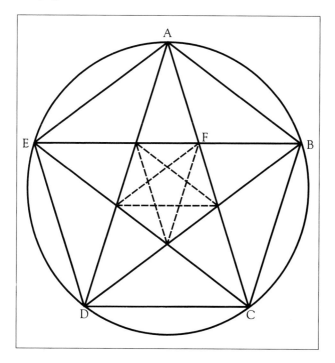

In addition, there is a rectangle which has a very strong and special relationship with a regular pentagon:

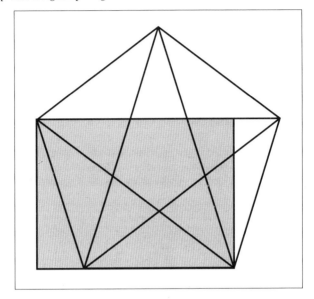

The very precise ratio of height to width in this 'pentagonal' rectangle was used by Poussin for his painting of *The Shepherds of Arcadia*. It is this precisely chosen shape which enabled Professor Cornford to identify the pentagonal geometry.

A comparison of the diagram above with that on page 196 shows that the 'pentagonal' rectangle can be identified in the landscape. It is defined by Rennes-le-Château, Point X, la Soulane and Point Y. The eastern face of David Wood's extended pentagram figure (which I term P2), runs from Bugarach, through la Soulane and Point X to the apex at Point O. The length X–la Soulane (the shorter side of the rectangle), is equal to O–X – as is the distance between la Soulane and the church of Bugarach. It is therefore clear that the eastern face of P2 is governed by the dimensions of the original Pentacle of Mountains. The exact length of the shorter side of the rectangle is repeated – once to the north and once to the south.

The pentagonal mountain configuration can also be clearly recognised as a controlling factor in the placing of some of the other structures.

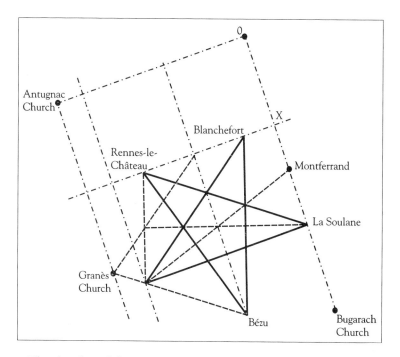

The churches of Granès and Antugnac, as well as the castle of Montferrand, conform elegantly to the extensions of the pentagonal design and are an early indication of the possible existence of an underlying grid pattern.

THE GRID

If the Rennes-le-Château landscape configurations are part of a conscious, planned and purposeful layout, then a basic, underlying and controlling grid pattern should be expected to show itself. And such is, indeed, the case. As the above diagram shows, the structural alignments are beginning to define right angles.

I have already pointed out that a search upon a 1:25000 scale map of any comparable area will show that an alignment of even three churches, or other significant structures, over such short distances, is rarely to be encountered. To find such alignments lying evenly spaced and forming right angles, is even less likely to occur by chance. But here, alignments, angular orientation and fixed measure can all be demonstrated.

The eastern face of David Wood's P2 runs from Bugarach Church, through la Soulane, the outer point of the Pentacle of Mountains and through the castles of Montferrand and Serres. It also passes precisely through the 'Trig Point' marking the peak of Cardou, the dominating mountain to the east of Rennes-le-Château and it culminates at Point O – which is a three-way track junction.* It is a 'strong' alignment and lies at a perfect right angle to the northern face of the Pentacle of Mountains. This northern face is an equally 'strong' alignment, passing through the churches of Campagne-sur-Aude and Rennes-le-Château, the castle of Blanchefort and the church of Arques. (Projected yet further to the east, it arrives at a way-side cross at a site which is, interestingly, labelled 'The Templar Camp'.)

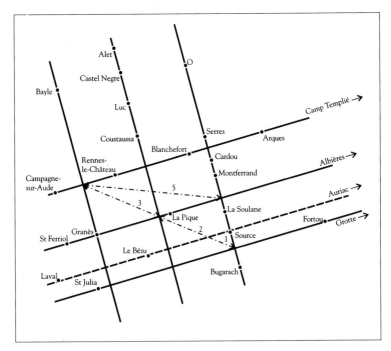

---

* It also includes other and subtler points of interest, which are detailed in *The Holy Place*. H.L.

To the south of this line is another, which passes through the churches of St Ferriol and Granès, the 'Trig Point' marking the height of la Pique (the sixth mountain at the centre of the Pentacle) and reaches the church of Albières, almost ten miles further to the east. This line is exactly parallel to the Rennes-le-Château/Arques line and thus, of course, is also at a right angle to the face of P2.

The diagram opposite illustrates the astonishing regularity in the layout. Not only are the lines equidistant, they are also separated by controlled distances which demonstrate the use of a fixed unit of measure. As the diagram shows, the diagonal across one box of the grid is equal to three units of measure. A diagonal across two horizontally adjacent boxes is equal to five units.

Any reader who takes the trouble to reproduce the above diagram upon the map will easily confirm the regularity of the unit divisions I have indicated. For those seeking no more than a rough confirmation, the unit upon the 1:25000 map measures an invisible fraction less than six and a half millimetres – and this will suffice as a rudimentary general statement. (For the pedantic, however, a more exact definition is 6.437376 mm.)

Chapter Fourteen
NEW FINDINGS

BORNHOLM

IT IS MY HOPE that the evidence thus far presented will have sufficed to establish that the phenomenon we are confronting is anything but a simple matter of random chance. That possibility was made even more remote by the independent findings made on the island of Bornholm by Erling Haagensen. Here there is no question of a 'choice' of structures. There are only fifteen churches on the island and *all* conform to the geometric layout. Plate 8 shows a pentagonal part of the design. Other layers are more complex, producing carefully controlled six- and seven-sided figures.

The quality and subtlety of the Bornholm designs hint at a more sophisticated undertaking. This does not seem to be a case of the unintentional preservation of ancient sacred sites. Some of the evidence indicates that the mediaeval church builders were conscious of the underlying plan. On Bornholm, for the first time, one begins to glimpse the simple, but very clever, techniques which were used to ensure the extreme accuracy which the builders evidently considered to be necessary.

The island's four round churches have now been adorned with conical roofs which enclose a rotunda placed around a circular central tower. Both rotunda and tower are pierced by very narrow slit windows, which are carefully aligned. Before the roof was added, these windows, of course, looked out over the surrounding landscape.

We were able to demonstrate in our film, *The Secret*, how a beacon burning within the tower of Østerlars Church would only be visible along an extremely narrow line defined by the placing of the windows. From a key position in the geometry, which lies upon the highest point in the

Østerlars Church before the addition of the roof.

island, the tiniest lateral movement serves to 'switch' the light on and off. Such a system would help to ensure extremely accurate angular alignments across many miles of undulating territory.

Østerlars, the central key to the design, even preserves a carefully arranged 'calendar'. The wall of the central tower has a circular mark placed with precision to catch, through two of these impeccably aligned slit windows, the first rays of the rising sun on Midsummer Day.

The full complexity of the Bornholm design seems to be displaying the virtuoso work of a master builder. The precision which Erling Haagensen has found is awe-inspiring. It is as if we are in the presence of a skilled teacher who is showing us how to solve a complex problem. As a relatively straightforward illustration of the degree of accuracy involved, I will provide only one example.

The geometry requires Østerlars Church to be equidistant from the churches of Nylars and Rutsker. The co-ordinates provided by the Danish Government Bureau of Land Surveying for the crosses which crown their pointed roofs establish that the distance from Østerlars to Nylars is 14335.585 metres. The distance from Østerlars to Rutsker is 14335.71 metres. The discrepancy is 125 mm – a little more than four-and-a-half inches over a measured distance of almost nine miles. The design also dictates that the church of Nylars should lie four times further from Øster-lars than from the church of Vestermarie. One is almost disappointed to discover that the Nylars/Vestermarie co-ordinates define a distance which is 128 cm (just over four feet) from perfection. But then ... Vestermarie was rebuilt in 1896. It would seem that the nineteenth-century builders did not have the same preoccupations as their twelfth-century predecessors.

BRITTANY

The Bornholm discovery had suddenly presented the possibility that the Rennes-le-Château geometry might be identified elsewhere. But how to undertake such a search? For one man, it would be an enormous undertaking – and incredibly time-consuming. However, as word of the landscape-structuring spread, I began to receive excited communications. Many were of highly unreliable findings. Sloppily irregular geometric figures were sent, traced over enormous areas on motoring maps and even atlases. But, among the fanciful, some more positive results were appearing in France. It would obviously be valuable to tap, in some way, the growing interest and enthusiasm.

In 1994, I was given the opportunity to institute a more widespread search. *France Magazine* is a quarterly publication, produced in Britain and aimed specifically at a Francophile readership.* With every reader having a guaranteed interest in the country, and many with homes in France, it seemed likely that a large number would also possess 1:25000 scale maps of their favoured area. I accordingly wrote an article for the magazine, explaining the findings in general and that I was not, as some people still seemed to imagine, seeking ley-lines, nor imaginary configurations, such as the Glastonbury Zodiac, but for very precisely measured distances between landscape features. I asked the readership's assistance in a hunt on their maps – but only for the 188 mm church measure. Examples were immediately forthcoming from numerous locations across France. From the southeast, above Nice, through the Dordogne, and up into the north, the

---

* *France Magazine* Ltd, Stow-on-the-Wold, Glos GL54 1BN, England.

'church measure' began to appear. It was Brittany, however, which produced the most spectacular result.

Patricia Hawkshaw is an English mathematics teacher with a second home in France, just inland from Quimper. She was able to identify, in her local area, no less than 162 repetitions of the measure, linking churches, *Calvaires* and hilltops. A more thorough examination of the map* produced the extraordinary configuration of Plate 7.

Not only is this, yet again, the Rennes-le-Château circle radius measure of 2 miles, 1618 yards. Here, once more is the link between hexagon and pentagon. That the design extends beyond the circles is elegantly indicated by the placing of two churches to the northeast and northwest. They lie where projections of the hexagon and pentagon faces intersect.

NORWAY

I have repeatedly stressed that the lines produced by the Rennes-le-Château geometry are short-distance and that extremely long lines are necessarily less 'provable'. However, with the evident links with Brittany – and particularly Bornholm – the likelihood of long-distance connections should, at least, be considered. Long-distance alignments have been identified by Harald Boehlke in Norway. These are worth recording because they bring an extraordinary additional assembly of 'coincidences' which cannot be ignored. His findings can be summed up as follows:

Until about a thousand years ago, Norway was pagan. The population was scattered in small settlements throughout the country, with some trading-posts mainly along the coasts. Historians have noted a marked change with the arrival of Christianity. The older trading centres disappeared and new towns of a more permanent nature were established by the Church. There seems to be a degree of puzzlement among Norwegian historians concerning the new settlements.

> ... It is hard to explain why [Oslo] was established in what was until then a backwater, outside the old established trade routes.
> Erik Schia, *Oslo Innerst i Viken*. Aschehaug 1991.

---

* IGN Blue Series; 0618 *ouest* – Châteauneuf-du-Faou.

KEY TO THE SACRED PATTERN

... We do not really know why Stavanger was chosen to become a cathedral city around 1100. A. W. Brøgger contends that (it) must have been elected for a specific reason.
Norge Vart Land, Gyldendal 1984.

Tønsberg [is] possibly younger than others. The first settlements seem to be from the end of the eleventh century.
Aschehaugs Norges Historie, 1995.

The elimination of the trading posts and the establishment of the towns of the tenth and eleventh centuries must ... be seen as deliberate policy ...
Per Sveaas Andersen.
Samlingen av Norge og Kristningen av landet 800–1130, Universitetsforlaget 1977.

The few mediaeval towns of Norway appear from approximately 997 to 1152 AD. Trondheim (997); Oslo (1000); Bergen (1070); Tønsberg (c. 1090); Stavanger (1125); Hamar (1152). All were established by the Church and Tønsberg has the only round church in Norway. It has been suggested that there was a second, now vanished, round church at Trondheim. The ancient seal of the monastery depicts such a church. Interestingly, the two towns associated with round churches lie due north/south, on the same line of longitude.

Using the mediaeval monasteries as his base points, Harald Boehlke found the following conjunctions of matched pairs of distances:

Tønsberg to Stavanger = 170.37 miles.   Tønsberg to Halsnøy = 170.96 miles.

Oslo to Stavanger = 190.12 miles.   Oslo to Bergen = 190.57 miles.

Hamar to Halsnøy = 197.36 miles.   Hamar to Bergen = 196.57 miles.

He has been able to establish a very interesting pentagonal geometry stemming from the monastery layout. Certainly, over such wide spans, the discrepancies in measure are not large. Nevertheless, they require extreme caution when attempting to draw firm conclusions. In pursuing a curious legend associated with one of his pentagonal points, he has extended his pentagram with intriguingly 'coincidental' results. The northwestern point of his design is fixed by the Dollstein Cave on an island called *Sandøy*. The Sagas tell of a visit by Ragnvald, Earl of Orkney, to this cave in 1127. In an echo of Rennes-le-Château, he was searching for a 'lost treasure'. Legends report that the cave continues under the sea to Scotland. As Harald Boehlke says:

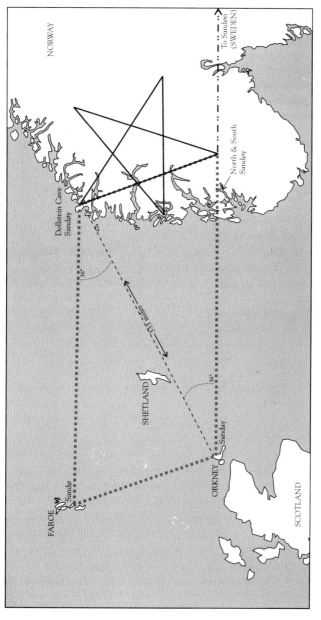

The line from Sanday in the Orkneys to Sandøn in Sweden is divided by the Pentagonal Golden Section Division 1:1.618 at North and South Sandøy. Harald Boehlke's diagram.

That a treasure might be hidden in the Dollstein Cave is not impossible. But that the cave is connected to Scotland seems to be the kind of legend it is better to ignore. But ... the Dollstein Cave is on the island of *Sandøy*, while west across the sea are the Faroe Islands – and another *Sandø*. We draw a line from *Sandøy* in Norway to *Sandø* in the Faroe Islands. Looking south to Earl Ragnvald's Orkneys, we discover *Sanday*. We draw the line from the Faroes to *Sanday* in the Orkneys. From there, a line eastwards to the southern point of the pentagram completes a perfect parallelogram. The diagonal from the Dollstein Cave on *Sandøy* to *Sanday* in the Orkneys 'connects' the cave to Scotland. The distance is 333 miles. The internal angles of the parallelogram are 36°.*

Further extensions of his geometry fix upon a Swedish island called *Sandøn*. The pentagonal Golden Division of the very long line from Swedish *Sandøn* to *Sanday* in the Orkneys, falls upon a small group of islands in the Oslo fjord – where are *North Sandøy* and *South Sandøy*.

Coincidences piled upon coincidences. And one cannot but be intrigued by the fact that Utstein monastery at Stavanger, one of Harald Boehlke's original key-points, is on a small group of islands, the largest of which is called Rennes Island. Here is yet another felicitous 'coincidence' to add to Rønne on Bornholm.

THE MEASURE

I have already said that the definition of the measure-system used by the creators of the Rennes-le-Château controlled landscape will present a thorny problem. It was even suggested by a Cambridge academic that, although he could not argue with the evidence thus far, I should suppress what follows, as he found it very difficult to accept. However, I consider it to be my task to observe, record and report.

Like it or not, accept it or not, the unit measure which I have described above in relation to the grid pattern is the English mile. 1760 yards. 5280 feet. 63360 inches. 320 poles. This, I accept, seems a ridiculous impossibility. The English measure was not a fixed and rational system at the time

---

* A 'pentagonal' angle. H.L.

of the construction of the churches, let alone in even earlier times. Or so we are taught. To suggest otherwise is, as one expert in measure would have it, 'mathematical romanticism and diffusionism run mad'. To suggest – as I do – that the system demonstrates Berriman's proposition that 'the earth was measured in remote antiquity', is to court the scorn and derision of those who 'know' better. And yet I have encountered such an accumulation of curiously precise indications in support of the idea, that to remain silent would be as cowardly as it would be unscholarly.

I must first, however, make a small digression in order to draw attention to a curiosity with regard to the definition of what is known as the English Statute Mile. This is fixed by law in a statute of 1592/3. One would anticipate that this statute should concern itself with the definition of measures. It does no such thing.

The statute is 'An Acte against newe Buyldinges'. In great and considerable detail it describes directives 'For the reformynge of the great Mischiefes and Inconveniences that daylie growe and increase by reason of the pesteringe of Houses with diverse Famylies … whereby great Infection of Sicknes & dearthe of Victualles and Fewell hath growen and ensued …'

Nine extremely lengthy sections of regulation follow, with the jolting irrelevance of a single sentence interpolated into the penultimate paragraph: 'And that a Myle shalbe [sic] reckoned and taken in this manner and noe otherwise, That is to saye, a Myle to conteyne Eight Furlongs, and everie Furlonge to conteyne Fortie Luggs or Poles, and every Lugg or Pole to conteyne sixteen Foote and Halfe.' The statute then reverts to further detail concerning the housing regulations.

The archivist, whom I consulted at the Palace of Westminster, agreed that this interpolation of an apparent total irrelevancy was, to say the least, odd. He was also able to inform me that Parliament was not sitting in that year. Who, he wondered, was responsible for this strange manner of fixing our mile? And why?

David Wood was the first to notice the appearance of the mile measure in the Rennes-le-Château geometry, as he pursued the alignments contributing to his extended pentagram. As I explored the further complexities of the geometry, I was able to confirm, again and again, that the English mile and its recognised sub-divisions, were unquestionably present. With the precise co-ordinates available on Bornholm, Erling Haagensen was able to strengthen the available data. As an example only, I can cite the separation between the churches of Ibsker and Povlsker which, the geometry dictated, should be 7 miles – or 11265.1 metres. The Danish Government Bureau of Land Surveying gives the separation of the crosses on the church roofs as 11263.512 metres. A discrepancy of 1.896 metres or 6 feet and just over 2½ inches.

In *The Holy Place*, I enumerated many examples of the presence of the English mile in the geometric configurations. I also explained my reasoning in regard to the use of the measure and its relationship to the dimensions of the Earth. In brief, the first 'fixed measure' was, presumably, the metre and was defined as one ten-millionth of the distance from the Pole to the Equator.* In my work, I had noticed the appearance of what I termed 'the Cromlech Pole' – which was just under half-an-inch longer than our present pole measure of 198 inches. A kilometre (which is acknowledged as an exact proportion of the Earth's surface), is equal to 39370 inches. The square root of 39370 is 198.41874 – just under half-an-inch longer than our present pole measure of 198 inches. Therefore the 'Cromlech Pole' is also an exact proportion of the Earth's surface.

The pole – or rod – or perch is a unit of measure with which, today, the man-in-the-street is unfamiliar. This quaint unit of one 320th of a mile is hardly in common usage. Having stumbled upon it, I began to experiment with the measure and found that it became more strange and more interesting. True, it is said that numbers can be used to prove anything. But not, I suggest, with the consistency, coherence and, one might almost say eloquence, of what I found.

As unfamiliar as the 198 inches of the present pole is the Pentagonal Golden Division number of 1.618. But the two interact with our mile to curious effect. In *The Holy Place* I described, in a somewhat jokey manner, how the accumulating information might have been used to devise the mile system by a mathematical genius of the past. (This is not to be interpreted as a suggestion that some super-human, super-intelligent agency appeared upon our planet in order to instruct the primitive human race. It is beyond question that some human beings are born with an innate and well nigh supra-normal understanding of number. As there is, to my knowledge, absolutely no evidence to the contrary, I prefer to rest with such a supposition rather than the alternative – and I suspect less likely – idea of supernatural or extra-terrestrial agencies.) I must ask the reader to bear with

---

* The decision to adopt the metric system was taken by the French National Assembly in 1791. H.L.

the apparent 'lunacy' which follows. There is an unquestionable method in this 'madness'.

The first step of our hypothetical mathematical genius is to measure the Earth and take one ten-thousandth of the distance from the Pole to the Equator. This, in inches, is 39370. The square root of this number is 198.41874. Such fractions are incomprehensible to all but the mathematically educated and so, for the simple folk, he rounds off the number to 198. Thus the number of inches in the pole.

Our genius now multiplies 198 by the Golden Division number – 1.618. Result: 320.364. Rounding off and simplifying yet again, he loses the fraction to be left with 320 – the number of poles in a mile.

Having fixed his mile at 320 poles of 198 inches each, he has arrived at a mile of 63360 inches which, divided by the Golden Division 1.618 results in 39159.456 inches. The nearest round number is 39160 – which is quite close to the original measure of 39370, which was taken from the Earth's surface. The difference is 210 inches – enough to make a pole with 12 inches left over to define the useful small measure of one foot.

Presented in a thus flippant manner, the underlying system can yet be glimpsed. But is it really there? Or have I simply juggled numbers into a desired pattern? Consider the following:

There is a now defunct unit of English measure known as the Domesday league. This was equivalent to one-and-a-half miles – or 2640 yards. How can this commonplace little measure relate to the dimensions of the Earth?

2640^2 (2640 Domesday leagues of 2640 yards) = 6969600 yards – which (divided by 1760) = 3960 miles.

Any standard reference work will confirm that the mean radius of the Earth is just under 3959 miles. (The equatorial radius is generally given as 3964 miles and the polar radius as 3949.) Can we allow our ancestor a discrepancy of a mile or so in his measurement of the Earth? Or – is the *fact* that the radius of the Earth is equal to the square of the Domesday league to be dismissed as yet another coincidence?

The Domesday league's rather dull-looking number 2640 has proved to relate to our English measure system in a number of fascinating ways, based upon these simple divisions:

Half of 2640 is 1320. One-and-a-half times 2640 is 3960.
(Or 1320 × 2 = 2640; 1320 × 3 = 3960.)

KEY TO THE SACRED PATTERN

1320 **INCHES** = 6.66 **POLES**

1320 **YARDS** × 2 = 2640 (**THE DOMESDAY LEAGUE**)

1320 **MILES** × 3 = 3960 (**THE EQUATORIAL RADIUS**)

1320 **INCHES** × 4 = 5280 (**FEET IN THE MILE**)

These numbers interact in many ways.

198 is the number of INCHES in a POLE. 198 × 2 = 396

The FOOT – 12 inches × 11 × 10 = 1320

The number of INCHES in 10 MILES is 633600 which, multiplied by 11 = 6969600 – noted above as the number of YARDS in the Earth's radius (= 2640^2)

And so on. But I have no wish, in this book, to submerge the non-mathematician in intimidating pages of calculation. The permutations are many and revolve around the simple numbers 1320 / 2640 / 3960.

TEACHING THE UNTUTORED APPRENTICE

In *The Holy Place*, I also attempted to grope towards an understanding of how such complex matters might have been conveyed by my hypothetical genius, the Teacher of Mathematics – (let us call him T.o.M.) – to an illiterate and innumerate work-force. I was able to show that, by following very simple instructions, it is possible to ensure that somebody with no knowledge of geometry whatsoever, could yet be taught how to construct accurate angles of 90°, or even the more complicated 'pentagonal' angles of 36° and 72°. I also showed how uncomplicated were the instructions necessary to divide a length into the Golden Division Proportions of 1:1.618. My encounter with the Domesday league of 2640 yards presented yet further opportunities for the passing on and preservation of even more abstruse information in a plain and easily remembered manner.

Since the Middle Ages, we have been accustomed to the idea of the passing down of information from master to student in the trade guilds. Certain elements of such ordinary teaching were preserved as 'trade secrets' – only to be acquired after a long and careful apprenticeship and withheld from the 'uninitiated'. The builders of the great cathedrals, for instance, guarded complex mathematical and geometric 'secrets' of their craft. The following imaginary scenario is of a similar nature and even includes a piece of 'secret information' which could be kept as a privilege only for the 'initiated'.

T.o.M. wishes to convey the essential numbers of his system to his 'artisans' who can neither write nor count. They must be conveyed in a manner which is both easy to pass on and difficult to modify inadvertently. How to set about it? His 'students' may be illiterate and innumerate, but they are not stupid. Even so, his method must be of the utmost simplicity – and there is nothing difficult about the concept of 'One'.

'I will teach you at the Sacred Grove', he might say, 'Bring with you a stone.'

To a second student: 'Bring with you a stone in each hand.'

As their teacher, he undertakes the more difficult task of bringing two stones in one hand and one in the other. The stones are laid upon the ground:

O	O O	O O O

The students can easily see that together they have brought the same number of stones as their teacher. The exercise is then repeated, with the result:

O	O O	O O O
O	O O	O O O

And again:

O	O O	O O O
O	O O	O O O
O	O O	O O O

As can be seen, T.o.M. has imparted, in three simple steps, the idea of

1	2	3
2	4	6
3	6	9

The little block of numbers are fixed – without risk of confusion.

The craft secret – to be passed on only at the time of initiation – is that the block of numbers must be altered by the simple expedient of moving the right hand column into the centre:

1	3	2
2	6	4
3	9	6

And now the numbers which create the mile measure system and hold its definition of the size of our planet are fixed and unforgettable. Whether the student understood the matter or not, the information was preserved.

I do not, for one moment, suggest that any such scene was ever played out. My purpose is merely to demonstrate an underlying simplicity in what appears to be a relatively complex matter.

1.618

Some of my mythical students would be more mathematically gifted and could be given more complicated memory aids. The importance and significance of pentagonal geometry has been amply demonstrated throughout this investigation. Any study of the pentagon and its Golden Division properties will create a familiarity with the number 1618. It was for this reason that I chose the easily remembered 2 miles and 1618 yards as my approximation for the Church Circle radius measure, which I knew was 'just under three miles'. Having chosen 2 miles, 1618 yards as my *aide-memoire*, I was startled to realise that I had defined an astonishingly close approximation of what is to be found in the landscape.

This was startling, as I had arrived at the radius measure by postulating a 'round-figure' unit of 1000 poles and multiplying it by the Golden Division to arrive at 1618 *poles*. (I had noticed that this seemed to be the length of a chord which fitted three times into the Church Circle and, from this, was able to calculate the circle's radius.)* David Wood's more complex methods involve taking the number of degrees in a circle (360), dividing by the Golden Division and taking five-sixths of the resulting number. This produces 185410.1956 which, in inches, is equal to 2 miles 1630.27 yards. Erling Haagensen found that his Circle radius was exactly one-third of the distance between Østerlars and Bodilsker Churches.

The Danish Land Survey co-ordinates give a distance of 14101.474 metres. This, divided by 3, is 2 miles 1620.5194 yards. It can be seen that my 'guessed' Golden Division number of 2 miles and 1618 yards is very close to the numbers being found by more sophisticated methods. As such, it is a remarkably simple and convenient *aide-memoire*.

Another astonishing property of the number 1.618 lies in its 'square'. Multiplied by itself, $1.618 \times 1.618 = 1.618 + 1$. Put another way, 1.618^2 is equal to 2.618. All numbers impossible for those who are 'pentagonally aware' to forget.

To this section I must add one other extraordinary coincidence. The 'holiness' of the Rennes-le-Château landscape stems from its pentagonal (and therefore Golden Section) configuration of mountains, which reflect on Earth, the movements of Venus in the Heavens. Earth's year consists of 365 and a quarter days. 365.25 divided by 1.618 = 225.74. Rounding off in my hypothetical T.o.M.'s habitual manner leaves us with 225 – the number of days in Venus's year.†

WHY?

We are confronting a mystery. The structured landscape of Rennes-le-Château and its association with the English mile (as well as the mile's apparent link with the dimensions of the Earth), are easily demonstrated, with a multitude of confirming instances. The measure and the geometry

---

* See *The Holy Place*, pp. 117–18. H.L.

† Venus goes through one complete cycle of phases (her synodic period) in 584 days. 584 divided by 1.618 = 360.9, which, rounded off, reflects the Ancient Egyptian year of 12 months of 30 days, i.e. 360 plus 5 'added' days. Or the 360 degrees in a circle. Additionally, Mercury and Saturn, the inner and outermost planets of the mediaeval Cosmos, show Golden Section relationships in orbit and size to within 99 per cent accuracy. Such additional coincidences of number, however, while food for thought, should not be allowed to lead into yet more mystically supernatural byways! H.L.

are evident. The patterns are repeatable. The designs are meaningful. All of this was created in a remote past, upon which the phenomenon is shedding a new light. The evidence therefore requires the serious attention of historians and archaeologists. But the confirming data lie mostly in a realm beyond their expertise and which they confess to finding difficult to accept.

On this matter, Professor Christopher Cornford commented: 'Historians have no knowledge of geometry ... and why should they? But if they were aware of the elegance and coherence of these geometric designs and still believed them to be the result of pure chance – then it would be necessary to accept a coincidence of such astronomical rarity as would, in itself, be an amazing wonder.'

Until historians and other experts turn their attention to these matters, the mystery will remain unexplained. I am aware that I will be expected, by some readers, to provide an explanation. There is a great yearning for 'proofs' of the existence of supernatural agencies at work among us or of global 'conspiracies' to keep us in ignorance of important facts. I do not share that yearning. Nor do I think that what I have discovered owes its creation to anything more than the ingenuity of *homo sapiens*. I *do not know* what led our ancestors to undertake the enormous labour which I have uncovered. That they did so is implicit in the patterns and in the dimensions. In guise of explanation, I can make no more than a vague guess. Other people's guesses will have as much validity.

My 'guess' therefore is the rather undramatic one that we are confronting an elaborate and skilful exercise in mapping. Long before the invention of maps, human beings still had need to travel from one place to another. To find their way across mountains and rivers, through forests and across empty moorlands. Beyond one's own familiar home territory, a recognisable system of markers would have been a valuable asset. Such a system may, perhaps, have been marked out by Standing Stones. There is, for instance, such a Standing Stone, crowning the crest above St Salvayre, six miles to the north of Rennes-le-Château. It is now a tiny, lost speck in a vast and empty landscape. This guess at least provides some sort of explanation for its otherwise enigmatic placing. Stone Circles were, perhaps, in key locations, with the extensive network known in detail only to an 'initiated' few. If those few were trained and skilled in the accurate gauging of short distances (2 miles 1618 yards?), a network of 'guides' could have developed with very specialist knowledge.

The above idea provides, at least, an understandable motivation. However, there is no evidence whatsoever to substantiate the guess. Apart, of course, from the hints uncovered by this investigation. I must also add that I am not utterly convinced by the hypothesis. As I have said: we are confronting a mystery. For what need was there, even for these conjectural guides, to know the dimensions of the Earth? This aspect is more easily melodramatised. Yet what I have found, as well as the work of Berriman and other scholars, seems to indicate that the English units of measure preserve an echo of that need.

'The present English units have roots in deep antiquity and have remained virtually unchanged,' said Professor H. F. Bowsher.* If this is, indeed the case, it is perhaps not surprising to have stumbled, at last, upon tangible evidence of the early use of those units.

There is, too, the 'occult' significance of the natural Pentagon of Mountains. The phrase 'As above – so below' has echoed down through the centuries. It cannot be denied that this physical manifestation, here on Earth, of the star-shape in the Heavens, would have imbued this place with holiness for those people who, long ago, realised that it was there. The mountains themselves preserve the measure. Perhaps the system was developed from attempts to mark out the site for the Holy Place that it was seen to be?

Rennes-le-Château has provided glimpses of even more difficult concepts than those which I have detailed above. In *The Holy Place*, I gave numerous instances of the geometric configurations being locked to the French prime meridian of longitude. As history teaches us that this meridian was not established until the eighteenth century, the very suggestion again invites derisory dismissal. But the evidence is there. Such yet more unlikely-seeming notions increase the difficulty of acceptance of the entire thesis. I am aware of this. But what purpose would be served in concealing them?

Prof. David H. Kelley said: ... *It seems to me futile to argue that 'can't be' is a stronger position than 'is'. Empirical reality takes precedence over theoretical objections, however strong the latter may seem* a priori.†

It is to be hoped that theoretical objections will give place to attempts to *prove* the data in this book to be wrong. If they *are* wrong, then the task of proof should be a quick and easy one. If they are *not* wrong ...?

* *Technikatörténeti Szemle* (ix. 1977).
† In *Neara Journal*, vol. XXVIII, 3 & 4.

Three decades of work have enabled me to glimpse the trace of gold buried beneath the thick dross of imagination and fantasy. The truth of Rennes-le-Château is no longer hidden behind a curtain of obscurity. But this truth is not the *only* truth of this story, though it is, I believe, the most important and the most profound. Certainly it is the most solid – resting, as it does, upon solid and irrefutable facts. Nevertheless, that truth remains a Mystery. And yet other, if lesser mysteries also remain.

What, if anything, did Saunière find? Who created the strange parchments with their incredible ciphers? And why? What was Poussin's secret 'that kings would have pains to draw from him'? Who placed so many obstacles and confusions in the path of my research? And why? Where lies the necessity for so much secrecy?

Many people crave the answers to these – and other – questions which litter the pathway to an understanding of the Mystery of Rennes-le-Château. But now, for me, they have no more than fleeting interest. For the end of my research is no more than a new beginning. What I have found is clear, demonstrable and without dispute. Even so – I remain uncomfortably aware that it lacks an explanation.

The great stone monuments of Stonehenge and Carnac are there for all to see. But no one can tell us why they were built, nor whence come the skills which built them. Rennes-le-Château has shown us their hidden, but precise, counterpart in a clear and recognisable mastery of mathematics and geometry.

At last we have in our hands the Key which will unlock a treasure house of lost knowledge.

At Rennes-le-Château, the ancient surveyors, measurers and mappers have left us the empirical reality of their amazing labours. They have left us the evidence of their skills and knowledge which, through many long centuries has been lost and forgotten. They speak to us across the years in the language of number and measure. No written words survive, yet their call to us is clear and confident and proud. It is time for us to listen – and to learn.

SELECT BIBLIOGRAPHY

Michael Baigent, Richard Leigh and Henry Lincoln, *The Holy Blood & The Holy Grail*, Jonathan Cape, London, 1982.

Michael Baigent, Richard Leigh and Henry Lincoln, *The Messianic Legacy*, Jonathan Cape, London, 1986.

A. E. Berriman, *Historical Metrology*, Dent, London, 1953.

R. D. Connor, *The Weights and Measures of England*, HMSO Books, Norwich, 1987.

Erling Haagensen, *Bornholms Mysterium*, Bogans Forlag, Denmark, 1993.

John Martineau, *A Book of Coincidences*, Wooden Books, Powys, 1995.

Richard Morris, *Churches in the Landscape*, Dent, London, 1989.

Abbé Sabarthès, *Dictionnaire Topographique du Département de l'Aude*, Imprimerie Nationale, Paris, 1912.

Hugh Schonfield, *The Essene Odyssey*, Element Books, 1984.

G. de Sède, *Le Trésor Maudit*, Editions J'ai Lu, Paris, 1968.

G. de Sède, *Rennes-le-Château*, Robert Laffont, Paris, 1988.

J. R. Smith, *From Plane to Spheroid*, Landmark, California, 1986.

Ian Stewart, *Nature's Numbers*, Weidenfeld & Nicolson, London, 1995.

Alexander Thom, 'The Geometry of Megalithic Man', *Mathematical Gazette*, 45, 1961.

Tom Williamson and Liz Bellamy, *Ley Lines in Question*, World's Work, 1983.

Dom Joseph Vaissete, *Abrégé de l'Histoire de Languedoc*, Paris, 1749.

David Wood, *Genisis*, Baton Press, Tunbridge Wells, 1985.

David Wood and Ian Campbell, *Geneset*, Bellevue Books, Sunbury on Thames, 1994.

INDEX

Numbers in *italic* type indicate illustrations

KEY TO THE SACRED PATTERN

KEY TO THE SACRED PATTERN